Adobe® Illustrator® 9.0

Classroom in a Book®

Adobe

www.adobe.com/adobepress

Contents

Getting Started

Adobe® Illustrator® is the industry-standard illustration program for print, multimedia, and online graphics. Whether you are a designer or technical illustrator producing artwork for print publishing, an artist producing multimedia graphics, or a creator of Web pages or online content, the Adobe Illustrator program offers you the tools you need to get professional-quality results.

About Classroom in a Book

Adobe Illustrator 9.0 Classroom in a Book® is part of the official training series for Adobe graphics and publishing software developed by experts at Adobe Systems. The lessons are designed to let you learn at your own pace. If you're new to Adobe Illustrator, you'll learn the fundamental concepts and features you'll need to master the program. If you've been using Adobe Illustrator for a while, you'll find Classroom in a Book teaches many advanced features, including tips and techniques for using the latest version of Adobe Illustrator.

Although each lesson provides step-by-step instructions for creating a specific project, there's room for exploration and experimentation. You can follow the book from start to finish or do only the lessons that correspond to your interests and needs. Each lesson concludes with a review section summarizing what you've covered.

Prerequisites

Before beginning to use *Adobe Illustrator 9.0 Classroom in a Book*, you should have a working knowledge of your computer and its operating system. Make sure you know how to use the mouse and standard menus and commands and also how to open, save, and close files. If you need to review these techniques, see the printed or online documentation included with your system.

Installing the program

You must purchase the Adobe Illustrator software separately. For complete instructions on installing the software, see the Introduction to the *Adobe Illustrator 9.0 User Guide*.

Installing the Classroom in a Book fonts

To ensure that the lesson files appear on your system with the correct fonts, you may need to install the Classroom in a Book font files. The fonts for the lessons are located in the Fonts folder on the Adobe Illustrator 9.0 Classroom in a Book CD. If you already have these on your system, you do not need to install them. If you have ATM® (Adobe Type Manager®), see its documentation on how to install fonts. If you do not have ATM, installing it from the CIB CD will automatically install the necessary fonts.

You can also install the Classroom in a Book fonts by copying all the files in the Fonts folder on the Adobe Illustrator 9.0 Classroom in a Book *CD to the Fonts folder within the folder in which you installed Adobe Illustrator 9.0 on your hard disk. Doing so makes the fonts available to Adobe Illustrator but not to other applications.*

Copying the Classroom in a Book files

The Classroom in a Book CD includes folders containing all the electronic files for the lessons. Each lesson has its own folder. You must install these folders on your hard drive to use the files for the lessons.

To save room on your drive, you can install the folders for each lesson as you need them.

To install the Classroom in a Book files:

1 Insert the Adobe Illustrator Classroom in a Book CD into your CD-ROM drive.

2 Create a folder named AICIB on your hard drive.

3 Copy the lessons you want to the hard drive:

• To copy all of the lessons, drag the Lessons folder from the CD into the AICIB folder.

• To copy a single lesson, drag the individual lesson folder from the CD into the AICIB folder.

If you are installing the files in Windows®, you must unlock them before using them. You don't need to unlock the files if you are installing them in Mac OS®.

4 In Windows, unlock the files you copied:

• If you copied all of the lessons, double-click the unlock.bat file in the AICIB/Lessons folder.

• If you copied a single lesson, drag the unlock.bat file from the Lessons folder on the CD into the AI CIB folder. Then double-click the unlock.bat file in the AICIB folder.

Restoring default preferences

The preferences file controls how palettes and command settings appear on your screen when you open the Adobe Illustrator program. Each time you quit Adobe Illustrator, the position of the palettes and certain command settings are recorded in the preferences file. If you want to restore the tools and palettes to their original default settings, you can delete the current Adobe Illustrator 9.0 preferences file. (Adobe Illustrator creates a preferences file if one doesn't already exist the next time you start the program and save a file.)

Important: If you want to save the current settings, rename the preferences file rather than throwing it away. When you are ready to restore the settings, change the name back and make sure that the file is located in the Illustrator 9.0 folder (Windows) or the Preferences folder (Mac OS).

1 Locate the AIPrefs file in the Illustrator 9.0 folder (Windows) or the Adobe Illustrator 9.0 Prefs file in the Adobe Illustrator 9.0 folder in the System folder (Mac OS).

If you can't find the file, choose Find from the Start menu and then choose Files or Folders (Windows), or choose Find from the desktop File menu (Mac OS). Type **AIPrefs** or **Adobe Illustrator 9.0 Prefs** in the text box, and click Find Now (Windows) or Find (Mac OS).

Note: If you still can't find the file, you probably haven't started Adobe Illustrator for the first time yet. The preferences file is created after you quit the program the first time, and it's updated thereafter.

2 Delete or rename the AIPrefs file (Windows) or the Adobe Illustrator 9.0 Prefs file (Mac OS).

3 Start Adobe Illustrator.

💡 *To locate and delete the Adobe Illustrator preferences file quickly each time you begin a new project, create a shortcut (Windows) or an alias (Mac OS) for the Illustrator 9.0 or Preferences folder.*

Additional resources

Adobe Illustrator 9.0 Classroom in a Book is not meant to replace documentation that comes with the program. Only the commands and options used in the lessons are explained in this book. For comprehensive information about program features, refer to these resources:

• The User Guide. Included with the Adobe Illustrator software, the User Guide contains a complete description of all features. For your convenience, you will find excerpts from these guides, including the Quick Tours for the software, in this Classroom in a Book.

• The Quick Reference Card, a useful companion as you work through the lessons.

• Online Help, an online version of the User Guide and Quick Reference Card, which you can view by choosing Help > Contents. (For more information, see Lesson 1, "Getting to Know the Work Area.")

• The Adobe Web site (www.adobe.com), which you can view by choosing File > Adobe Online if you have a connection to the World Wide Web.

Adobe certification

The Adobe Training and Certification Programs are designed to help Adobe customers improve and promote their product proficiency skills. The Adobe Certified Expert (ACE) program is designed to recognize the high-level skills of expert users. Adobe Certified Training Providers (ACTP) use only Adobe Certified Experts to teach Adobe software classes. Available in either ACTP classrooms or on site, the ACE program is the best way to master Adobe products. For Adobe Training and Certification Programs information, visit the Partnering with Adobe Web site at http://partners.adobe.com.

A Quick Tour of Adobe Illustrator

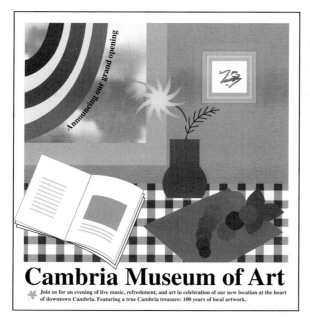

This interactive demonstration of Adobe Illustrator is designed to give an overview of key features of the program in about one hour.

Getting started

You'll work in one art file during this tour. Before you begin, you need to restore the default preferences for Adobe Illustrator. Then you'll open the finished art file for this lesson to see what you'll create.

1 To ensure that the tools and palettes function exactly as described in this tour, delete or deactivate (by renaming) the Adobe Illustrator 9.0 preferences file. See "Restoring default preferences" on page 3.

2 Start Adobe Illustrator.

3 To open the finished art file, choose File > Open, and open the TourEnd.ai file in the Lesson00 folder, located inside the Lessons folder within the AICIB folder on your hard drive.

4 If you like, choose View > Zoom Out to make the finished artwork smaller, and leave it on your screen as you work. If you don't want to leave the image open, choose File > Close.

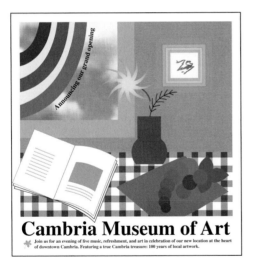

For an illustration of the finished artwork in this lesson, see the color section.

Now open the start file to begin the tour.

5 To open the start file, choose File > Open, and open the TourStrt.ai file in the Lesson00 folder, located inside the Lessons folder within the AICIB folder on your hard drive.

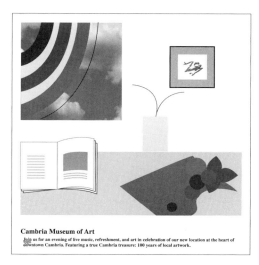

Cambria Museum of Art
Join us for an evening of live music, refreshment, and art in celebration of our new location at the heart of downtown Cambria. Featuring a true Cambria treasure: 100 years of local artwork.

6 Choose File > Save As, name the file **Cambria.ai**, and select the Lesson00 folder. Leave the Format option set to Adobe Illustrator® Document, and click Save. In the Illustrator Native Format Options dialog box, select Illustrator 9.0 Compatibility and click OK.

Creating basic shapes

Adobe Illustrator includes a variety of tools and commands for creating basic geometric shapes, as well as specialized tools for precision drawing and patterns.

You'll begin this tour by adding some basic shapes to the artwork.

Drawing a star

First, you'll draw a star and modify the shape to create the flower.

1 Double-click the zoom tool (Q) in the toolbox to enlarge the view to 100%.

2 Hold down the mouse button on the ellipse tool (○) in the toolbox to display a group of tools. Select the star tool (☆), and then click once at the top left of the flower stem.

Clicking once with the star tool rather than dragging it in the artwork lets you precisely specify the shape's dimensions.

3 In the Star dialog box, specify the shape of the star. (We specified 60 points for Radius 1, 15 points for Radius 2, and 10 for the number of points on the star.) Click OK.

Now you'll change the direction of the star points.

4 In the toolbox, select the twirl tool (🌀) from the same group as the rotate tool (◐). In the artwork, select the top point of the star but don't release the mouse button. Drag the point to the right or left. Release the mouse button when you are satisfied with the effect.

Painting the fill and stroke

In Illustrator, color within an object is called a *fill* and color on a line is called a *stroke*. The current fill and stroke colors are shown in the large Fill and Stroke boxes near the bottom of the toolbox and in the Color palette.

Now you'll paint the flower's fill and remove the stroke.

1 With the flower still selected, click the Stroke box in the toolbox and click the None button to remove the stroke. Then click the Fill box to specify you want to edit the fill of the star.

A. *Stroke box selected*
B. *None button selected*
C. *Fill box selected*
D. *Color button selected*

2 Click the Swatches tab to bring the Swatches palette to the front of its group or choose Window > Show Swatches.

The Swatches palette contains a premade set of colors, gradients, and patterns that you can edit, save, and apply.

3 Click any swatch in the palette to change the flower's color. (We chose the Yellow & Orange Radial gradient.)

For information on how to create your own gradients, see Lesson 8, "Blending Shapes and Colors."

Now you'll change the stroke weight of the flower stem.

4 Select the selection tool (↖) in the toolbox, and then click the left line of the stem to select it. If the Stroke palette is not visible, click the Stroke tab to bring the palette to the front of its group or choose Window > Show Stroke.

5 In the Stroke palette, type a larger value in the Weight text box (we increased it to 3 points) and press Enter or Return to apply the change.

6 Choose File > Save.

Combining shapes

Adobe Illustrator includes numerous tools and commands that let you modify the shapes of objects. The Pathfinder commands change the shapes of objects by adding and subtracting the outlines, or *paths,* around them.

Uniting shapes into one

Now you'll add a circle shape to the rectangular flower vase and unite the shapes into one object.

1 Choose View > Smart Guides to turn them on. Smart Guides give you information about the objects as you point to them.

2 Choose Edit > Deselect All to deselect the artwork, and then click the Default Fill and Stroke button in the toolbox to deselect the current settings of the flower stem.

Default Fill and Stroke button

3 Select the ellipse tool (○) from the same group as the star tool (☆) in the toolbox. Hold down Shift+Alt (Windows) or Shift+Option (Mac OS) and drag to draw a circle that's almost as tall as the rectangular flower vase. (Holding down Shift constrains the ellipse to a circle. Holding down Alt/Option draws from the center rather than from the left side.)

4 Click the selection tool ( ) to select the circle, select its center point, but don't release the mouse button. Drag the circle to the center of the rectangle. When you release the mouse button, the Smart Guides snap the circle's center to the center of the rectangle.

5 Now select the circle's center point and slowly drag the circle straight down the vertical guide until its center reaches the intersect point of the table. Then release the mouse button.

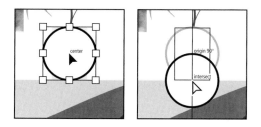

Now you'll unite the circle and rectangle into one object.

6 With the circle still selected and using the selection tool, Shift-click the rectangle to select both objects. Choose Window > Show Pathfinder, and click the Unite button ( ) in the Pathfinder palette.

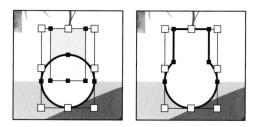

Sampling a color

Now you'll paint the vase with a color from the window curtain.

1 With the vase still selected, select the eyedropper tool (🖊) in the toolbox and click the middle stripe of the curtain to pick up, or *sample,* its dark blue color. Sampling a color copies the color's fill and stroke into the Color palette and into any objects that are currently selected.

Subtracting one shape from another

Now you'll use a Pathfinder command to change the shape of the bottom of the flower vase.

1 Select the rectangle tool (□), and draw a rectangle over the bottom portion of the vase.

2 Click the selection tool (▶) to select the rectangle, and Shift-click the vase to select both objects.

3 In the Pathfinder palette, click the Minus Front button (⬚).

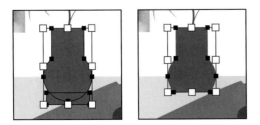

The rectangle shape (the front shape) is subtracted from the round shape of the vase, creating a straight line at the base.

Creating blends

Adobe Illustrator lets you blend shapes and colors of objects together into a new object that you can modify. Now you'll blend two different sized and colored circles to create a bunch of grapes.

1 Click the largest circle on the napkin to select it, and then Shift-click the smallest circle to select it.

2 Choose Object > Blend > Blend Options. In the Blend Options dialog box, for Spacing choose Specified Steps, type **5** for the number of steps, and click OK.

3 Choose Object > Blend > Make to create five intermediate objects that blend the colors and size of the two circles.

Editing your drawing

Adobe Illustrator has tools that let you edit, erase, and smooth what you draw, and a Navigator palette to help you move around in the artwork as you work.

Zooming in

Now you'll use the Navigator palette to zoom in closer on the blended grapes so you can change the direction of its path.

1 If it isn't visible, click the Navigator tab to bring the palette to the front of its group or choose Window > Show Navigator.

2 In the Navigator palette, move the slider or click the Zoom In button (⌃) to zoom in closer to the artwork (to about 300%) and use the hand pointer to move the red view box over the grapes.

Diverting a path

You can change the straight path of the blended grapes to a curved path by moving the direction points of an anchor on the path.

1 Select the convert-anchor-point tool (⌐) from the same group as the pen tool (✎) in the toolbox, and experiment with moving the path of the grapes by selecting an end anchor point and dragging it to the left or right. You can also drag the direction handles on the anchor point.

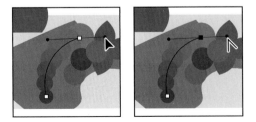

2 Press Shift+Ctrl+A (Windows) or Shift+Command+A (Mac OS) to deselect the artwork, and then choose File > Save.

Editing a shape

Now you'll use the pencil tool to change the shape of the table napkin under the grapes.

1 Select the selection tool ( ) in the toolbox, and click the napkin to select it.

2 Select the pencil tool ( ) in the toolbox, and position the pointer over the anchor point at the right corner of the napkin. (If necessary, scroll to the right to see it.)

3 Press the mouse button and drag the pencil tool down along the right side of the napkin to straighten out the shape, starting from the right corner and ending on the bottom corner of the napkin. When you release the mouse button, the napkin is reshaped.

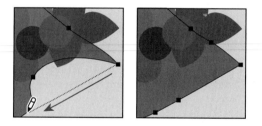

4 If you make a mistake, choose Edit > Undo and then redraw the shape.

5 When you've finished, choose Edit > Deselect All to deselect the napkin.

6 In the Navigator palette, click the Zoom Out button ( ) a few times to zoom back out to 100%, and then move the view box to the center of the artwork.

Drawing straight lines

Now you'll draw some straight lines to create a window frame on two sides of the window.

1 Click the Default Fill and Stroke button ( ) in the toolbox to deselect the settings of the napkin.

2 Choose View > Outline, and then select the pen tool ( ) from the same group as the convert-anchor-point tool ( ) in the toolbox.

3 Make sure that the Smart Guides are turned on in the View menu, and click the anchor point on the bottom left corner of the window to begin drawing the first straight line. Then hold down Shift and click directly beneath the window to end the line.

Each time you click, you create an anchor point, and Illustrator connects the anchor points with a straight line. Holding down Shift constrains the line to vertical, horizontal, or diagonal paths.

4 Shift-click five more times to draw the window frame in a counterclockwise direction, ending with the same anchor point you started with. As you move the pen tool over your starting point, the pen tool displays a small circle, indicating that your last click will close the object's path.

5 Click the selection tool ( ) to select the frame, and then Shift-click the top of the wall to the right to select it also.

6 Choose View > Preview. Notice the window frame you just drew is on top of the flower. Objects are tiled in the order that they're created with the most current on top.

7 Choose Object > Arrange > Send to Back.

Many of the objects in this illustration were created using the pen tool. For information on drawing with the pen tool, see Lesson 4, "Drawing with the Pen."

Painting

In Adobe Illustrator, you can paint an object in many ways. So far, you've painted the flower with a color or gradient from the Swatches palette and copied a color from the curtain to the flower vase using the eyedropper tool. You can paint objects in Illustrator artwork with black, white, shades of gray, process and spot colors, gradients, and patterns. You can also use the Brushes palette to apply patterns to the stroke or path of an object.

Painting with a spot color

Now you'll paint the wall and the window frame with the same spot color and change the tint.

1 With both the window frame and the wall still selected, make sure the Fill box is selected in the toolbox. (The Fill box appears in front of the Stroke box to indicate that it's selected.)

2 If it's not visible, click the Swatches tab to bring the palette to the front of its group or choose Window > Swatches.

3 Position the hand pointer over the swatches to see their names, and select the Aqua swatch in the fourth row. You can identify this swatch as a spot color by the triangle and dot in the bottom right corner of the swatch.

In Illustrator, a color swatch can be a predefined spot color (such as a PANTONE® color) or any color you save and name in your artwork.

4 Shift-click the wall to deselect it and keep the window frame selected.

5 In the Color palette, drag the Tint slider to the left to lighten the color. (We used 65%.)

6 In the Color palette, drag the None button up and drop it over the Stroke box to remove the window frame's stroke. (This action keeps the Fill box selected.)

Painting with brushes

You can paint with four types of brushes—Calligraphic, Scatter, Art, and Pattern. You can also create your own brushes to draw with or to apply to existing paths. Now you'll apply a custom-made Art brush to the flower's stem and a Pattern brush to the picture frame on the wall.

1 Click the right side of the flower stem to select it, and choose Window > Show Brushes, or click the Brushes tab behind the Swatches palette to bring the Brushes palette to the front.

2 Position the mouse button over the triangle in the top right corner of the Brushes palette, press the mouse button to display the palette menu, and choose View By Name. The names of the brushes are grouped by type (Calligraphic, Scatter, Art, or Pattern) and then listed alphabetically with each group. Scroll down to the list of Art brushes and select the Leaf Art brush.

3 Now click the outer edge of the picture frame on the wall to select it, and select the Picframe Pattern brush in the Brushes palette.

See Lesson 5, "Working with Brushes," for information on creating your own custom brushes and using the Brushes palette.

Painting with a pattern swatch

Now you will use the Swatches palette to add a pattern fill to the tablecloth.

1 Click inside the tablecloth to select it. If necessary, click the Fill box in the toolbox to select the tablecloth's fill.

2 Click the Swatches tab to bring the palette to the front of its group, click the Show Pattern Swatches button at the bottom of the Swatches palette, and click the pattern you want. Try out the other different pattern fills for the tablecloth. (We used Tablecloth Pattern #1.)

Scaling and rotating objects

You can easily scale, rotate, and shear objects—either by dragging or by specifying precise values. Now you'll scale and rotate the book to enlarge it and turn it at an angle.

1 To scale the book, first click the book to select its bounding box. Then hold down Shift and slowly drag the bottom right corner of the bounding box about halfway to the napkin.

Holding down Shift as you drag increases the size of the book proportionally while keeping the left side of the book in its original position.

2 To rotate the book, move the cursor down to the bottom right corner of the book, just outside the bounding box. (The pointer changes from a scale symbol to a rotate symbol.) Press the mouse button and drag the pointer down and to the left to rotate the book in a clockwise direction.

3 Choose Edit > Deselect All to deselect the artwork, and then choose File > Save.

Using layers

The Layers palette in Adobe Illustrator lets you organize artwork into layers, groups, and objects that can be selected, displayed, edited, and printed individually or together.

1 If the Layers palette is not visible, click the Layers tab to bring the palette to the front of its group or choose Window > Show Layers.

The artwork has been organized into four layers. New objects are created on the layer that is selected in the Layers palette. You can view, select, and edit each layer, group, or object within a layer using the Layers palette.

2 In the Layers palette, click the triangle to the left of the Draw&Paint layer name. The list expands to display the thumbnails of the paths that are on the Draw&Paint layer.

3 Click the triangle again to collapse the Draw&Paint layer's path list.

4 In the Layers palette, click Photo to select that layer. Then drag the Photo layer up, just above the Curtain layer but below the Draw&Paint layer, to move the photo to the front of the window.

5 Notice how the curtain is hidden behind the clouds in the window. Now drag the Curtain layer in the Layers palette back up to just above the Photo layer to bring the curtain to the front of the artwork.

Moving layers in the Layers palette changes the order in which objects appear in the artwork, with the layer at the top of the palette containing the frontmost objects.

You can also change the transparency or apply effects to layers or nested layers.

6 In the Layers palette, click the hollow circle to the right of the Curtain layer name.

Curtain layer selected

Selecting the circle changes it to a hollow double-circle, indicating that all objects on the Curtain layer are now selected and will be affected by changes to their appearance or transparency.

7 Click the Transparency tab to bring the Transparency palette to the front of its group or choose Window > Show Transparency.

8 Change the Opacity setting to 70%. All objects on the Curtain layer are now slightly transparent. Notice that the double-circle now appears solid, indicating that the layer has appearance attributes applied to it.

70% opacity   *Appearance attributes applied*   *Result*

See Lesson 10, "Working with Layers," for information on creating layers and nested layers, and using the Layers palette.

Applying bitmap image filters

Adobe Illustrator includes special-effects filters that you can apply to embedded bitmap images (also known as *raster images*) for a range of effects.

Filtering a bitmap image

Now you'll apply a filter to the embedded bitmap image of the sky to make it look less like a photo.

1 In the Layers palette, click the lock icon next to the Photo layer to unlock the layer, letting you modify artwork on that layer.

2 Click Photo to select the Photo layer. Hold down Alt (Windows) or Option (Mac OS) and click the eye icon in the column to the left of the Photo layer.

Holding down Alt/Option as you click the eye icon hides all of the other layers. Hiding layers is a useful way to isolate detailed artwork as you work.

3 Select the selection tool (▶), and click the photo image of the sky to select it.

The image is an imported TIFF file from Adobe Photoshop®. You can import artwork in a wide variety of formats from other applications.

 For information on embedding or linking image files to your artwork, see "Opening and Placing Artwork" in online Help or Chapter 2 in the Adobe Illustrator User Guide.

4 Choose Filter > Sketch > Water Paper. Experiment with changing the filter values. When the preview in the Water Paper dialog box appears the way you like, click OK to apply the filter to the bitmap image.

Original   *Water Paper filter applied*

5 In the Layers palette, Alt-click (Windows) or Option-click (Mac OS) the eye icon again to show all the layers.

Applying a live effect

Now you'll give the wall next to the window a textured surface by applying an effect to it. The effect is called a live effect because, unlike the filter you applied to the image above, you can edit or change the effect at any time by using the Appearance palette.

1 Click the Appearance tab to bring the Appearance palette to the front of its group or choose Window > Show Appearance.

2 Click the wall to select it. The appearance attributes of the wall are displayed in the Appearance palette.

3 Choose Effect > Artistic > Rough Pastels. Experiment with different values, and then click OK.

4 Notice that the appearance attributes have changed in the Appearance palette.

Original   *Effect applied*   *Appearance palette*

5 With the wall shape still selected, choose Effect > Artistic > Film Grain. Experiment with different values, and then click OK. (We used the default values.)

You can alter the appearance of an object by changing the order of the effects in the Appearance palette.

6 In the Appearance palette, drag the Rough Pastels effect beneath the Film Grain effect. Notice how the effect changes when you apply the Film Grain effect before the Rough Pastels.

7 Choose File > Save to save the changes.

You're now ready to work with type.

Adding type

Adobe Illustrator lets you easily create type on a path or at any point in your artwork, as well as create and import text in columns or in other containers.

Now you'll add a headline to a path along the edge of the curtain.

1 In the Layers palette, drag the Text layer to the top of the palette.

A curved line has been drawn along the edge of the window curtain.

2 Select the path type tool (✎) from the same group as the type tool (**T**) in the toolbox, and click once on the bottom end of the curved line to position the insertion point.

When you click a line with the path type tool, the line is converted to an invisible path (without any fill or stroke color) and a blinking insertion point appears.

3 Type **Announcing our grand opening**.

The default characteristics of the type are Helvetica* Regular 12 Points.

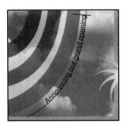

Sampling type

Now you'll sample the type characteristics of the title at the bottom of the artwork and apply them to the new type.

1 Click the selection tool ( ). Clicking the selection tool after typing automatically selects the entire block of type.

2 Select the eyedropper tool ( ) in the toolbox, and click anywhere within the words *Cambria Museum of Art*.

Sampling type with the eyedropper tool applies the characteristics to any selected type objects. It also copies the type characteristics to the Paragraph and Character palettes and the fill colors to the Color palette.

Changing type characteristics

Now you'll open the Character palette and change the character size of the poster's title to make it bigger.

1 Select the selection tool ( ), and click the title "Cambria Museum of Art" to select the block of type.

2 Choose Type > Character to display the Character palette. Double-click to select 15 pt in the Size box and type **44**. Press Enter or Return to apply the change.

Wrapping text around objects

Now you'll wrap the type at the bottom of the artwork around the linked image of a cloverleaf.

1 Click the cloverleaf image to select it, and then Shift-click the text to the right of the image.

2 Choose Type > Wrap > Make to wrap the type around the cloverleaf image.

3 Choose File > Save to save the artwork. Choose File > Close to close the file.

You can save Illustrator files in different formats depending on how you want to use the artwork. See "Saving and Exporting Artwork" in online Help or Chapter 14 in the Adobe Illustrator User Guide.

Congratulations! You've completed the Illustrator tour. Now you're ready to create your own Illustrator artwork.

Lesson 1

Getting to Know the Work Area

To make the best use of the extensive drawing, painting, and editing capabilities in Adobe Illustrator, it's important to learn how to navigate the work area. The work area consists of the artboard, the scratch area, the toolbox, and the default set of floating palettes.

In this introduction to the work area, you'll learn how to do the following:

• Open an Adobe Illustrator file.

• Select tools from the toolbox.

• Use viewing options to enlarge and reduce the display of a document.

• Work with palettes.

• Use online Help.

Getting started

You'll be working in one art file during this lesson, but before you begin you'll need to restore the default preferences for Adobe Illustrator. Then you'll open the finished art file for this lesson to see what you'll be creating.

1 To ensure that the tools and palettes function exactly as described in this lesson, delete or deactivate (by renaming) the Adobe Illustrator 9.0 preferences file. See "Restoring default preferences" on page 3.

2 Double-click the Adobe Illustrator icon to start the Adobe Illustrator program.

When you start Adobe Illustrator, the menu bar, the toolbox, and five palette groups appear on the screen.

Now open the start file to begin the lesson.

3 Choose File > Open, and open the L1start.ai file in the Lesson01 folder, located inside the Lessons folder within the AICIB folder on your hard drive.

For an illustration of the finished artwork in this lesson, see the color section.

4 Choose File > Save As, name the file **Parrots.ai**, and select the Lesson01 folder. Leave the Format option set to Adobe Illustrator® Document, and click Save. In the Illustrator Native Format Options dialog box, select Illustrator 9.0 Compatibility and click OK.

About the work area

In Adobe Illustrator, the work area occupies the entire space within the Illustrator window and includes more than just the printable page containing your artwork. The printable and nonprintable areas are represented by a series of solid and dotted lines between the outermost edge of the window and the printable area of the page.

__Imageable area__ is bounded by the innermost dotted lines and represents the portion of the page on which the selected printer can print. Many printers cannot print to the edge of the paper.

__Nonimageable area__ is between the two sets of dotted lines representing any nonprintable margin of the page. This example shows the nonimageable area of an 8.5" x 11" page for a standard laser printer.

__Edge of the page__ is indicated by the outermost set of dotted lines.

__Artboard__ is bounded by solid lines and represents the entire region that can contain printable artwork. By default, the artboard is the same size as the page, but it can be enlarged or reduced. The U.S. default artboard is 8.5" x 11", but it can be set as large as 227" x 227".

__Scratch area__ is the area outside the artboard that extends to the edge of the 227-inch square window. The scratch area represents a space on which you can create, edit, and store elements of artwork before moving them onto the artboard. Objects placed onto the scratch area are visible on-screen, but they do not print.

– From the Adobe Illustrator User Guide, Chapter 2

__A.__ Imageable area __B.__ Nonimageable area
__C.__ Edge of page __D.__ Artboard __E.__ Scratch area

Viewing artwork

When you open a file, it is displayed in Preview view, which displays artwork the way it will print. When you're working with large or complex illustrations, you may want to view only the outlines, or *wireframes*, of objects in your artwork, so that the screen doesn't have to redraw the artwork each time you make a change.

1 Choose View > Outline. Only the outlines of the objects are displayed.

2 Choose View > Preview to see all the attributes of the artwork.

3 Choose View > Overprint•Pixel Closeup to zoom in to a preset area of the image. This custom view was added to the document.

Note: To save time when working with large or complex documents, you can create your own custom views within a document to quickly jump to specific areas and zoom levels. You set up the view that you want to save and then choose View > New View. Name the view; it is saved with the document.

4 Choose View > Overprint Preview to view any lines or shapes that are set to overprint.

5 Choose View > Pixel Preview to view how the artwork will look when it is rasterized and viewed on-screen in a Web browser.

Artwork view *Preview view* *Overprint preview* *Pixel preview*

Working with tiled artwork

The artboard's dimensions do not necessarily match the paper sizes used by printers. As a result, when you print a file, the program divides the artboard into one or more rectangles that correspond to the page size available on your printer. Dividing the artboard to fit a printer's available page size is called tiling.

As you work with tiled artwork, be sure to consider how the artwork relates to the boundaries of the page grid and to the total dimensions of the artboard. For example, if the artwork is tiled onto six pages, part of the artwork will print on a separate sheet of paper that corresponds to page 6. If you specify printing only from pages 1 to 5, the part of the artwork that is on page 6 won't print.

If you have set up the file to view and print multiple pages, the file is tiled onto pages numbered from left to right and from top to bottom, starting with page 1. (The first page is always page 1; you cannot change the page 1 designation in Adobe Illustrator.) These page numbers appear on-screen for your reference only; they do not print. The numbers enable you to print all of the pages in the file or specify particular pages to print.

The page or set of pages is aligned with the upper left corner of the artboard by default. However, you can reposition pages on the artboard by using the page tool.

– From the Adobe Illustrator User Guide, Chapter 2

For more information on tiling, see "Tiling artwork and adjusting page boundaries" in online Help.

Using the Illustrator tools

The Illustrator toolbox contains selection tools, drawing and painting tools, editing tools, viewing tools, and the Fill and Stroke color selection boxes. As you work through the lessons, you'll learn about each tool's specific function.

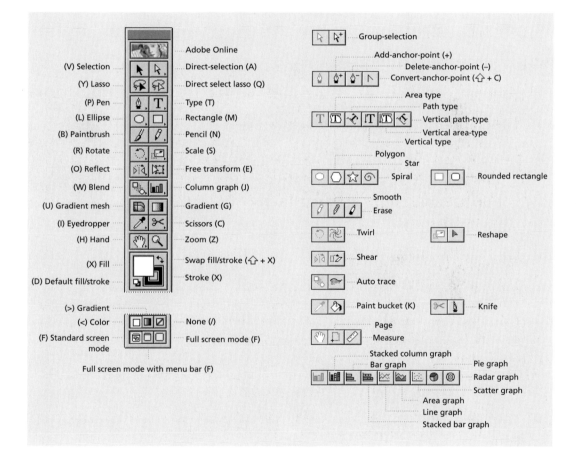

For an overview of the toolbox, see figure 1-1 in the color section.

1 To select a tool, either click the tool in the toolbox or press the tool's keyboard shortcut. For example, you can press M to select the rectangle tool from the keyboard. Selected tools remain active until you click a different tool.

2 If you don't know the keyboard shortcut for a tool, position the pointer over the tool to display the tool's name and shortcut. (All keyboard shortcuts are also listed in the Quick Reference section in online Help. You'll learn to use online Help later in this lesson.)

Some of the tools in the toolbox display a small triangle at the bottom right corner, indicating the presence of additional hidden tools.

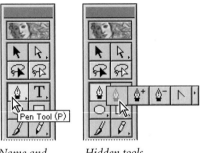

Name and   Hidden tools
shortcut

3 Select hidden tools in either of the following ways:

• Click and hold down the mouse button on a tool that has additional hidden tools. Then drag to the desired tool, and release the mouse button.

• Hold down Alt (Windows) or Option (Mac OS), and click the tool in the toolbox. Each click selects the next hidden tool in the hidden tool sequence.

Note: *When you click a viewing tool to change the screen display of a document, you must return to the Standard screen mode to see the default work area displayed.*

Standard
screen mode

Changing the view of artwork

You can reduce or enlarge the view of artwork at any magnification level from 3.13% to 6400%. Adobe Illustrator displays the percentage of the artwork's actual size in the title bar, next to the filename, and at the lower left corner of the Adobe Illustrator window. Using any of the viewing tools and commands affects only the display of the artwork, not the actual size of the artwork.

Using the View commands

To enlarge or reduce the view of artwork using the View menu, do one of the following:

• Choose View > Zoom In to enlarge the display of the Parrots.ai artwork.

• Choose View > Zoom Out to reduce the view of the Parrots.ai artwork.

Each time you choose a Zoom command, the view of the artwork is resized. Additional viewing options appear at the lower left corner of the window in a hidden menu, indicated by a triangle next to the percentage.

You can also use the View menu to fit the artwork to your screen.

1 Choose View > Fit in Window. A reduced view of the entire document is displayed in the window.

2 To display artwork at actual size, choose View > Actual Size. The artwork is displayed at 100%. (The actual size of your artwork determines how much of it can be viewed on-screen at 100%.)

3 Choose View > Fit in Window before continuing to the next section.

Using the zoom tool

In addition to the View commands, you can use the zoom tool to magnify and reduce the view of artwork.

1 Click the zoom tool ($\mathcal{Q}$) in the toolbox to select the tool, and move the cursor into the document window. Notice that a plus sign appears at the center of the zoom tool.

2 Position the zoom tool over the parrot in the upper left corner of the illustration and click once. The artwork is displayed at a higher magnification.

3 Click two more times over the upper left parrot. The view is increased again, and you'll notice that the area you clicked is magnified. Next you'll reduce the view of the artwork.

4 With the zoom tool still selected, position the pointer over the upper left parrot and hold down Alt (Windows) or Option (Macintosh). A minus sign appears at the center of the zoom tool (⊖).

5 Click in the artwork twice; the view of the artwork is reduced.

In addition to clicking the zoom tools, you can drag a marquee to magnify a specific area of your artwork.

6 With the zoom tool still selected, hold down the mouse button and drag over the area of the illustration you want to magnify; then release the mouse button.

7 Drag a marquee around the lower parrot.

The percentage at which the area is magnified is determined by the size of the marquee you draw with the zoom tool (the smaller the marquee, the larger the level of magnification).

Area selected   Resulting view

Note: *Although you can draw a marquee with the zoom tool to enlarge the view of artwork, you cannot draw a marquee to reduce the view of artwork.*

You can also use the zoom tool to return to a 100% view of your artwork, regardless of the current magnification level.

8 Double-click the zoom tool in the toolbox to return to a 100% view.

Because the zoom tool is used frequently during the editing process to enlarge and reduce the view of artwork, you can select it from the keyboard at any time without deselecting any other tool you may be using.

9 Before selecting the zoom tool from the keyboard, click any other tool in the toolbox and move it into the document window.

10 Now hold down spacebar+Ctrl (Windows) or spacebar+Command (Mac OS) to select the zoom tool from the keyboard. Click or drag to zoom in on any area of the artwork, and then release the keys. The tool you selected in the previous step is displayed.

11 To zoom out using the keyboard, hold down spacebar+Ctrl+Alt (Windows) or spacebar+Command+Option (Mac OS). Click the desired area to reduce the view of the artwork, and then release the keys.

12 Double-click the zoom tool in the toolbox to return to a 100% view of your artwork.

Scrolling through a document

You use the hand tool to scroll to different areas of a document.

1 Click the hand tool (✍) in the toolbox.

2 Drag downward in the document window. As you drag, the artwork moves with the hand.

As with the zoom tool, you can select the hand tool from the keyboard without deselecting the active tool.

3 Before selecting the hand tool from the keyboard, click any other tool in the toolbox and move the pointer into the document window.

4 Hold down the spacebar to select the hand tool from the keyboard, and then drag to bring the artwork back into view.

You can also use the hand tool as a shortcut to fit all the artwork in the window.

5 Double-click the hand tool to fit the document in the window.

Using the Navigator palette

The Navigator palette lets you scroll a document at different magnification levels without scrolling or resizing artwork in the document window.

1 Make sure that the Navigator palette is at the front of its palette group. (If necessary, click the Navigator palette tab, or choose Window > Show Navigator.)

2 In the Navigator palette, drag the slider to the right to about 200% to magnify the view of the parrots. As you drag the slider to increase the level of magnification, the red outline in the Navigator window decreases in size.

3 In the Navigator palette, position the pointer inside the red outline. The pointer becomes a hand.

Dragging slider to 200%   *200% view of image*   *View in Navigator palette*

4 Drag the hand to scroll to different parts of the artwork.

You can also drag a marquee in the Navigator palette to identify the area of the artwork you want to view.

5 With the pointer still positioned in the Navigator palette, hold down Ctrl (Windows) or Command (Mac OS), and drag a marquee over an area of the artwork. The smaller the marquee you draw, the greater the magnification level in the document window.

Using the status bar

At the bottom left edge of the Illustrator window is the status bar. The status bar can display information about any of the following topics:

• The current tool in use.

• The date and time.

• The amount of virtual memory (Windows) or free RAM memory (Mac OS) available for your open file.

• The number of undos and redos available.

• The document's color profile.

To specify the type of information you want to display in the status line, do the following:

1 Position the pointer over the triangle in the status bar, and hold down the mouse button.

2 Drag to choose the type of information you want from the pop-up menu.

Working with palettes

Palettes help you monitor and modify artwork. By default, they appear in stacked groups. To show or hide a palette as you work, choose the appropriate Window > Show or Window > Hide command. Show displays the selected palette at the front of its group; Hide conceals the entire group.

You can reorganize your work space in various ways. Try these techniques:

• To hide or display all open palettes and the toolbox, press Tab. To hide or display the palettes only, press Shift+Tab.

• To make a palette appear at the front of its group, click the palette's tab.

Click the Attributes tab to move the palette to the front.

• To move an entire palette group, drag its title bar.

• To rearrange or separate a palette group, drag a palette's tab. Dragging a palette outside of an existing group creates a new group.

Palettes are grouped.   *Drag a palette by its tab to separate the palette from its group.*

• To move a palette to another group, drag the palette's tab to that group.

• To display a palette menu, position the pointer on the triangle in the upper right corner of the palette, and hold down the mouse button.

• To change the height of a palette (except the Align, Attributes, Color, Info, Options, Pathfinder, or Transform palette), drag its lower right corner.

Click to collapse or expand palette.
A. *Windows* **B.** *Mac OS*

• To collapse a group to palette titles only, click the minimize/maximize box (Windows) or the resize box (Mac OS); click the box again to expand the palette group.

• To cycle through the available sizes for a palette, double-click a palette's tab or single-click on the double triangles to the left of the palette name. You can still access the menu of a collapsed palette.

Using context menus

In addition to the menus at the top of your screen, context-sensitive menus display commands relevant to the active tool, selection, or palette.

To display context-sensitive menus, position the pointer over the artwork or over an item in a palette list. Then click with the right mouse button (Windows) or press Ctrl and hold down the mouse button (Mac OS). (In Windows, you can also use context-sensitive Help. See "Using online Help" on page 44.)

Here we've used the pen tool. Options for the pen tool are displayed in the tool's context-sensitive menu. (You access these same options by selecting the Edit or Object menu.)

Calibrating your monitor

Whether preparing artwork for print or online use, you should begin by calibrating your monitor. This will ensure the closest possible match between your colors on-screen and those produced by a printer, a video display, or a different computer monitor, and also between your colors in Adobe Illustrator and in other software applications. If your monitor isn't calibrated, the resulting colors may not even be close to what you originally saw on it.

Creating an ICC monitor profile

Your monitor will display color more reliably if you use color management and accurate ICC profiles. The Adobe Gamma™ utility, which is automatically installed into your Control Panels folder, lets you calibrate and characterize your monitor to a standard and then save the settings as an ICC-compliant profile available to any program that uses your color management system. This calibration helps you eliminate any color cast in your monitor, make your monitor grays as neutral as possible, and standardize image display across different monitors.

Although Adobe Gamma is an effective calibration and profiling utility, hardware-based utilities are more precise. If you have a hardware-based utility that can generate an ICC-compliant profile, you should use that instead of Adobe Gamma.

Depending on your workflow scenario, an ICC monitor profile can be either a source profile, a destination profile, or both.

Note: *Adobe Gamma can characterize, but not calibrate, monitors used with Windows NT®. In addition, the ICC profile you create with Adobe Gamma can be used as the system-level profile in Windows NT. Its ability to calibrate settings in Windows 98 depends on the video card and video driver software. In such cases, some calibration options documented here may not be available.*

– From the Adobe Illustrator User Guide, Chapter 7

To calibrate your monitor with Adobe Gamma, do the following:

1 Make sure that your monitor has been turned on for at least a half hour to stabilize the monitor display.

2 Set the room lighting at the level you plan to maintain.

3 Turn off any desktop patterns and change the background color on your monitor to a neutral gray. This prevents the background color from interfering with your color perception and helps you adjust the display to a neutral gray. (For more on how to do this, refer to the manual for your operating system.)

4 Set your monitor to display thousands of colors or more.

5 Launch the Adobe Gamma utility:

• In Windows, double-click Adobe Gamma in Program Files > Common Files > Adobe > Calibration.

• In Mac OS, from the Apple® Menu, choose Control Panels > Adobe Gamma.

6 Click to reflect one of the following options:

• Step by Step (Assistant) and click Next for a version of the utility that will guide you through each step of the process. This version is recommended if you're inexperienced creating color profiles. If you choose this option, follow the instructions described in the utility.

• Control Panel and click Next for a version of the utility that is contained in a single dialog box. This version is recommended if you have experience creating color profiles.

Using online Help

For complete information about using palettes and tools, you can use online Help. Online Help includes all of the information from the *Adobe Illustrator 9.0 User Guide*, plus keyboard shortcuts and additional information, including full-color galleries of examples not included in the printed user guide. All of the illustrations in online Help are in color.

Online Help is easy to use, because you can look for topics in these ways:

• Scanning a table of contents.

• Searching for keywords or phrases.

• Using an index.

• Jumping from topic to topic using related topic links.

Displaying the online Help contents

First you'll look for a topic using the Contents screen.

To properly view online Help topics, you need Netscape Communicator 4.0 (or later) or Microsoft® Internet Explorer 4.0 (or later). You must also have JavaScript active.

1 To display the Help Contents menu, choose Help > Illustrator Help, or press F1 (Windows).

2 Drag the scroll bar or click the arrows to navigate through the contents. The contents are organized in a hierarchy of topics, much like the chapters of a book.

Illustrator Help Contents screen

3 Position the pointer on the Looking at the Work Area chapter, and click it to display its contents.

4 Locate the Toolbox Overview (1 of 5) topic, and click to display it. An illustration of the selection tools and shortcut information appears.

The online Help system is interactive. You can click any blue text, called a *link*, to jump to another topic. The pointer icon indicates links and appears when you move the mouse pointer over a link or a hotspot.

Using keywords, links, and the index

If you can't find the topic you are interested in by scanning the Contents page, then you can try searching using Search. You can search using keywords or phrases.

1 Click Search, and type **Brushes** in the text box. Click the Search button to go to that topic. A list appears of the items containing information about brushes.

2 Click Creating Brushes to learn about creating brushes. Notice that there are several subtopics available for further research.

3 Click Creating a Calligraphic Brush to read step-by-step instructions on how to create a calligraphic brush.

You can also search for a topic using the Index.

4 Click Index to go to an alphabetical listing of topics. You will see an alphabet.

5 Click the letter H to get a listing of all the topics starting with H.

6 Click the 1 or 2 next to the hand tool entry to get information about the hand tool and its functions.

Click Index for alphabet.   Click Letter for topics; then click number.

Using Adobe online services

Another way to get information on Adobe Illustrator or on related Adobe products is to use the Adobe online services.

Visiting the Adobe Web site

If you have an Internet connection and a Web browser installed on your system, you can access the U.S. Adobe Systems Web site (at http://www.adobe.com) for information on services, products, and tips pertaining to Illustrator.

1 If you have an Internet connection, from Adobe Illustrator, choose Help > Adobe Online, or click the icon at the top of the toolbox.

2 Click Refresh.

3 If a message appears asking if you want to update Adobe Online components, click Yes.

A progress bar indicates that the Adobe Online components are being updated for the Illustrator program.

4 The splash screen for Adobe Illustrator 9.0 online services appears, with buttons above the Adobe Illustrator title linking to topics on the Adobe web site.

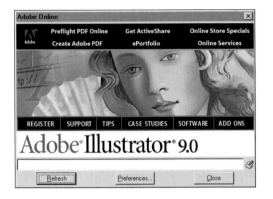

5 Click a topic button to go to the Adobe Web site. If your browser is not already running, it will launch.

You can easily find information specifically on Illustrator—including tips and techniques, galleries of artwork by Adobe designers and artists around the world, the latest product information, and troubleshooting and technical information. Or you can learn about other Adobe products and news.

6 When you have finished browsing the Adobe page, close and exit the browser.

Changing Internet settings for Illustrator

Illustrator uses the default Internet configuration settings on your computer unless you change the settings. If you want to change the Internet configuration settings for Illustrator, do the following:

1 From Illustrator, choose Help > Adobe Online or click the icon at the top of the toolbox to open the Adobe Online dialog box.

2 Click Preferences.

General preferences affect how Adobe Online interacts with all Adobe products installed on your system. Application preferences affect how Adobe Online interacts with Illustrator. To see an explanation of each preference option, click Setup and follow the prompts. You also can set up an automatic refresh using the Update Options.

Note: *You can also set Adobe Online preferences by choosing Edit > Preferences > Online Settings.*

3 When you have finished using Adobe Online, click Close to return to Illustrator.

4 Choose File > Save. Choose File > Close to close your file.

Now you're ready to begin creating and editing artwork.

Review questions

1 Describe two ways to change your view of a document.

2 How do you select tools in Illustrator?

3 Describe three ways to change the palette display.

4 Describe two ways to get more information about the Illustrator program.

Review answers

1 You can select commands from the View menu to zoom in or out of a document, or fit it to your screen; you can also use the zoom tools in the toolbox, and click or drag over a document to enlarge or reduce the view. In addition, you can use keyboard shortcuts to magnify or reduce the display of artwork. You can also use the Navigator palette to scroll artwork or change its magnification without using the document window.

2 To select a tool, you can either click the tool in the toolbox or press the tool's keyboard shortcut. For example, you can press V to select the selection tool from the keyboard. Selected tools remain active until you click a different tool.

3 You can click a palette's tab or choose Window > Show Palette Name to make the palette appear. You can drag a palette's tab to separate the palette from its group and create a new group, or drag the palette into another group. You can drag a palette group's title bar to move the entire group. Double-click a palette's tab to cycle through a palette's various sizes. You can also press Shift+Tab to hide or display all palettes.

4 Adobe Illustrator contains online Help, with all the information in the *Adobe Illustrator 9.0 User Guide*, plus keyboard shortcuts and some additional information and full-color illustrations. Illustrator also has context-sensitive help about tools and commands, and online services, including a link to the Adobe Systems Web site, for additional information on services, products, and Illustrator tips.

Lesson 2

Creating Basic Shapes

Many objects in the Adobe Illustrator program can be created by starting with basic shapes and then editing them to create new shapes. In this lesson, you will use some basic shapes to create a logo.

In this lesson, you'll learn how to do the following:

- Use tools and commands to create basic shapes.
- Copy and combine objects to create new shapes.
- Use selection tools to select and change parts of objects.
- Paint objects.
- Scale objects using the bounding box.

Getting started

Before you begin, you'll need to restore the default preferences for Adobe Illustrator and then you'll open the finished art file for this lesson to see what you'll be creating.

1 To ensure that the tools and palettes function exactly as described in this lesson, delete or deactivate (by renaming) the Adobe Illustrator 9.0 preferences file. See "Restoring default preferences" on page 3 in the Introduction.

2 Start Adobe Illustrator.

3 Choose File > Open, and open the L2end.ai file in the Lesson02 folder, located inside the Lessons folder within the AICIB folder on your hard drive.

4 If you like, choose View > Zoom Out to make the finished artwork smaller, adjust the window size, and leave it on your screen as you work. (Use the hand tool (✋) to move the artwork where you want it in the window.) If you don't want to leave the image open, choose File > Close.

⬤ For an illustration of the finished artwork in this lesson, see the color section.

Now create the start file to begin the lesson.

5 Choose File > New to open a new untitled document. Leave the Color Mode and Artboard Size at the default settings.

6 Choose File > Save As, name the file **Logo.ai**, and select the Lesson02 folder. Leave the Format option set to Adobe Illustrator® Document, and click Save. In the Illustrator Native Format Options dialog box, select Illustrator 9.0 Compatibility and click OK.

Setting up the document

You'll begin the lesson by setting the ruler units to inches, displaying a grid to use as a guideline for drawing, and closing the palettes that you won't use.

1 Close all of the palettes by clicking their close boxes or by holding down Shift and pressing Tab once. For now, you won't need to use them.

You can also hide or show the palettes individually by choosing Window > Hide Navigator, Window > Hide Color, Window > Hide Swatches, Window > Hide Layers, and Window > Hide Transform, or choosing the corresponding Show commands. (Pressing Shift+Tab switches between hiding and showing the palettes. Pressing Tab alone hides or shows the toolbox.)

2 Choose View > Show Grid to display a grid that's useful for measuring, drawing, and aligning shapes. This grid won't print with the artwork.

3 Choose View > Show Rulers to display rulers along the top and left side of the window. The ruler units by default are set to points.

You can change ruler units for all documents or for only the current document. The ruler unit of measure applies to measuring objects, moving and transforming objects, setting grid and guide spacing, and creating ellipses and rectangles. (It does not affect the units in the Character, Paragraph, and Stroke palettes. These are controlled by the options in the Units & Undo Preferences dialog box.)

4 Choose File > Document Setup to change the ruler units for only this document. In the Document Setup dialog box, for Units choose Inches, leave the other settings unchanged, and click OK.

You can also set the default ruler units for all documents by choosing Edit > Preferences > Units & Undo.

Using basic shape tools

In this lesson, you'll create a simple logo using the basic shape tools. The shape tools are organized in two groups in the toolbox, under the ellipse and rectangle tools. You can tear these groups off the toolbox to display in their own palettes.

1 Hold down the mouse button on the ellipse tool (○) until a group of tools appears, and then drag to the tear-off triangle at the end and release the mouse button.

Tearing off tool group

2 Move the ellipse tool group away from the toolbox, and then repeat step 1 to tear off the rectangle tool (□) group.

Drawing the pencil shape

In Adobe Illustrator, you control the thickness and color of lines that you draw by setting *stroke attributes*. A *stroke* is the paint characteristics of a line or the outline of an object. A *fill* is the paint characteristics of the inside of an object. The default settings will let you see the objects you draw in white with a black outline.

First you'll draw a series of rectangles and triangles that make up the pencil. You'll display Smart Guides to align your drawing.

1 Select the zoom tool (🔍) in the toolbox, and click in the middle of the window to zoom in to 150%. (Notice that 150% is displayed in the bottom left corner of the window.)

2 Choose View > Smart Guides to turn them on. Smart Guides automatically snap the edges of objects to nearby objects or their intersect points as you move them.

3 Select the rectangle tool (□), and drag it to draw a rectangle that's **3/4 inch** wide and **1 inch** tall. (Use the rulers and the grid as guides.) This will be the body of the pencil.

When you release the mouse button, the rectangle is automatically selected and its center point appears. All objects created with the shape tools have a center point that you can drag to align the object with other elements in your artwork. You can make the center point visible or invisible (using the Attributes palette), but you cannot delete it.

You'll draw another rectangle centered inside the first one to represent the two vertical lines on the pencil.

4 With the rectangle tool still selected, position the pointer over the center point of the rectangle, hold down Alt (Windows) or Option (Mac OS), and drag out from the center point to draw a rectangle that's centered inside it—release the mouse button when the rectangle is the same height as the first rectangle (1 inch).

Holding down Alt or Option as you drag the rectangle tool draws the rectangle from its center point rather than from its top left corner. Smart Guides will indicate when you've snapped to the first rectangle's edge.

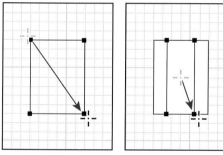

Drag to draw first rectangle.

Alt/Option-drag to draw second rectangle.

Besides dragging a tool to draw a shape, you can also click with it to open a dialog box of options. Now you'll create a rounded rectangle for the eraser by setting options in a dialog box.

5 Select the rounded rectangle tool (○), and click once in the artwork to open the Rounded Rectangle dialog box. Type **.75** in the Width text box, press Tab, and type **.75** in the Height text box. Then press Tab again, and type **.20** in the Corner Radius text box (the radius is the amount of the curve on the corners). Click OK.

💡 *To automatically enter identical Width and Height values in the Ellipse or either Rectangle dialog box, enter a Width or Height value, and then click the name of the other value to enter the same amount.*

You'll use Smart Guides to help you align the eraser to the top of the pencil body.

6 Choose View > Hide Bounding Box to hide the bounding boxes of selected objects. This will prevent you from accidentally distorting the eraser shape when you move and align it.

7 With the rounded rectangle tool still selected, hold down Ctrl (Windows) or Command (Mac OS) to select the selection tool ( ) temporarily. Select the right edge of the eraser without releasing the mouse button, and then drag the eraser to the right side of the pencil body (Smart Guides indicate the path of the right side). Release the mouse button to drop the eraser on top of the pencil body.

8 Then hold down Ctrl (Windows) or Command (Mac OS), select the bottom edge of the eraser, and drag it up to the intersect point at the top of the pencil body. Release the mouse button.

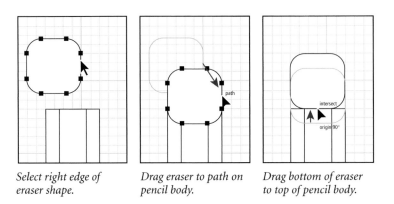

Select right edge of eraser shape. *Drag eraser to path on pencil body.* *Drag bottom of eraser to top of pencil body.*

Next you'll create two shapes to represent the metal bands connecting the eraser to the pencil.

9 To create the first band, click once in the artwork to open the Rounded Rectangle dialog box again. Type **.85** in the Width text box, **.10** in the Height text box, and **.05** in the Corner Radius text box. Click OK.

10 Click the selection tool to select the band, select the bottom left anchor point, and move the band to the top of the pencil body. Release the mouse button. (Smart Guides snap the anchor point to the top corner of the pencil body.)

11 With the band still selected, hold down Alt (Windows) or Option (Mac OS), select the anchor point again, drag straight up to make a copy, and move it above the original band. Release the mouse button. (Smart Guides snap the anchor point of the new copy to the top of the original band.)

Move first metal band between eraser and pencil body. *Alt/Option-drag a copy above first metal band.* *Smart Guides snap objects into position.*

You've been working in Preview view. This default view of a document lets you see how objects are painted (in this case, with a white fill and black stroke). If paint attributes seem distracting, you can work with just the wireframe view of an object.

Now you'll draw two triangles to represent the pencil tip and lead point using Artwork view.

12 Choose View > Outline to switch from Preview view to Outline view.

Illustrator lets you control the shape of polygons, stars, and ellipses by pressing certain keys as you draw. You'll draw a polygon and change it to a three-sided triangle.

13 Select the polygon tool (○), and position the pointer over the center point of the two rectangles. Drag to begin drawing a polygon, but don't release the mouse button. Press the Down Arrow key three times to reduce the number of sides on the polygon to a three-sided triangle, and move the mouse in an arc to rotate one side of the triangle to the top. Before you release the mouse button, hold down the spacebar and drag the triangle down to position it below the pencil body.

Drag to draw polygon; don't release mouse button.

Press Down Arrow key three times.

Drag to rotate triangle.

Hold down spacebar and move triangle.

Now you'll create the second triangle for the pencil's lead tip using the scale tool.

14 With the triangle still selected, select the scale tool (▱) in the toolbox and then Alt-click (Windows) or Option-click (Mac OS) the bottom corner point of the triangle.

Clicking the corner point of the triangle sets the reference point from which the new triangle will scale. Holding down Alt/Option as you click displays the Scale dialog box.

15 In the Scale dialog box, type **30%** in the Scale text box and click Copy. (Don't click OK.)

Click to set scaling reference point.

Set scale value.

Result

16 Choose File > Save to save your work.

Drawing the piece of stationery

You can draw the diamond-shaped piece of stationery for the logo in a couple of ways. One way is to draw four-sided polygons (using the same methods you used to draw the triangles for the pencil tip). Another way, that you'll try now, is to draw using the rectangle tool, the rotate tool, and the Transform palette.

1 Select the rectangle tool (□) in the toolbox, and position the pointer over the center point of the pencil body. Hold down Shift+Alt (Windows) or Shift+Option (Mac OS) and drag the tool to draw a rectangle of any size from the center of the pencil.

Holding down Shift as you drag the rectangle tool constrains the rectangle to a square. Holding down Alt/Option draws the rectangle from its center point rather than from the top left corner.

Now you'll use the Transform palette to enter precise dimensions for the square.

2 Choose Window > Show Transform to open the Transform palette.

3 Type **2.25** in the W (width) text box and **2.25** in the H (height) text box. Press Enter or Return to apply the changes.

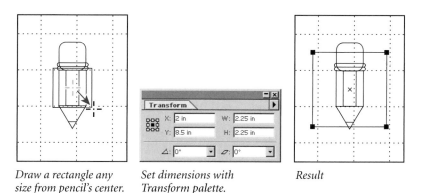

Draw a rectangle any size from pencil's center.   *Set dimensions with Transform palette.*   *Result*

Next you'll create a smaller square that's centered inside the first one.

4 With the square still selected, choose Edit > Copy to copy the square to the Clipboard. Then choose Edit > Paste in Front to paste the copy of the square directly on top of the first one.

5 In the Transform palette, type **1.5** in the W (width) text box and **1.5** in the H (height) text box. Press Enter or Return to apply the changes.

For information on using the transform tools and Transform palette in Illustrator, see Lesson 6, "Transforming Objects."

Now you'll rotate the squares to create the diamond shape.

6 Select the selection tool (▶) to automatically select the new square, and Shift-click to select the larger square.

7 Select the rotate tool (○) in the toolbox and position the pointer over the bottom right corner of the larger square. Drag the corner to the left or right until a corner is at the top. (Smart Guides help to constrain the rotation to 45°.)

Use Transform palette to set dimensions of pasted copy.   *Use rotate tool to turn selected objects 45°.*

8 With the two squares still selected, hold down Ctrl (Windows) or Command (Mac OS), and drag the top corner point of the larger square to move the squares down to just below the metal eraser bands on the pencil.

9 Choose View > Preview, and then choose Object > Arrange > Send to Back to move the squares behind the pencil.

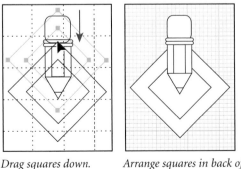

Drag squares down.   *Arrange squares in back of pencil.*

10 Click away from the artwork or choose Edit > Deselect All to deselect the artwork, and then choose File > Save to save your work.

Decorating the stationery border

You'll decorate the border of the piece of stationery with a circle, a spiral, and some star shapes, using different methods to create the shapes.

1 Click 150% in the status bar in the bottom left corner of the window, type **200**, and press Enter or Return to zoom in to a 200% view of the artwork.

2 Select the ellipse tool (○), and position the pointer in the left corner of the stationery border. Hold down Shift+Alt (Windows) or Shift+Option (Mac OS) and drag the tool to draw a small circle.

Holding down Shift as you drag the ellipse tool constrains the shape to a circle; holding down Alt/Option draws it from its center point.

3 Now select the spiral tool (⊚), and position it in the bottom left side of the stationery about midway between the two corners. Drag the tool to draw a small spiral, and then use the arrow keys to adjust its position.

Press Shift+Alt/Option   *Draw spiral.*
and drag to draw circle.

You can drag the spiral tool to draw spirals or click once to open the Spiral dialog box and specify the characteristics before drawing the spiral. Illustrator lets you specify the radius, number of segments, and percent of decay (amount that the spiral uncoils).

Drawing spirals

The spiral tool creates a spiral-shaped object of a given radius and number of winds; that is, the number of turns that the spiral completes from start to finish.

Spirals

To draw a spiral by specifying dimensions:

1. Select the spiral tool, and click where you want to place the center of the spiral.

By default, the Spiral dialog box displays the dimensions of the last spiral you drew. The unit of measure is determined by the unit of measure set in the Document Setup or Units & Undo Preferences dialog box.

2. In the Radius text box, enter the distance from the center to the outermost point in the spiral.

3. In the Decay text box, enter the amount by which each wind of the spiral should decrease relative to the previous wind.

4. Click the arrows or enter the number of segments in the Segments text box. Each full wind of the spiral consists of four segments.

5. For Style, select the counterclockwise or clockwise option to specify the direction of the spiral, and click OK.

– From the Adobe Illustrator User Guide, Chapter 3

Now you'll draw some stars using different methods.

4 Select the star tool (☆), and position the pointer in the bottom corner of the stationery. Drag the tool to draw the first star shape. By default, the star tool draws a five-pointed star.

5 With the star tool still selected, click in the bottom right side of the stationery (midway between the two corners) to create a second star. By default, the Star dialog box displays the dimensions of the last star you drew. In the Star dialog box, type **4** in the Points text box, and click OK.

6 To draw the last star, start dragging the star tool in the right corner of the stationery, but don't release the mouse button. As you drag, press the Up Arrow key to increase the number of points on the star (we created an eight-sided star), and then before releasing the mouse button, hold down the spacebar and move the star into position in the corner of the border.

Draw star.   *Press Up Arrow key to add star points.*

7 Ctrl-click (Windows) or Command-click (Mac OS) away from the artwork to deselect the star, and choose File > Save.

Tips for drawing polygons, spirals, and stars

You can control the shapes of polygons, spirals, and stars by pressing certain keys as you draw the shapes. As you drag the polygon, spiral, or star tool, choose any of the following options to control the shape:

• To add or subtract sides on a polygon, points on a star, or number of segments on a spiral, press the Up Arrow key or the Down Arrow key before releasing the mouse button. The tool remains set to the last value you specified until you reset the number.

• To rotate the shape, move the mouse in an arc.

• To keep a side or point at the top, hold down Shift.

• To keep the inner radius constant, hold down Ctrl (Windows) or Command (Mac OS).

• To move a shape as you draw it, hold down the spacebar. (This also works for rectangles and ellipses.)

Now you're ready to add a fresh coat of paint.

Painting the logo

In Adobe Illustrator, you can paint both the fill and the stroke of shapes with colors, patterns, or gradients. You can even apply various brushes to the path (or stroke) of the shapes. For this logo, you'll use a simple method to reverse the default fill and stroke of your shapes, painting the fill with black and the stroke with white.

1 Select the selection tool (⭡) in the toolbox, and then click the eraser shape to select it.

2 Click the Swap Fill and Stroke button in the toolbox.

Select eraser shape.   *Swap fill and*   *Result*
                           stroke.

The black stroke of the rounded rectangle is transposed with the rectangle's white fill.

3 Click one of the two rectangles that make up the pencil body to select it, and then Shift-click to select the other rectangle. Click the Swap Fill and Stroke button in the toolbox to swap the white fills of the pencil body with the black strokes.

4 Click the outer rectangle (not the inner rectangle) of the stationery border to select it, and then click the Swap Fill and Stroke button.

Now you'll paint the pencil's lead tip with both a black fill and a black stroke.

5 Click the small triangle that represents the lead tip to select it, and choose Window > Show Color to open the Color palette.

6 In the Color palette, make sure that the Fill box is selected (in front of the Stroke box); then click the black color box to the right of the color bar to paint the triangle's fill with black.

A. Fill box *B.* Stroke box *C.* Color bar
D. White color box *E.* Black color box

To complete the design, you'll draw a curvy line using the pencil tool.

7 Click away from the artwork to deselect it and, with the Fill box selected, click the None button in the toolbox to indicate no fill setting. Then click the Stroke box to make it active.

8 Select the pencil tool (✐) in the toolbox and draw a curvy line below the pencil's tip in the logo.

The curvy line remains selected after you draw it.

9 To adjust the path of the curvy line, drag the pencil tool along part of the selected line and then continue dragging to draw the new path.

10 If the Stroke palette isn't visible, choose Window > Show Stroke to display it, and then increase the stroke weight of the selected line to **3** points in the Weight text box. Press Enter or Return.

⊡ For information on drawing and editing shapes with the pencil tool, see "Drawing and editing freeform paths" in online Help or Chapter 3 in the Adobe Illustrator User Guide.

Copying and scaling shapes

A final step for creating logos is to scale the artwork to a 1-inch square and make sure that the resized logo still presents a clear image. You'll use the bounding box feature in Illustrator to make a scaled copy of the logo.

1 Double-click the zoom tool (🔍) to zoom out to 100%.

2 Choose View > Show Bounding Box to display the bounding boxes of selected objects.

3 Choose Edit > Preferences > General, and select the Scale Strokes & Effects option. Leave the other settings as they are, and click OK.

The Scale Strokes & Effects preference scales stroke weights and effects automatically, whether you scale objects by dragging or by using the Scale dialog box. You can also choose this command from the Transform palette menu.

4 Choose Edit > Select All to select all the objects in the logo, and then click the selection tool (▶) in the toolbox to select their bounding box.

5 Hold down Alt (Windows) or Option (Mac OS) and drag the pointer from the center of the objects to the outside of the bounding box to make a copy of the logo.

6 Position the copy of the logo below the original, and line up the left corner point on the logo with a grid line to make it easier to measure as you scale the copy.

7 Using the selection tool, select the bottom right corner point of the bounding box, hold down Shift, and drag the corner up and to the left to scale down the logo—release the mouse button when the logo is about an inch wide.

Holding down Shift as you drag the corner of the bounding box scales the objects proportionally.

Shift-drag to scale   *Result*
proportionally.

You can use various zoom options to zoom in on the smaller logo and check its clarity. Illustrator's Navigator palette is useful for moving around in the artwork at a higher magnification.

8 Choose Window > Show Navigator to open the Navigator palette, and then click the Zoom In button at the bottom of the palette several times to zoom to 600%. As you click, the artwork in the window disappears and the red box in the Navigator palette becomes smaller.

The red square shows you where objects are located in relation to the artwork in the window. You can drag the red square to move the focus, or you can click where you want the red square to go.

9 In the Navigator palette, position the pointer so the hand is pointing to the smaller logo and click to move the red square over it.

Click to zoom in.   *Click to move red view box.*

For more information on using the Navigator palette, see Lesson 1, "Getting to Know the Work Area."

10 Choose View > Hide Grid to hide the grid and clear the background of the artwork.

11 Double-click the hand tool ($\text{\small 🖐}$) to fit the artwork in the window.

12 Choose File > Save to save your artwork. Choose File > Close to close the file.

You've completed the basic shapes lesson and created the logo artwork.

For information on different ways you can add color to the logo, see Lesson 3, "Painting."

Review questions

1 What are the basic shape tools? Describe how to tear or separate a group of shape tools away from the toolbox.

2 How do you draw a square?

3 How do you draw a triangle?

4 Describe three ways to specify the size of a shape.

5 What is a quick way to transpose the color of an object's stroke with its fill color?

Review answers

1 There are six basic shape tools: ellipse, polygon, star, spiral, rectangle, and rounded rectangle. To separate a group of tools from the toolbox, hold the pointer over the tool that appears in the toolbox and press the mouse button until the group of tools appears. Without releasing the mouse button, drag to the triangle at the end of the group, and then release the mouse button to tear off the group.

2 To draw a square, select the rectangle tool (□) in the toolbox, hold down Shift and drag to draw the square, or hold down Alt (Windows) or Option (Mac OS) and click to enter equal dimensions for the width and height in the Rectangle dialog box.

3 To draw a triangle, select the polygon tool (○) in the toolbox, start dragging to draw the shape, and press the Down Arrow key to reduce the number of sides to three. Or Alt/Option-click to enter the radius and number of sides in the Polygon dialog box.

4 To specify the size of a shape, you can do any of the following:

• Select the shape and specify new dimensions in the W (width) and H (height) text boxes in the Transform palette.

• Select the shape and then select the scale tool (▱) in the toolbox. Alt/Option-click to set the point of origin and specify the dimensions in the Scale dialog box (click Copy to make a scaled copy of the selected object).

• Select the shape, and drag a side or corner handle of the shape's bounding box to resize its width, height, or both. (Shift-drag a corner handle to resize the selection proportionally.)

5 A quick way to transpose the color of an object's stroke with its fill color is to select the object and then click the Swap Fill and Stroke button in the toolbox.

Lesson 3

Painting

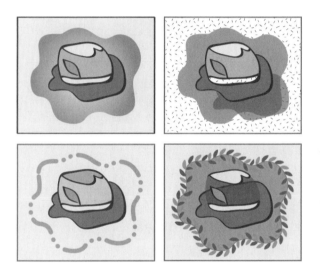

The Color and Swatches palettes let you apply, modify, and save colors in your artwork. You can paint with HSB, RGB, Web-safe RGB, or CMYK colors, grayscale, global process and spot colors, patterns, and gradients of blended colors. With the new Brushes palette, you can apply art or patterns to the path of an object.

In this lesson, you'll learn how to do the following:

- Paint with, create, and edit colors.
- Name and save colors, and build a color palette.
- Copy paint and appearance attributes from one object to another.
- Adjust the saturation of a color.
- Paint with gradients, patterns, and brushes.

Getting started

In this lesson, you'll learn about the variety of paint options in the Adobe Illustrator program as you paint an illustration of four hats. Before you begin, you'll need to restore the default preferences for Adobe Illustrator and then you'll open the finished art file for this lesson to see what you'll be creating.

1 To ensure that the tools and palettes function exactly as described in this lesson, delete or deactivate (by renaming) the Adobe Illustrator 9.0 preferences file. See "Restoring default preferences" on page 3.

2 Start Adobe Illustrator.

3 Choose File > Open, and open the L3end.ai file in the Lesson03 folder, located inside the Lessons folder within the AICIB folder on your hard drive.

4 If you like, choose View > Zoom Out to make the finished artwork smaller and leave it on your screen as you work. (Use the hand tool (✋) to move the artwork where you want it in the window.) If you don't want to leave the image open, choose File > Close.

For an illustration of the finished artwork in this lesson, see the color section.

Now open the start file to begin the lesson.

5 Choose File > Open, and open the L3start.ai file in the Lesson03 folder, located inside the Lessons folder within the AICIB folder on your hard drive.

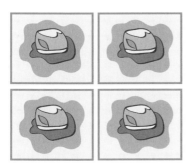

6 Choose File > Save As, name the file **Hats.ai**, and select the Lesson03 folder. Leave the Format option set to Adobe Illustrator® Document, and click Save. In the Illustrator Native Format Options dialog box, select Illustrator 9.0 Compatibility and click OK.

Filling with color

Painting objects with colors, gradients, or patterns is done using a combination of palettes and tools—including the Color palette, the Swatches palette, the Gradient palette, the Stroke palette, and the paint buttons in the toolbox, which let you select and change an object's paint and line attributes.

You'll begin by filling an object with color. Filling an object paints the area enclosed by the path.

When you reset the defaults, the Color palette and Swatches palette appear automatically on-screen when starting Adobe Illustrator.

1 Click the Swatches tab to bring the palette to the front of its group. (If the Color and Swatches palettes aren't visible, display them by choosing Window > Show Color and Window > Show Swatches.)

2 Click the close box or choose Window > Hide Layers to close the Layers palette. You won't need this palette for this lesson.

3 Choose View > Hide Bounding Box. The bounding box is useful for moving and resizing objects. You won't need this option for this lesson.

4 Select the selection tool (▸) in the toolbox, and then click the rectangular border around the top left block in the artwork to select the object.

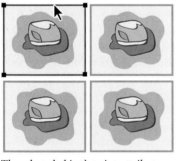

The selected object's paint attributes appear in the toolbox.

In the toolbox, notice that the Fill box appears in the foreground, indicating that it is selected. (This is the default.) The box has a fill of a warm gray color. The Color button appears depressed, indicating that it is selected. In the background behind the Fill box, the Stroke box has a turquoise outline, indicating that the rectangle is outlined in turquoise. When the Stroke box or Fill box is in the background, its color is not the current selection.

The fill and stroke attributes of the selected object also appear in the Appearance palette. Appearance attributes can be edited, deleted, saved as styles, and applied to other objects, layers, and groups. You'll use this palette later in this lesson.

The Transparency palette displays the selected object's opacity and blending mode—both of which can affect the color of your artwork. You'll change transparency and blending modes later in this chapter. For more information on the Transparency palette, see "Using the Transparency palette" in online Help or Chapter 8 in the Adobe Illustrator User Guide.

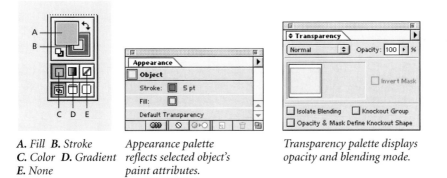

A. Fill B. Stroke
C. Color D. Gradient
E. None

Appearance palette
reflects selected object's
paint attributes.

Transparency palette displays
opacity and blending mode.

The Color palette displays the current color for the fill and stroke as well, and its CMYK sliders show the color's percentage of cyan, magenta, yellow, and black. At the bottom of the Color palette is the color bar. Now you'll use it to select a fill color of yellow.

5 In the Color palette, position the eyedropper pointer over the color bar. Hold down the mouse button and drag the eyedropper across the colors. As you drag, the color updates in the Fill boxes in the toolbox, Color palette, and Appearance palette.

A. Fill box B. Stroke box C. Out of Web Color Warning
D. None button E. Color bar
F. Black color box G. White color box

The color bar lets you quickly pick a fill or stroke color from a spectrum of colors and select colors visually. You can also choose white or black by clicking the white color box or black color box on the right end of the color bar.

6 Now click a yellow color in the color bar to select the color. You can adjust the color by dragging the CMYK sliders in the Color palette. (We selected a yellow color with these values: C = 3.53%, M = 4.31%, Y = 48.63%, and K = 0%.) The color is updated in the Fill boxes in the toolbox and the Color palette, and in the artwork.

The paint attributes you choose are applied to all new objects you create until you change the attributes again. Depending on the last paint attribute applied, either the Fill box or the Stroke box appears selected and frontmost in the toolbox.

Stroking with color

Next, you'll outline the squiggly area around the bottom left hat. Painting just the outline of an object is called *stroking*.

1 Using the selection tool ( ), click the squiggly shape around the hat in the bottom left rectangle to select it.

Select squiggly shape in bottom left rectangle.

The Fill box in the toolbox displays a pale green color. The Stroke box in the background has a red slash, indicating the squiggly shape's stroke is unpainted (a stroke of "None").

You'll start by swapping the fill color with the stroke color.

2 Click the Swap Fill and Stroke button to reverse the colors of the selected object's fill and stroke.

The Fill box now has no fill (a fill of "None") and the Stroke box has a pale green color. (The color will become apparent in the next step.) With a fill of None, you can see through to the fill underneath—in this case, the gray color of the rectangle's fill.

Now you'll change the weight of the line that you just stroked using the Stroke palette. *Stroke weight* is the thickness of a line. In the Stroke palette (beneath the Transparency palette), the line has a weight of 1 point.

3 Click the Stroke tab to bring the palette to the front of its group. Then type **7** in the Weight text box and press Enter or Return to change the stroke weight to 7 points. The squiggly line now stands out.

Next you'll use the Stroke palette's options to change the line from solid to dashed.

4 First, drag the Swatches palette by its tab to move the palette down and away from the Stroke palette.

5 In the Stroke palette, hold down the mouse button on the triangle in the upper right corner of the palette and choose Show Options from the palette menu. (You use this same technique for choosing options from other palette menus.)

You use the Stroke palette options to specify how to cap the ends, join the corners, and make lines dashed or dotted.

6 In the Stroke palette, select the Dashed Line option. The Dash and Gap text boxes become active.

To create a dashed or dotted line, you specify the length of the dash (or dot) and then the gap, or spacing, between the dashes. You can create a dashed or dotted line with as few as two values or as many as six values. The more values you enter, the more complex the pattern.

7 Type the following values in the Dash and Gap text boxes, pressing Tab to advance to the next text box: **12, 0, 12, 0, 12**. Leave the last Gap box empty. Press Enter or Return to apply the change.

Now you'll select a cap for the lines to create a dotted-line effect.

8 In the Cap options area of the Stroke palette, click the Round Cap button (the middle button). Click away from the artwork to deselect it and see the result.

Select Round Caps for   *Result*
dashed line.

[?] For examples of other effects you can create, and information on stroking lines, see "Using the Stroke palette" in online Help or Chapter 6 in the Adobe Illustrator User Guide.

You can select objects by a common paint attribute (such as their stroke color or weight) and change them all at once.

9 Select the border of one of the rectangles, and click the Stroke box in the toolbox to select the rectangle's stroke.

10 Choose Edit > Select > Same Stroke Weight to select the strokes of all the objects that have the same stroke weight in the artwork (in this case, all of the rectangles).

11 In the Stroke palette, type **2** in the Weight text box and press Enter or Return to globally change the stroke weight to 2 points.

12 Click away from the artwork to deselect it, and choose File > Save.

Building a custom palette

Now you'll learn how to create your own custom palettes by mixing colors, naming them, and saving them in the Swatches palette.

Mixing your own color

You'll start to create a custom palette by mixing a color using the CMYK sliders in the Color palette. First you'll mix a fill color.

1 In the toolbox, click the Fill box to make it active.

2 Using the selection tool ( ), click the middle of the hat in the bottom left rectangle to select it.

*Select middle of hat in bottom
left rectangle.*

In the Color palette, notice that the hat color is grayscale—that is, a percentage of black—and only a K (black) slider shows a value. The color bar changes to display a scale ramp from white to black.

Now you'll change the color model to CMYK so that you can mix colors.

3 In the Color palette, choose CMYK from the palette menu.

The Color palette lets you edit and mix colors—either colors that you create or colors that you have selected from the Swatches palette, from an object, or from a color library. In this case, you're choosing colors using the CMYK color model.

Now you'll select an orange color for the middle of the hat.

4 In the Color palette, drag the CMYK sliders to select a light orange color or type values in the % text boxes and press Enter or Return to apply the changes. (We specified 0% cyan, 25% magenta, 54% yellow, and 0% black.)

You can use the different color models in conjunction with the Color palette sliders to select a color precisely by its different color values. However, if you mix color models (such as CMYK and RGB) in the same file, Illustrator will convert the colors to whatever mode the file is saved in.

For information on the color models that Illustrator uses, see "Color Modes and Models" in online Help or Chapter 6 in the Adobe Illustrator User Guide.

5 Click away from the artwork to deselect it, and choose File > Save.

Saving colors

The Swatches palette stores the colors, gradients, and patterns that have been preloaded into Adobe Illustrator, as well as those you have created and saved for reuse. New colors added to the Swatches palette are saved with the current file. Opening a new artwork file displays the default set of swatches that comes with the Adobe Illustrator program.

You'll add the light orange color you just mixed to the Swatches palette so it will be stored with this artwork file. You can select a color to add from either the Fill or Stroke boxes in the toolbox, or from the Color palette. Even though you deselected the artwork, the light orange color is still the current color in the Fill box in the toolbox and in the Color palette.

1 Drag the orange color from the Fill box and drop it in the Swatches palette. It appears in the first empty spot in the palette.

As you drag a color into the Swatches palette, an outline appears around the palette, indicating that it is active and that you are about to drop the color.

Now you'll add another color to the Swatches palette.

2 Using the selection tool (▲), select the top left rectangle that you painted with a yellow fill.

3 Make sure that the Fill box is selected in the toolbox, and then click the New Swatch button at the bottom of the Swatches palette to store the color.

You can make your own custom set of swatches for the file by deleting swatches from the Swatches palette that you don't use.

4 Click away from the artwork to deselect it, and then click the black swatch (C=0, M=0, Y=0, K=100) in the Swatches palette to select it. Click the Delete Swatch button at the bottom of the Swatches palette, and then click Yes in the warning dialog box to delete the swatch.

If you want to add a color back into the Swatches palette, you can drag the color directly from the Color palette or from the Fill or Stroke boxes in the toolbox. You can also restore the default set of colors to your artwork.

5 Choose Window > Swatch Libraries > Default_CMYK to retrieve the default set of swatches for CMYK files. (These swatches may look different from the swatches in your Swatches palette.)

6 In the Default palette, select the black color swatch you deleted in step 4, and then choose Add to Swatches from the palette menu to copy the selected swatch back to your customized Swatches palette. The color appears as the last color in the bottom row of the Swatches palette.

You can add swatches from any color library palette to the Swatches palette.

7 Click the close box of the Default palette to close it, and choose File > Save.

Naming a color

You can name colors and refer to that name as you paint. All colors—whether process colors or spot colors—can be named while still retaining all of the characteristics of the color mode (for example, RGB, Web Safe RGB, HSB, or Grayscale modes).

1 Double-click the yellow swatch you saved in the Swatches palette, or select it and choose Swatch Options from the Swatches palette menu.

2 In the Swatch Options dialog box, name the color (for example, "background-yellow") and click OK.

The Swatches palette lets you name, store, and select three types of colors: individual and global process colors (these include grayscale and CMYK, RGB, Web Safe RGB, and HSB color models), and global spot colors. Spot colors are special premixed colors used instead of, or in addition to, process color inks; they require their own separations and their own plates on press.

Working with process colors, spot colors, and registration color

It is important to understand the different types of color used in Adobe Illustrator—global process color, non-global process color, spot color, and registration color—because the color type determines how colors are updated throughout the document, and how they are separated and printed.

Process colors are the four inks used in traditional color separations: cyan, magenta, yellow, and black. In Illustrator, all five color models that are used in a CMYK file—that is, CMYK, RGB, Web Safe RGB, HSB, and Grayscale—will result in process colors. Avoid using process colors in documents intended for online viewing only, because CMYK has a smaller color gamut than a typical monitor.

Global process colors are process colors that automatically update throughout the document when the swatch is edited; that is, every object containing such a color changes when the corresponding swatch is modified.

Non-global process colors also can be assigned any of the five color models (CMYK, RGB, Web Safe RGB, HSB, and Grayscale), but do not automatically update throughout the document when the color is edited. Process colors are non-global by default; a non-global process color can be changed to a global process color using the Swatch Options dialog box.

Spot colors are special premixed colors that are used instead of, or in addition to, CMYK inks, and that require their own separations and their own plates on a printing press. When a spot color swatch is edited, the color is updated globally throughout the document.

You can assign any of the five color models to a spot color. Spot colors may or may not fall within the CMYK gamut; for example, a spot color may be a neon or metallic ink that is not within the CMYK gamut, or it may be a shade of green that falls within the gamut.

Registration colors are applied to objects that you want to print on all plates in the printing process, including any spot color plates. Registration colors are typically used for crop marks and trim marks.

For an illustration of global and non-global process colors, see figure 3-1 in the color section.

Now you'll change the display of the Swatches palette so that you can locate the color by its name.

3 Choose Name View from the Swatches palette menu to display the swatches by name and see the swatch you just named.

You can change how swatches are displayed in the palette—as large or small swatches, or by name. When you display swatches by name, the Swatches palette also displays icons indicating the color model and color type (individual process color, global process color, or global spot color).

Copying paint attributes

Adobe Illustrator lets you copy paint attributes of objects (such as their fill and stroke color) in various ways and apply the attributes to other objects.

You'll use the eyedropper tool to copy colors from your artwork into the Color palette. Also called *sampling*, copying colors lets you replicate paint attributes even when you don't know their exact values.

1 Select the eyedropper tool (🖊) in the toolbox.

2 In the bottom left rectangle, click the orange brim of the hat to sample its color. This action picks up the fill and stroke attributes of the hat brim and displays them in the Color palette.

By default, the eyedropper tool affects all paint attributes of an object. However, you can restrict which attributes are affected (by double-clicking the eyedropper tool and selecting options in the dialog box).

3 To quickly apply the current paint attributes to the top of the hat, hold down Alt (Windows) or Option (Mac OS) to temporarily select the paint bucket tool (🖐), and then click inside the top of the hat to apply the paint.

Select attributes with   *Apply with paint bucket.*
eyedropper.

Copying appearance attributes

Adobe Illustrator lets you copy appearance attributes that include both the fill and the stroke of an object as well as its transparency and effects.

You'll create a drop shadow shape and change its transparency. Then you'll apply the shadow's appearance to another shape using the Appearance palette. You can save and name appearance attributes using the Styles palette.

1 Select the selection tool (▶) in the toolbox, and click the hat brim in the upper right rectangle.

2 Hold down Alt (Windows) or Option (Mac OS) and drag the brim slightly down and to the right. Release the mouse button to leave a copy of the hat brim. This copy will become a drop shadow.

3 Choose Object > Arrange > Send Backward to move the shadow shape underneath the hat brim. You should still be able to see both the shadow shape and the hat brim.

4 With the object still selected, use the Color palette to change its stroke to None.

5 Change the fill to a medium brown. (We specified 49% cyan, 65% magenta, 100% yellow, and 0% black.)

Move a copy of the brim and paint it brown.

6 Click the Transparency tab to bring the palette to the front of its group. Then choose Show Options from the palette menu to expand the palette.

7 With the shadow shape still selected, in the Transparency palette type **50** in the Opacity percentage box or use the slider, and press Return or Enter to change the opacity of the shape to 50%.

Change shadow's transparency to 50%.

8 In the Appearance palette, click the Object thumbnail to select it. Drag the Object thumbnail from the Appearance palette until the pointer is over the bottom right hat side. Release the mouse button to apply the appearance to the hat side. Notice that the hat side is now a transparent brown.

Drag Object thumbnail onto the hat side of bottom right hat.

Release mouse button to apply appearance.

9 Click away from the artwork to deselect it, and choose File > Save.

For more information on using the Appearance and Style palettes, see Lesson 9, "Using Appearance Attributes, Styles, and Effects," or see that topic in online Help or Chapter 10 of the Adobe Illustrator User Guide.

Saturating colors

Next, you'll adjust the saturation of the new color you added to the hat's top by changing the percentage of black in the color.

1 Using the selection tool ( ), click the top of the hat in the bottom left rectangle to select it. Make sure that the Fill box in the toolbox is selected.

Select top of hat.

Shift-drag left to desaturate magenta mix.

2 In the Color palette, hold down Shift and drag the M slider to the left to desaturate the color. Notice that as you Shift-drag, the sliders move in tandem, and the intensity of the color changes. Adjusting the saturation lets you change the strength of a color without affecting the hue. (However, if you drag a slider that is set to 0%, you will change the hue or color rather than the saturation.)

3 Click away from the artwork, and choose File > Save.

Painting with patterns and gradients

In addition to process and spot colors, the Swatches palette can contain pattern and gradient swatches. Adobe Illustrator provides sample swatches of each type in the default palette and lets you create your own patterns and gradients.

To learn how to create your own gradients, see Lesson 8, "Blending Shapes and Colors."

[?] For information on how to create patterns, see "Creating and working with patterns" in online Help or Chapter 8 in the Adobe Illustrator User Guide.

Now you'll fill some objects with a pattern, working with the hat in the top right rectangle.

1 Using the selection tool ( ), click in the center of the inner shape of the hat ribbon in the top right rectangle. The Fill box in the toolbox shows that the shape's current fill is gray.

*Select inner shape of hat ribbon
in top right rectangle.*

The buttons at the bottom of the Swatches palette let you display swatches grouped as solid colors, gradients, or patterns.

2 In the Swatches palette, click the Show Pattern Swatches button (the fourth button from the left). All of the pattern swatches appear.

A. Show All Swatches *B.* Show Color
Swatches *C.* Show Gradient
Swatches *D.* Show Pattern Swatches
E. New Swatch *F.* Delete Swatch

3 Click a pattern in the palette to select it, and fill the hat ribbon. (We selected the Confetti pattern.)

4 Now select the background of the top right rectangle. Make sure that the Fill box is selected, and paint the rectangle's fill with the same pattern.

Fill hat ribbon with a pattern.   *Select background of top right rectangle.*   *Fill background with same pattern.*

Now you'll apply a gradient to the first block in the illustration.

5 In the top left rectangle, select the squiggly line around the hat, and make sure that the Fill box is selected in the toolbox.

6 In the Swatches palette, click the Show Gradient Swatches button (third button from the left) to show only gradient swatches in the palette.

7 Click a gradient to apply it to the fill of the squiggly shape. (We selected the Yellow & Orange Radial gradient.)

Painting with a Pattern brush

Brushes can be applied to existing paths or objects. There are four types of brushes in the Brushes palette: Calligraphic, Scatter, Art, and Pattern. For information on how to create your own custom brushes, see Lesson 5, "Working with Brushes."

Now you'll paint the stroke of a shape with a Pattern brush.

1 Use the selection tool ( ) to select the squiggly shape around the hat in the bottom right rectangle.

2 Choose Window > Show Brushes or click the Brushes tab behind the Swatches palette to display the Brushes palette.

3 Choose View By Name from the Brushes palette menu, and scroll down to see the Pattern brushes. Click a name to select a brush, and apply it to the squiggly shape around the hat. (We selected the Laurel Pattern brush.)

The type of brush (Calligraphic, Scatter, Art, or Pattern) is indicated by an icon to the right of the brush name.

Select the squiggly shape in bottom right rectangle.

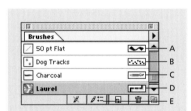

A. Calligraphic B. Scatter C. Art D. Pattern E. Options of Selected Object

Apply a Pattern brush.

You can change the size and other characteristics of the pattern after it is applied to the selected object.

4 With the squiggly shape still selected, in the Brushes palette click the Options of Selected Object button (second button from the left) at the bottom of the palette.

5 In the Stroke Options (Pattern Brush) dialog box, select the Preview option to view different settings applied to the artwork without closing the dialog box.

6 Try out different settings to see how they affect the pattern on the squiggly shape, pressing Tab to move between the options. (We entered 75% in the Scale text box.) When you're satisfied with the settings, click OK to apply them to the artwork.

7 Choose File > Save.

8 Close the file.

You've completed painting the hat artwork using a variety of painting tools.

See these topics to learn more on the following painting techniques:

• For how to paint objects with colors that blend in multiple directions, see Lesson 11, "Creating Airbrush Effects."

• For how to create other blending effects, see Lesson 8, "Blending Shapes and Colors."

• For more on transparency, styles, appearance attributes, and effects, see Lesson 9, "Using Appearance Attributes, Styles, and Effects".

Review questions

1 Describe three ways to fill an object with color.

2 How can you save a color?

3 How do you name a color?

4 How do you restore the original set of colors in the Swatches palette?

5 How do you paint a shape with a transparent color?

6 How can you desaturate a color?

7 What is a quick way to view all the pattern swatches in the Swatches palette?

8 What are the four types of brushes that you can paint the fill or stroke of objects with?

Review answers

1 To fill an object with color, select it and select the Fill box in the toolbox. Then do one of the following:

• Click a color in the color bar in the Color palette.

• Drag the color sliders or type in values in the % text boxes in the Color palette.

• Click a color swatch in the Swatches palette.

• Select the eyedropper tool (🖊), and click a color in the artwork.

• Drag and drop an appearance thumbnail onto a shape in the artwork.

• Choose Window > Swatch Libraries to open another color library, and click a color swatch in the color library palette.

2 You can save a color for painting other objects in your artwork by adding it to the Swatches palette. Select the color, and do one of the following:

• Drag it from the Fill box and drop it over the Swatches palette.

• Click the New Swatch button in the bottom of the Swatches palette.

• Choose New Swatch from the Swatches palette menu.

You can also add colors from other color libraries by selecting them in the color library palette and choosing Add to Swatches from the palette menu.

3 To name a color, double-click the color swatch in the Swatches palette or select it and choose Swatch Options from the palette menu. Type the name for the color in the Swatch Options dialog box.

4 To restore the original set of colors in the Swatches palette, choose Window > Swatch Libraries > Default. This palette contains all of the original swatches that appear by default before you customize the Swatches palette.

5 To paint a shape with a transparent color, select the shape and fill it with any color. Then adjust the opacity percentage in the Transparency palette to less than 100%.

6 To desaturate a color, select the color and Shift-drag a slider to the left in the Color palette. Shift-dragging the slider causes the other sliders to move in tandem so the hue won't change.

7 A quick way to view all the pattern swatches in the Swatches palette is to click the Show Pattern Swatches button at the bottom of the palette.

8 The four types of brushes are Calligraphic, Scatter, Art, and Pattern.

Lesson 4

Drawing with the Pen Tool

The pen tool is a powerful tool for drawing straight lines, Bézier curves, and complex shapes. Although the pencil tool is easier for drawing and editing lines, the pen tool can be more precise. You'll practice drawing with the pen tool by creating an illustration of a pear.

In this lesson, you'll learn how to do the following:

• Draw straight lines.

• End path segments and split lines.

• Draw curved lines.

• Select curve segments and adjust them.

• Draw different types of curves, smooth and pointed.

• Edit curves, changing from smooth to pointed and vice versa.

Getting started

In this lesson, you'll create an illustration of a pear pierced by an arrow. Before you begin, you'll need to restore the default preferences for Adobe Illustrator and then you'll open the finished art file for this lesson to see what you'll be creating.

1 To ensure that the tools and palettes function exactly as described in this lesson, delete or deactivate (by renaming) the Adobe Illustrator 9.0 preferences file. See "Restoring default preferences" on page 3.

2 Start Adobe Illustrator.

3 Choose File > Open, and open the L4end.ai file in the Lesson04 folder, located inside the Lessons folder within the AICIB folder on your hard drive.

4 Choose View > Zoom Out to make the finished artwork smaller and leave it on your screen as you work. (Use the hand tool (✋) to move the artwork where you want it in the window.) If you don't want to leave the image open, choose File > Close.

🔵 For an illustration of the finished artwork in this lesson, see the color section.

Now open the start file to begin the lesson.

5 Choose File > Open, and open the L4start.ai file in the Lesson04 folder, located inside the Lessons folder within the AICIB folder on your hard drive.

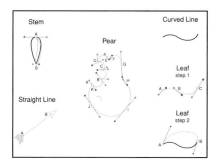

6 Choose File > Save As, name the file **Pear.ai**, and select the Lesson04 folder. Leave the Format option set to Adobe Illustrator® Document, and click Save. In the Illustrator Native Format Options dialog box, select Illustrator 9.0 Compatibility and click OK.

7 Hold down Shift and press Tab once to hide all of the palettes. (Pressing Shift+Tab toggles between hiding and displaying the palettes. Pressing Tab alone hides or shows the toolbox as well.)

Drawing straight lines

You draw straight lines by using the pen tool to create a starting anchor point and an ending anchor point. You can create straight lines that are vertical, horizontal, or diagonal by holding down Shift as you click with the pen tool. This is called *constraining* the line.

We've created a template layer in this file so you can practice using the pen tool by tracing over the template. (See Lesson 10, "Working with Layers," for information on creating layers.)

You'll begin by drawing the straight line for the arrow.

1 Choose View > Straight Line to zoom into the left corner of the template.

Separate views that show different areas of the template at a higher magnification were created for this document and added to the View menu.

To create a custom view, choose View > New View. For information, see "Viewing artwork" in online Help or Chapter 1 in the Adobe Illustrator User Guide.

2 Choose View > Hide Bounding Box to hide the bounding boxes of selected objects. Select the pen tool () in the toolbox, and move the pointer to the dashed line in the artwork. Notice that the pen tool pointer has a small x next to it. This indicates that clicking will begin a new path.

3 Click point A at the left end of the line to create the starting anchor point—a small solid square.

4 Click point B at the right end of the line to create the ending anchor point.

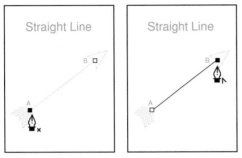

Click once to begin a straight line.   *Click again to end it.*

When you click a second time, a caret (^) appears next to the pen tool. The caret indicates that you can split the anchor point to create a direction line for a curve by dragging the pen tool from this anchor point. The caret disappears when you move the pen tool away from the anchor point.

You must end the path before you can draw other lines that aren't connected to the path.

5 End the path using one of the following methods:

• Hold down Ctrl (Windows) or Command (Mac OS) to activate the current selection tool, and click away from the path to deselect it.

• Choose Edit > Deselect All.

• Click the pen tool in the toolbox.

Now you'll make the straight line thicker by changing its stroke weight.

6 Select the selection tool (▶) in the toolbox, and click the straight line to select it.

7 Choose Window > Show Stroke to display the Stroke palette.

8 In the Stroke palette, type **3** points in the Weight text box and press Enter or Return to apply the change.

Splitting a path

To continue creating the arrow for this illustration, you'll split the path of the straight line using the scissors tool and adjust the segments.

1 With the straight line still selected, select the scissors tool (✁) in the toolbox and click in the middle of the line to make a cut.

Cuts made with the scissors tool must be on a line or a curve rather than on an endpoint.

Where you click, you see a new selected anchor point. The scissors tool actually creates two anchor points each time you click, but because they are on top of each other, you can see only one.

2 Select the direct-selection tool (▹) in the toolbox, and position it over the cut. The small hollow square on the pointer indicates that it's over the anchor point. Select the new anchor point, and drag it up to widen the gap between the two split segments.

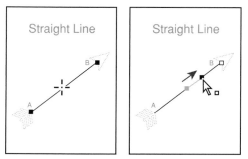

Click with the scissors   Drag to separate the
tool to cut the line.   new line segments.

Adding arrowheads

Adobe Illustrator lets you add premade arrowheads and tails to open paths by applying a Stylize filter. Now you'll add an arrowhead to the ending point of one line segment and a tail to the starting point of the other line segment.

1 With the top line segment selected, choose Filter > Stylize > Add Arrowheads.

Note: Choose the top Filter > Stylize command. The second Filter > Stylize command applies painted or impressionistic effects to bitmap images.

2 In the Add Arrowheads dialog box, leave the Start section set to None. For the end, click an arrow button to select the number 2 style of arrowhead (a thumbnail preview appears in the dialog box), and click OK.

Illustrator adds the arrowhead to the end of the line (the last anchor point created on the uncut line).

3 Using the direct-selection tool ( ), select the bottom line segment, and choose Filter > Add Arrowheads to open the dialog box again. Select the number 18 style of arrowhead from the Start section, select None for the End section, and click OK to add a tail to the starting point of the line.

You can reapply the same arrowhead style to other selected objects by choosing Filter > Apply Add Arrowhead.

4 Choose Edit > Deselect All to deselect the artwork, and then choose File > Save.

Drawing curves

In this part of the lesson, you'll learn how to draw smooth curved lines with the pen tool. In vector drawing programs such as Adobe Illustrator, you draw a curve, called a Bézier curve, by setting anchor points and dragging to define the shape of the curve. Although drawing curves this way takes some getting used to, it gives you the most control and flexibility in computer graphics.

You'll draw the pear, its stem, and a leaf. You'll examine a single curve and then draw a series of curves together, using the template guidelines to help you.

Selecting a curve

1 Choose View > Curved Line to display a view of a curved line on the template.

2 Using the direct-selection tool (⬉), click one of the segments of the curved line to view its anchor points and its direction lines, which extend from the points. The direct-selection tool lets you select and edit individual segments in the curved line.

A. *Anchor point* **B.** *Direction line*
C. *Direction point (or handle)*

As their names imply, the anchor points anchor the curved segments, and the direction lines control the direction of the curves. You can drag the direction lines or their endpoints, called *direction points* or *handles*, to adjust the shape of the curve.

Anchor points, direction points, and direction lines are aids to help you draw. They always appear in the current layer color—in this case, red. Anchor points are square, and, when selected, appear filled; unselected, they appear unfilled, like hollow squares. Direction points are round. These lines and points do not print with the artwork.

By selecting the curve, you also select the paint attributes of the curve so that the next line you draw will have the same attributes. For more on paint attributes, see Lesson 3, "Painting."

Drawing the leaf

Now you'll draw the first curve of the leaf.

1 Choose View > Leaf or scroll down to see the guides for Leaf step 1.

Instead of dragging the pen tool to draw a curve, you drag it to set the starting point and the *direction* of the line's curve. When you release the mouse button, the starting point is created and two direction lines are formed. Then you drag the pen tool to end the first curve and to set the starting point and direction of the next curve on the line.

2 Select the pen tool () and position it over point A on the template. Press the mouse button and drag from point A to the red dot. Then release the mouse button.

Next you'll set the second anchor point and its direction lines.

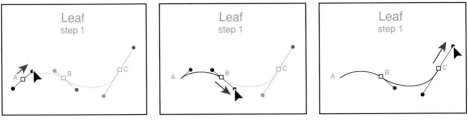

Drag to start the line and set
direction of first curve.

Drag to end first curve and set
direction of second curve.

Drag to end second curve and
adjust its direction.

3 Press the mouse button and drag from point B to the next red dot. Then release the mouse button. Illustrator connects the two anchor points with a curve that follows the direction lines you have created. Notice that if you vary the angle of dragging, you change the amount of curve.

If you make a mistake as you draw, you can undo your work by choosing Edit > Undo. Adobe Illustrator by default lets you undo a series of actions—limited only by your computer's memory—by repeatedly choosing Edit > Undo. (To set the minimum number of undoes, choose Edit > Preferences > Units & Undo.)

4 To complete the curved line, drag the pen tool from point C on the template to the last red dot and release the mouse button.

5 Ctrl-click (Windows) or Command-click (Mac OS) away from the line to indicate the end of the path. (You must indicate when you have finished drawing a path. You can also do this by clicking the pen tool in the toolbox, or by choosing Edit > Deselect All.)

Drawing different kinds of curves

Now you'll finish drawing the leaf by adding to an existing curved segment. Even if you end a path, you can return to the curve and add to it later. The Alt key (Windows) or Option key (Mac OS) lets you control the type of curve you draw.

1 Scroll down to the instructions on the template for Leaf step 2.

You'll add a *corner point* to the path. A corner point lets you change the direction of the curve. A *smooth point* lets you draw a continuous curve.

2 Position the pen tool over the end of the line at point A. The slash next to the pen tool indicates that you'll continue the path of the line rather than start a new line.

3 Hold down Alt (Windows) or Option (Mac OS) and notice that the status bar in the lower left corner of the window displays "Convert Anchor Point." Now Alt/Option-drag the pen tool from anchor point A to the red dot. Then release the mouse button.

A slash indicates pen tool is aligned with anchor.

Alt/Option-dragging creates corner point.

So far, all of the curves you have drawn have been open paths. Now you'll draw a closed path, in which the final anchor point is drawn on the first anchor point of the path. (Examples of closed paths include ovals and rectangles.) You'll close the path using a smooth point.

4 Position the pointer over anchor point B on the template. A small open circle appears next to the pen tool indicating that clicking will close the path. Press the mouse button and drag from this point to the second red dot.

Notice the direction lines where you close the path. The direction lines on both sides of a smooth point are aligned along the same angle.

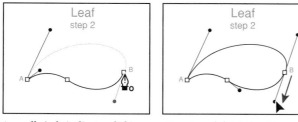

A small circle indicates clicking with pen tool closes the path.

Drag to red dot to lengthen curved line.

5 Ctrl-click (Windows) or Command-click (Mac OS) away from the line, and choose File > Save.

Changing a smooth curve to a corner and vice versa

Now you'll create the stem by adjusting a curved path. You'll convert a smooth point on the curve to a corner point and a corner point to a smooth point.

1 Choose View > Stem to display a magnified view of the stem.

2 Select the direct-selection tool ( ) in the toolbox, position the pointer over point A at the top of the curve to display a hollow square on the pointer, and then click the anchor point to select it and display its red direction lines for the smooth point.

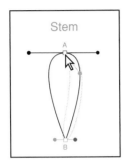

3 Select the convert-anchor-point tool ( ) from the same group as the pen tool in the toolbox.

(When the pen tool is the current tool, a shortcut to get the convert-anchor-point tool is to press Alt (Windows) or Option (Mac OS).)

4 Using the convert-anchor-point tool, select the left direction point (on top of the red dot) on the direction line and drag it to the gold dot on the template, and then release the mouse button.

Dragging with the convert-anchor-point tool converts the smooth anchor point to a corner point and adjusts the angle of the left direction line.

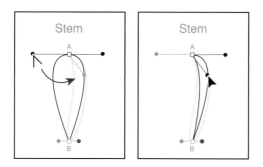

5 Using the convert-anchor-point tool, select the bottom anchor point and drag from point B to the red dot to convert the corner point to a smooth point, rounding out the curve, and then release the mouse button.

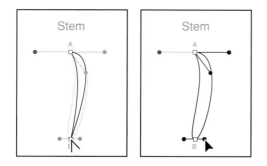

Two direction lines emerge from the anchor point, indicating that it is now a smooth point.

When using the convert-anchor-point tool, keep these guidelines in mind:

• Drag from the curve's anchor point for a smooth point and continuous curve.

• Click the curve's anchor point or drag a handle (direction point) of the curve for a corner point on a discontinuous curve.

6 Choose File > Save.

Drawing the pear shape

Now you'll draw a single, continuous object that contains smooth points and corner points. Each time you want to change the direction of a curve at a point, you'll hold down Alt (Windows) or Option (Mac OS) to create a corner point.

1 Choose View > Pear to display a magnified view of the pear.

First you'll draw the bite marks on the pear by creating corner points and changing the direction of the curve segments.

2 Select the pen tool ( ) from the same group as the convert-anchor-point tool ( ). Drag the pen tool from point A on the template to the red dot to set the starting anchor point and direction of the first curve. Release the mouse button.

3 Drag the pen tool from point B to the red dot—but don't release the mouse button— and hold down Alt (Windows) or Option (Mac OS) and drag the direction handle from the red dot to the gold dot. Release the mouse button.

4 Continue drawing to points C and D by first dragging from the anchor point to the red dot and then Alt/Option-dragging the direction handle from the red dot to the gold dot.

At the corner points B, C, and D, you first drag to continue the current segment, and then Alt/Option-drag to set the direction of the next curved segment.

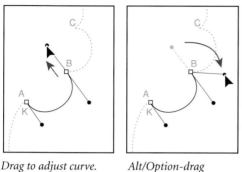

Drag to adjust curve.   *Alt/Option-drag direction point to set corner point.*

Next, you'll complete drawing the pear by creating smooth points.

5 Drag from each of the points E through J to their red dots, and then click anchor point K to close the pear shape. Notice that when you hold the pointer over anchor point K, a small open circle appears next to the pen, indicating that the path will close when you click.

6 Hold down Ctrl (Windows) or Command (Mac OS) and click away from the path to deselect it, and choose File > Save.

Editing curves

To adjust the curves you've drawn, you can drag the curve's anchor points or its direction lines. You can also edit a curve by moving the line.

1 Select the direct-selection tool ( ), and click the outline of the pear.

Clicking with the direct-selection tool displays the curve's direction lines and lets you adjust the shape of individual curved segments. Clicking with the selection tool selects the entire path.

  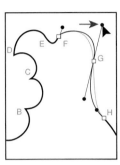

Use direct-selection tool   Select anchor point.   Adjust anchor point.
to select individual
segments.

2 Click the anchor point G at the top right of the pear to select it, and adjust the segment by dragging the top direction handle as shown in the illustration.

3 Now select the pen tool ( ) and drag to draw the small curve on the pear where the arrow will pierce it. (Use the dashed line on the template as a guide.)

4 Choose File > Save.

Tips for drawing curves

Keep the following guidelines in mind to help you draw any kind of curve quickly and easily:

• *Always drag the first direction point in the direction of the bump of the curve, and drag the second direction point in the opposite direction to create a single curve. Dragging both direction points in the same direction creates an S curve.*

• *When drawing a series of continuous curves, draw one curve at a time, placing anchor points at the beginning and end of each curve, not at the tip of the curve. Use as few anchor points as possible, placing them as far apart as possible.*

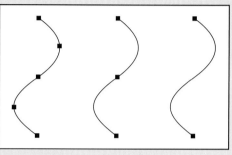

Drag in the opposite direction to create a smooth curve.   *Drag in the same direction to create an S curve.*   *Less to more efficient curves*

 For information on adding, deleting, and moving anchor points on a path, see "Drawing" in online Help or Chapter 3 in the Adobe Illustrator User Guide.

Finishing the pear illustration

To complete the illustration, you'll assemble the objects together, paint them, and position parts of the arrow to create the illusion of the pear being pierced.

Assembling the parts

1 Double-click the zoom tool ( ) to zoom to 100%.

2 Choose Window > Show Layers to display the Layers palette.

3 In the Layers palette, click the template icon ( ) that's next to the Template layer name to hide the template.

4 Select the selection tool ( ) in the toolbox, and Shift-click to select the two single curved lines that you no longer need for the leaf. Press Backspace (Windows) or Delete (Mac OS) to delete them.

Select and delete extra lines.

Now you'll make the leaf and stem smaller and rotate them slightly using the Transform commands.

5 Select the stem and choose Object > Transform > Scale. Enter **50%** in the Scale text box, select the Scale Strokes & Effects option, and click OK.

The Scale Strokes & Effects option scales stroke weights and effects automatically. You can also set this option as a preference (choose Edit > General > Preferences).

6 Choose Object > Transform > Rotate. Enter **45** degrees in the Angle text box, and click OK.

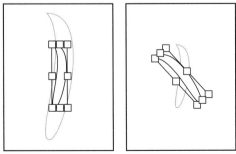

Scale stem 50%.   *Rotate stem 45°.*

Now you'll repeat the scaling and rotation on the leaf.

7 Select the leaf and choose Object > Transform > Scale. Leave the settings as they are, and click OK to scale the leaf by 50%. Then choose Object > Transform > Rotate, and enter **15** degrees in the Angle text box, and click OK.

You can also scale and rotate objects using the scale and rotate tools or the free transform tool to do both. For information, see Lesson 6, "Transforming Objects."

8 Move the stem and the leaf to the top of the pear.

9 Move the parts of the arrow over the pear to make it look as if the arrow is entering the front of the pear and exiting the back.

Objects are arranged in the order in which they are created, with the most recent in front.

10 Select the bottom part of the arrow, and choose Object > Arrange > Bring to Front to arrange it in front of the pear.

Painting the artwork

Now paint the objects as you like. We removed the stroke on the leaf, the stem, and the pear; and we painted the fills with custom-made gradients called Pear leaf, Pear stem, and Pear body, which are provided in the Swatches palette. We painted the arrow with a dark blue color, and then we added some detail lines to the leaf, the stem, and the round part of the pear using the paintbrush tool and the pen tool.

1 Choose Window > Show Swatches to display the Swatches palette.

2 Select an object, and then select a swatch in the Swatches palette to paint the object with a color, pattern, or gradient.

To learn how to create your own gradients, see Lesson 8, "Blending Shapes and Colors." To learn more about painting options in Illustrator, see Lesson 3, "Painting," and Lesson 11, "Creating Airbrush Effects."

3 In the Color palette, drag the None icon up and drop it on the Stroke box to remove the stroke of a selected object and still leave the Fill box selected.

4 Choose File > Save to save your work. Choose File > Close to close the file.

You've completed the lesson on drawing straight lines and curves. For additional practice with the pen tool, try tracing over images with it. As you practice more with the pen tool, you'll become more adept at drawing the kinds of curves and shapes you want.

Exploring on your own

Now that you've used the pen tool to draw precise Bézier curves on the pear, try drawing the pear using the pencil tool to create a hand-drawn look. You can edit lines that you draw using the pencil tool to change their shape, and you can use the smooth tool and erase tool to edit the drawing further.

1 Open the L4start.ai file again, and save it as Pear2.ai.

2 Select the pencil tool (✐) in the toolbox, and draw the pear in one continuous line without releasing the mouse button. To close the path, hold down Alt (Windows) or Option (Mac OS)—a small circle appears on the pointer—and continue dragging to draw the end of the line connected to the starting point.

Anchor points are set down as you draw with the pencil tool, and you can adjust them once the path is complete. The number of anchor points is determined by the length and complexity of the path and by the tolerance values set in the Pencil Tool Preferences dialog box. (Double-click the tool to display its preferences dialog box.)

Note: You can draw and edit brushed paths with the paintbrush tool by using the same methods as for paths drawn with the pencil tool. (See Lesson 5, "Working with Brushes.")

3 Use the pencil tool (✐) to edit the shape of the pear by redrawing segments on the path.

To change a path with the pencil tool:

1. If the path you want to change is not selected, select it with the selection tool (➤). Or Ctrl-click (Windows) or Command-click (Mac OS) the path to select it.

2. Position the pencil tool on or near the path to redraw, and drag the tool until the path is the desired shape.

   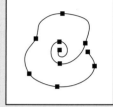

Using the pencil tool to edit a closed shape   *Using the pencil tool to create an open shape*

Depending on where you begin to redraw the path and in which direction you drag, you may get unexpected results. For example, you may unintentionally change a closed path to an open path, change an open path to a closed path, or lose a portion of a shape.

– From the Adobe Illustrator User Guide, Chapter 3

4 Use the smooth tool (✐) to round out the shape of a curved segment (deleting anchor points if necessary).

The number of anchor points is determined by the length and complexity of the new path and by the tolerance values set in the Smooth Tool Preferences dialog box.

Smoothing the path with the smooth tool

The smooth tool lets you smooth out an existing stroke or section of a path. The smooth tool retains the original shape of the path as much as possible.

Stroke before and after using the smooth tool

To use the smooth tool:

1. If the path to smooth is not selected, select it with the selection tool ( ). Or Ctrl-click (Windows) or Command-click (Mac OS) the path to select it.

2. Do one of the following:

• Select the smooth tool ( ).

• When the pencil or paintbrush tool is selected, hold down Alt (Windows) or Option (Mac OS) to change the pencil to the smooth tool.

3. Drag the tool along the length of the path segment you want to smooth out. The modified stroke or path may have fewer anchor points than the original.

4. Continue smoothing until the stroke or path is the desired smoothness.

5 Use the erase tool () to erase segments on the path of the pear, and then redraw them using the pencil tool ( ).

Erasing the path with the erase tool

The erase tool lets you remove a portion of an existing path or stroke. You can use the erase tool on paths (including brushed paths), but not on text or meshes.

Strokes before and after using the erase tool

To use the erase tool:

1. Select the erase tool ( ).

2. Drag the tool along the length of the path segment you want to erase (not across the path). For best results, use a single, smooth, dragging motion.

Anchor points are added to the ends of the new paths.

Review questions

1 Describe how to draw straight vertical, horizontal, or diagonal lines using the pen tool.

2 How do you draw a curved line using the pen tool?

3 How do you draw a corner point on a curved line?

4 How do you change a smooth point on a curve to a corner point?

5 What tool do you use to edit a segment on a curved line?

Review answers

1 To draw a straight line, you click twice with the pen tool—the first click sets the starting anchor point, and the second click sets the ending anchor point of the line. To constrain the straight line vertically, horizontally, or along a 45° diagonal, hold down Shift as you click with the pen tool.

2 To draw a curved line using the pen tool, you hold down the mouse button and drag to create the starting anchor point and set the direction of the curve, and then you click to end the curve.

3 To draw a corner point on a curved line, hold down Alt (Windows) or Option (Mac OS) and drag the direction handle on the end point of the curve to change the direction of the path, and then continue dragging to draw the next curved segment on the path.

4 Use the direct-selection tool (↕) to select the anchor point, and then use the convert-anchor-point tool (⌐) to drag a direction handle to change the direction.

5 To edit a segment on a curved line, select the direct-selection tool (↕) and drag the segment to move it, or drag a direction handle on an anchor point to adjust the length and shape of the segment.

Lesson 5

Working with Brushes

Adobe Illustrator offers four brush types —Calligraphic, Scatter, Art, and Pattern brushes—to create art along paths. You can use the paintbrush tool or the drawing tools to apply brushes to artwork. Use the brushes provided, or create new ones from artwork you make in Illustrator.

In this lesson, you'll learn how to do the following:

• Draw with each of the four brush types, using the paintbrush tool.

• Change brush color and adjust brush settings before and after applying brushes to artwork.

• Create new brushes from Adobe Illustrator artwork.

• Apply brushes to paths created with drawing tools.

Applying brushes to paths

Illustrator brushes let you apply artwork to paths to decorate paths with patterns, figures, textures, or angled strokes. You can choose from four brush types—Art, Calligraphic, Pattern, and Scatter. You'll learn about each of the brush types in this lesson. You can modify the brushes provided with Illustrator, and you can create your own brushes. Brushes appear in the Brushes palette.

You apply brushes to paths using the paintbrush tool or the drawing tools. To apply brushes using the paintbrush tool, you choose a brush from the Brushes palette and draw in the artwork. The brush is applied directly to the paths as you draw. To apply brushes using a drawing tool, you draw in the artwork, select a path in the artwork, and then choose a brush in the Brushes palette. The brush is applied to the selected path.

You can change the color, size, and other features of a brush. You can also edit paths after brushes are applied.

Getting started

In this lesson, you'll learn to use the four brush types in the Brushes palette, including how to change brush options and how to create your own brushes. Before you begin, you'll need to restore the default preferences for Adobe Illustrator. Then you'll open the finished art file for this lesson to see what you'll create.

1 To ensure that the tools and palettes function exactly as described in this lesson, delete or deactivate (by renaming) the Adobe Illustrator 9.0 preferences file. See "Restoring default preferences" on page 3.

2 Start Adobe Illustrator.

3 Choose File > Open, and open the L5end.ai file in the Lesson05 folder, located inside the Lessons folder in the AICIB folder on your hard drive.

4 If you like, choose View > Zoom Out to make the finished artwork smaller, adjust the window size, and leave it on your screen as you work. (Use the hand tool (🖐) to move the artwork where you want it in the window.) If you don't want to leave the image open, choose File > Close.

⬤ For an illustration of the finished artwork in this lesson, see the color section.

To begin working, you'll open an existing art file set up with guides to draw the artwork.

5 Choose File > Open to open the L5start.ai file in the Lesson05 folder inside the AICIB folder on your hard drive.

6 Choose File > Save As, name the file **Brushes.ai**, and select the Lesson05 folder. Leave the Format option set to Adobe Illustrator® Document, and click Save. In the Illustrator Native Format Options dialog box, select Illustrator 9.0 Compatibility and click OK.

Using Art brushes

Art brushes stretch artwork evenly along a path. Art brushes include strokes resembling various graphic media, such as the Charcoal and Marker brushes. Art brushes also include images, such as the Arrow brush, and text, such as the Type brush, which paints the characters *A-R-T* along a path. In this section, you'll use the Charcoal brush to draw the trunk and limbs of a tree.

The start file has been created with *guides* that you can use to create and align your artwork for the lesson. Guides are paths that have been converted using the View > Make Guides command. The guides are locked and cannot be selected, moved, modified, or printed (unless they are unlocked).

For more information on guides, see "Using guides and grids" in online Help or Chapter 4 in the Adobe Illustrator User Guide.

Drawing with the paintbrush tool

Now you'll use the paintbrush tool to apply a brush to the artwork.

1 In the toolbox, click the paintbrush tool ( ) to select it.

You select a brush in the Brushes palette to be applied to the artwork.

2 Click the Brushes tab to bring the Brushes palette to the front. (If the palette isn't visible on-screen, choose Window > Show Brushes.)

A. Displays Brushes palette menu
B. Remove Brush Stroke
C. Options of Selected Object
D. New Brush   E. Delete Brush

Brushes are arranged according to brush type, in the following order: Calligraphic, Scatter, Art, and Pattern.

By default, brushes appear as icons. You can also view brushes by name. When viewed by name, a small icon to the right of the brush name indicates the brush type.

3 In the Brushes palette, position the mouse button over the triangle in the top right corner of the Brushes palette, press the mouse button to display the palette menu, and choose View By Name.

You can choose which types of brushes are displayed in the Brushes palette to reduce the palette size and make it easier to find the brushes you want to use.

4 Choose Show Calligraphic Brushes, Show Scatter Brushes, and Show Pattern Brushes from the palette menu to deselect those options, leaving only Art brushes visible in the palette. A check mark next to the brush type in the Brushes palette menu indicates that the brush type is visible in the palette.

Showing and hiding brush types

5 Select the Charcoal art brush in the Brushes palette.

Brushes are applied to paths like stroke color. If you have a fill color selected when you apply a brush to a path, the path will be stroked with the brush and filled with the fill color. Use a fill of None when applying brushes to prevent the brushed paths from being filled. Later in this lesson you'll use a fill color with a brush. For more information on stroke and fill color, see Lesson 3, "Painting."

6 In the toolbox, click the Fill box and click the None box.

7 Draw a long, upward stroke to create the left side of the tree trunk, tracing over the guides as you draw. Don't worry if your stroke doesn't follow the guide exactly. You'll remove the guides at the end of the lesson, so they won't show through the finished artwork.

8 Draw a second upward stroke to create the right side of the tree trunk, using the guide to place your drawing.

Draw with the paintbrush tool.

Last path drawn remains selected.

Notice that each path remains selected after you draw it, until you draw another path. In the next section, you'll use the paintbrush tool to edit the path on the right side of the tree trunk.

9 Choose File > Save to save your work.

Editing paths with the paintbrush tool

As you saw in the previous section of this lesson, when you draw with the paintbrush tool the last path you draw remains selected by default. This feature makes it easy to edit paths as you draw. If you draw over the selected path with the paintbrush tool, the portion of the selected path that you drew over is edited. You can disable or set a tolerance for path editing in the Paintbrush Tool Preferences dialog box.

Now you'll use the paintbrush tool to edit the selected path.

1 Place the paintbrush tool ( ) near the top of the selected path (the right side of the tree trunk) and draw upward.

The selected path is edited from the point where you began drawing over it. The new path is added to the selected path (instead of becoming a separate path).

Draw over selected path to edit it.   *Selected path is edited.*

Sometimes when using the paintbrush tool you may want paths to remain unselected as you draw, so that you can draw over paths without altering them and create layered or overlapping strokes. You can change the paintbrush tool preferences so that paths remain unselected as you draw.

2 In the toolbox, double-click the paintbrush tool to display the Paintbrush Tool Preferences dialog box. You use this dialog box to change the way the paintbrush tool functions.

You'll turn off the Keep selected option, which is on by default.

3 Click the Keep Selected option to deselect it. Then click OK.

Now you'll draw the limbs of the tree.

4 Draw shorter strokes to create the limbs of the tree.

With the Keep Selected option turned off, paths remain unselected. You can draw overlapping paths without altering the earlier paths.

If you use the paintbrush tool with the Keep Selected option turned off, you can still edit a path with the paintbrush tool by selecting the path and then redrawing the path with the paintbrush tool. Use the selection tool to select an entire path. Use the direct-selection tool to select a segment or a point on the path, for greater control in the editing process.

5 Press Ctrl (Windows) or Command (Mac OS) to toggle to the selection tool ( ), and select a branch in the artwork that you want to redraw.

Pressing Ctrl/Command temporarily selects the selection tool (or the direct-selection or group-selection tool, whichever was used last) when another tool is selected.

Draw with the   *Path remains unselected.*   *Select path to edit it.*
paintbrush tool.

6 Use the paintbrush tool to draw over the selected path.

Use the selection tool to select paths to be edited with the paintbrush tool when you have the Keep Selected option turned off.

In addition to editing paths with the paintbrush tool, you can also use the smooth tool and the erase tool (located behind the pencil tool in the toolbox) to redraw or remove portions of a path drawn with the paintbrush tool. For information on using the smooth and erase tools, see "Exploring on your own" on page 118 in Lesson 4, "Drawing with the Pen Tool."

After you apply a brush to an object, it's easy to apply another brush to the paths to change the appearance of the object.

7 Select the selection tool ( ) and drag a marquee to select the tree trunk and branches.

8 In the Brushes palette, click the Marker brush. The new brush is applied to the selected paths in the artwork.

Charcoal strokes selected   *Selecting Marker brush*   *Marker brush applied*

9 Click outside the artwork to deselect it and view the tree without selection highlights.

10 Drag a selection marquee to select the tree again.

11 Click several other brushes in the Brushes palette to see the effects of those brushes in the artwork. When you have finished, click the Charcoal brush again to reapply that brush.

12 Click outside the artwork to deselect it.

13 Choose File > Save to save your work.

As you complete the rest of this lesson, use the methods you learned in this section to edit paths as you draw with the paintbrush tool. You can turn on the brushes, editing paths with the Keep Selected option if you want strokes to remain selected as you draw, or use the selection tool to select strokes to be edited.

Using Scatter brushes

Scatter brushes scatter an object, such as a leaf, a ladybug, or a strawberry, along a path. In this section, you'll use the Fall Leaf Scatter brush to create leaves on the tree. You'll start by adjusting options for the brush to change the appearance of the brush in the artwork.

Changing brush options

You adjust the settings of a brush in the Brush Options dialog box to change the appearance of the brush. You can adjust different settings for each brush type—Art, Calligraphic, Pattern, and Scatter—either before or after brushes have been applied to artwork. The changes you make appear when you apply the brush to artwork, but do not appear in the brush icon in the Brushes palette.

Now you'll open the Brush Options dialog box for the Fall Leaf Scatter brush and change the size and other features of the brush.

1 In the Brushes palette, choose Show Scatter Brushes from the palette menu to select that option. Then choose Show Art Brushes to deselect that option.

2 Double-click the Fall Leaf brush to open the Scatter Brush Options dialog box.

You'll adjust the Size, Spacing, Scatter, and Rotation options for the brush. These options can be set to Fixed or Random values. For Fixed options, you enter a single value. For Random options, you enter a range of values. (If you have a pressure-sensitive drawing tablet attached to your computer, you can set options to Pressure to determine values with the pressure of the stylus.) The options are as follows:

• The Size option indicates the size of the object in the brush, from 10% to 1000%, relative to the default size (indicated by 100%).

• The Spacing option indicates the distance between brush objects on a path relative to 100% (objects touching but not overlapping).

• The Scatter option indicates the deviation of objects to either side of the path, where 0% equals alignment on the path.

• The Rotation option indicates the orientation of the object in the brush, from −180° to 180° relative to either the page or the path.

3 For Size, Spacing, Scatter, and Rotation, choose Random or Fixed, then drag the sliders or enter values. We used the following values:

• For Size, Random values, 40% and 60%.

- For Spacing, Random values, 10% and 30%.

- For Scatter, Random values, −40% and 40%.

- For Rotation, Random values, −180° and 180°, relative to Page.

Select Fall Leaf brush.   *Set brush options.*

4 Click OK.

In addition to the features you adjusted in this section, you can also change the color of a brush. You'll change the color of the Fall Leaf brush and another brush later in this lesson.

Applying a scatter brush to paths

Now you'll use the Fall Leaf brush with its adjusted settings to draw leaves on the tree in the artwork. You'll start by selecting the tree and locking it. Locking an object prevents it from being altered while you work on other objects in the artwork.

1 Use the selection tool ( ) to drag a marquee around all parts of the tree to select them.

2 Choose Object > Lock.

The selection highlights and bounding box around the tree disappear, and the tree is locked.

3 Select the Fall Leaf scatter brush.

4 Use the paintbrush tool (✐) to draw strokes with the Fall Leaf brush above the tree branches, using the guides to help place your paths. Remember that if you want to edit paths as you draw, you can use the Keep Selected option for the paintbrush tool or select paths with the selection tool.

Drawing with paintbrush tool   *Fall Leaf brush applied to artwork*

5 Choose File > Save.

Changing the color attributes of brushes

You'll change the color of the Fall Leaf brush in the artwork.

Before you change the color of a brush, it's helpful to understand how Illustrator applies color to brushes. To change the color of Art, Pattern, and Scatter brushes, you use one of three *colorization methods,* models for applying color to the artwork in a brush. To change the color of Calligraphic brushes, you simply select the brush and choose a stroke color. (See Lesson 3, "Painting," for information on choosing a stroke color.) You can change the color attributes of a brush before and after you apply the brush to artwork.

For an illustration of brush colorization methods, see figure 5-1 in the color section.

To colorize Art, Pattern, and Scatter brushes, you choose from three colorization methods—Tints, Tints and Shades, and Hue Shift:

• Tints applies a single hue (the stroke color) to the brush, with the hue equal to black in the original brush, and white added to the hue for lighter colors—similar to creating a grayscale version of the brush, with the stroke color used in place of black. If the original brush contains no black, the colorized brush contains only tints of the hue, no fully saturated areas.

• Tints and Shades applies a single hue (the stroke color) to the brush, with the hue equal to 50% black in the original brush, and black or white added to the hue for darker or lighter colors. As with Tints, this method is similar to creating a grayscale version of the brush, except that the stroke color replaces the mid-range color (instead of replacing black) in the original brush. Tints and Shades creates a wider range of contrast than Tints.

• Hue Shift shifts a selected color in the brush to the current stroke color, and shifts all other colors in the brush correspondingly around the color wheel, to preserve the relationships between the original brush colors. For example, if the original brush is blue and orange (complementary colors) and you select the blue color and shift it to red, the orange color will shift correspondingly to green (red's complement). (If the original brush has only one color, the Hue Shift colorized brush also will contain only one color.)

You choose a colorization method in the Brush Options dialog box. Many brushes are set to a colorization method of None by default; for these brushes you must choose a colorization method before you can change the brush color. Some brushes are set to the Tints, Tints and Shades, or Hue Shift colorization method by default; for these brushes the current stroke color is applied automatically to the brush when you use it in the artwork. (To find a brush's default colorization setting, double-click the brush in the Brushes palette to view the Brush Options dialog box, and then check the setting in the Method pop-up menu in the Colorization section.)

Note: Brushes colorized with a stroke color of white may appear entirely white. Brushes colorized with a stroke color of black may appear entirely black. Results depend on the original brush colors.

Changing the brush color using Hue Shift colorization

Now you'll change the color of the Fall Leaf brush using the Hue Shift colorization method.

1 Select the selection tool ( ), and drag a selection marquee to select the Fall Leaf strokes in the artwork.

2 Click the Color palette tab to bring the palette to the front. (If the Color palette isn't visible on-screen, choose Window > Show Color.)

3 Select the Stroke box in the Color palette. Then click in the color bar to select a color for the Fall Leaf brush. (We chose a lavender color.)

4 In the Brushes palette, double-click the Fall Leaf brush to view the Brush Options dialog box for the brush.

5 In the Colorization section in the dialog box, choose Hue Shift from the Method pop-up menu.

The Key Color swatch in the Colorization section indicates the brush color that will shift to the new stroke color. The Key Color box displays the default key color unless you select another key color. For the Fall Leaf brush, the default key color is the leaf's red color.

To select a different key color to be shifted in a brush, you click the Key Color eyedropper, and then position the eyedropper on the desired color in the dialog box's brush example, and click. The new key color shifts to the stroke color when you use the brush in the artwork (and other colors in the brush will shift correspondingly). Selecting a new key color is useful if a brush contains several colors and you want to try out shifting different colors in the brush. For this lesson, you'll use the default key color.

6 Click Preview to preview the Hue Shift colorization.

The selected Fall Leaf strokes are colorized with the current stroke color (the color you selected in step 3). This color will appear when you apply the Hue Shift colorization method.

When you apply a brush to artwork, Illustrator uses the current stroke color for the brush. However, that color appears only if a colorization method is selected for the brush. For example, when you applied the Fall Leaf brush, the current stroke was black. But the brush appeared with its default colorization, not black, because the brush colorization method was set to None. Selecting brush strokes and choosing a new stroke color applies that new color to the brush. For more information on using stroke color, see Lesson 3, "Painting."

7 Click OK. An alert box appears, letting you apply your changes to the brush settings to the strokes in the artwork, or leave the existing strokes unchanged and change only subsequent brush strokes.

8 In the alert box, click Apply To Strokes to apply the colorization change to the strokes in the artwork.

Once you select a colorization method for a brush, the new stroke color applies to selected brush strokes and to new paths painted with the brush.

9 In the Color palette, click the color bar in several different places to try other stroke colors for the selected brush strokes.

10 When you are satisfied with the color of the Fall Leaf brush strokes, click away from the artwork to deselect it.

11 Choose File > Save.

Changing the brush color using Tints colorization

Now you'll apply a new color to the Marker brush in the Art Brushes section of the Brushes palette, and use the brush to draw blades of grass in the artwork.

You'll begin by selecting the brush in the Brushes palette.

1 In the Brushes palette menu, choose Show Art Brushes. Then choose Show Scatter brushes to hide those brushes.

You'll display the Brush Options dialog box for the Marker brush to see the default colorization settings for the brush.

2 In the Brushes palette, double-click the Marker brush.

3 In the Art Brush Options dialog box, note that the Marker brush is set to the Tints colorization method.

This method is the default because the brush's original color is black. The Tints method replaces black with the stroke color. The Tints and Shades and Hue Shift colorization methods do not work with black brushes; both methods replace the original black color with black, leaving the brush unchanged.

While the Art Brush Options dialog box is open, you'll also change the size of the brush so that the brush appears in the appropriate scale when you draw with it in the artwork.

4 In the Size section of the dialog box, enter **50%** for Width.

Marker brush selected   Marker brush with default Tints colorization method

5 Click OK to accept the settings and close the dialog box.

Now you'll select a color for the grass, and draw the grass with the Marker brush.

6 In the Color palette, click in the color bar to select a color for the grass. (We chose a bright green.)

7 Use the paintbrush tool ( ) to draw short, upward strokes around the base of the tree. Use the guides to place your drawing. The Marker brush uses the stroke color you selected in step 6.

Because the Marker brush is all one color, the Tints colorization applies the new stroke color as one color (rather than varied tints of the color). When the original brush contains several colors, the Tints colorization method applies a different tint for each color in the brush.

8 Press Ctrl (Windows) or Command (Mac OS) and click outside the artwork to deselect it.

9 Choose File > Save.

Using a fill color with brushes

When you apply a brush to an object's stroke, you can also apply a fill color to paint the interior of the object with a color. When you use a fill color with a brush, the brush objects appear on top of the fill color in places where the fill and the brush objects overlap.

Choose fill color. *Draw with paintbrush.* *Brush objects appear on top of fill.*

Now you'll use the paintbrush tool to draw a canoe at the edge of the grass with an Art brush applied to the canoe's stroke, and you'll fill the canoe with a color.

1 In the Brushes palette, select the Tapered Stroke brush.

Like the Marker brush you used earlier in this lesson, the Tapered Stroke brush uses the Tints colorization method by default. To change the color of the Tapered Stroke brush, you'll simply select a stroke color.

2 In the Color palette, make sure that the Stroke box is selected. Then click in the color bar to select a color for the edges of the canoe. (We chose a dark orange.)

Now you'll use the paintbrush tool to draw the edges of the canoe. Use the guides to align your drawing.

3 Use the paintbrush tool ( ) to draw a crescent shape to make the side and bottom of the canoe:

• Draw a long stroke from left to right to make the side edge of the canoe. Do not release the mouse button.

• While still holding down the mouse button, draw a second long stroke beneath the first, from right to left, connecting the two strokes at the right endpoint of the object, to make a crescent shape. When you have drawn the second stroke, release the mouse button.

You may have to draw the crescent shape more than once to create a shape with a single path. Remember that you can edit paths as you draw. Use the direct-selection tool to select a segment of the path that you want to redraw.

Don't worry if your drawing doesn't match the guides exactly. What's important is drawing the shape as one path, without releasing the mouse button, so that you can fill the object correctly. (If a shape is made of separate paths, the fill color is applied to each path separately, yielding unexpected results.)

4 Draw a third long stroke for the top side of the canoe. Then draw two shorter strokes for the crossbars. (Draw the top side and crossbars as separate paths, releasing the mouse button after each one.)

Draw crescent as one path.   *Add top.*   *Add crossbars.*

Now you'll fill the side of the canoe with a color.

5 Select the selection tool ( ), and select the crescent shape you drew for the lower side and bottom of the canoe.

6 In the Color palette, select the Fill box. Then click in the color bar to select a fill color for the canoe. (We chose a yellowish orange.)

Selected shape is filled.

7 Click outside the artwork to deselect it.

8 Choose File > Save.

Using Calligraphic brushes

Calligraphic brushes resemble strokes drawn with the angled point of a calligraphic pen. Calligraphic brushes are defined by an elliptical shape whose center follows the path. Use these brushes to create the appearance of hand-drawn strokes made with a flat, angled pen tip.

You'll use a Calligraphic pen to draw water in front of the canoe. You'll begin by selecting the brush, and then choose a color for the brush.

1 In the Brushes palette, choose Show Calligraphic Brushes from the palette menu to select that option. Then choose Show Art Brushes from the menu to deselect that option.

2 In the Brushes palette, select the 12 pt Oval brush.

3 In the Color palette, click the Stroke box. Then click in the color bar to select a new color for the water. (We chose a light blue.)

Calligraphic brushes use the current stroke color when you apply the brushes to artwork. You do not use colorization methods with Calligraphic brushes.

4 In the Color palette, click the Fill box and then click the None box.

Use a fill of None with brushes to prevent paths from being filled when you apply the brush.

5 Select the paintbrush tool (✐), and draw wavy lines for the water surface.

The paths you draw use the stroke color you selected in step 3.

Now you'll change the shape of the 12 pt Oval brush in the Brush Options dialog box to change the appearance of the strokes made with the brush.

6 In the Brushes palette, double-click the 12 pt Oval brush to display the Calligraphic Brush Options dialog box.

You can change the angle of the brush (relative to a horizontal line), the roundness (from a flat line to a full circle), and the diameter (from 0 to 1296 points) to change the shape that defines the brush's "tip," and change the appearance of the stroke that the brush makes. Now you'll change the diameter of the brush.

7 In the dialog box, select Preview to preview the changes you'll make.

8 Enter **8 pt** for Diameter. In the Name text box, enter **8 pt Oval**. Notice that the weight of the Calligraphic brush strokes in the artwork decreases.

9 Click OK. In the alert box, click Apply To Strokes to apply the change to the strokes in the artwork.

12 pt Oval brush   Selecting 8 pt Oval brush   Result

10 Press Ctrl (Windows) or Command (Mac OS) and click outside the artwork to deselect it.

11 Choose File > Save.

Using Pattern brushes

Pattern brushes paint a pattern made up of separate sections, or *tiles*, for the sides (middle sections), ends, and corners of the path. When you apply a Pattern brush to artwork, the brush applies different tiles from the pattern to different sections of the path, depending on where the section falls on the path (at an end, in the middle, or at a corner). You'll use the Rope Pattern brush to draw a rope from the canoe to the tree, with different tiles used for the rope's middle and end sections.

1 In the Brushes palette, choose Show Pattern Brushes from the palette menu to select that option. Then choose Show Calligraphic Brushes from the menu to deselect that option.

2 Double-click the Rope brush to display the Pattern Brush Options dialog box for the brush.

The Brush Options dialog box displays the tiles in the Rope brush. The first tile on the left is the Side tile, used to paint the middle sections of a path. The second tile on the right is the Start tile, used to paint the beginning section of a path. The last tile on the right is the End tile, used to paint the end of a path.

Pattern brushes can have up to five tiles—the Side, Start, and End tiles, plus an Outer Corner tile and an Inner Corner tile to paint sharp corners on a path. The Rope brush has no corner tiles because the brush is designed for curved paths, not sharp corners (just as a real rope creates loops or coils, not sharp angles). In the next section of this lesson, you'll create a Pattern brush that uses corner tiles.

Now you'll change the scale of the Pattern brush so that the brush is in scale with the rest of the artwork when you apply it.

3 In the Pattern Brush Options dialog box, enter **20%** in the Scale text box, and click OK.

Rope brush   *Rope brush with Side, Start, and End tiles scaled 20%*

4 Select the paintbrush tool (✏), and draw a path that loops around the base of the tree. Then draw a second path that leads from the loop around the tree to the canoe.

Draw the rope as two separate paths, rather than one path, to avoid creating a path with a sharp angle. (Because the Rope brush does not include corner tiles, the brush uses Side tiles to paint sharp angles. The Side tiles appear to sever at sharp corners, and the rope appears to be cut.)

Apply Rope brush as two separate paths.

Now you'll select a blade of grass you created earlier in the lesson and move it in front of the rope to make the rope appear to lie behind the grass.

5 Select the selection tool ( ), and then select a grass blade lying along the path of the rope. (Be careful not to select the rope along with the grass.)

If you like, you can Shift-click to select additional grass blades along the path of the rope.

6 Choose Object > Arrange > Bring to Front.

Selecting grass blade   *Bring grass to front.*

7 Choose File > Save.

Tips for using brushes

When you work with brushes, keep the following points in mind:

• *You can often use Scatter brushes and Pattern brushes to achieve the same effect. However, one way in which they differ is that Pattern brushes follow the path exactly, whereas Scatter brushes do not.*

• *If you apply a brush to a closed path and want to control the placement of the end of the path, select the scissors tool and split the path. To change again, select the endpoints, choose Object > Path > Join, and use the scissors again.*

• *To select all brushstroke paths in the current artwork, choose Edit > Select > Brush Strokes.*

• *For better performance when creating a brush from art that contains multiple overlapping paths filled with the same color and with no stroke, select the paths and click the Unite button in the Pathfinder palette before you create the brush.*

– From the Adobe Illustrator User Guide, Chapter 3

Creating brushes

You can create new brushes of all four brush types, using artwork in an Illustrator file as the basis for the brush. In this section, you'll use artwork provided with the lesson to create a new Pattern brush with three tiles—a cloud for the Side tile, and a sun for the Outer Corner tile and Inner Corner tile.

Creating swatches for a Pattern brush

You create Pattern brushes by first creating swatches in the Swatches palette with the artwork that will be used for the Pattern brush tiles. In this section, you'll use the cloud and sun drawings included with the artwork file to create swatches.

1 Use the scroll bars, the hand tool, or the Navigator palette to display the scratch area to the right of the artboard to view the cloud and sun drawings located there.

For information on moving to different areas of the document window, see Lesson 1, "Getting to Know the Work Area."

The cloud and sun were created using the Marker brush. (You can use any drawing tool to create artwork for new brushes.) Each piece was then expanded using the Object > Expand Appearance command. If you used a brush to create art for the swatch, you must first expand the art before you can create a swatch in the Swatches palette.

You'll unlock the sun and cloud artwork, and then use the artwork to create swatches. The objects were locked to prevent them from being altered while you completed the earlier sections of the lesson.

2 Choose Object > Unlock All.

Bounding boxes and selection highlights appear around the sun and cloud, indicating that the objects are unlocked and selected. The tree, which you locked earlier in the lesson, is also unlocked and selected. (The tree can be unlocked, because you've finished drawing in the area of the tree.)

3 Click outside the artwork to deselect the objects.

4 Click the Swatches palette tab to view the Swatches palette. (If the palette isn't visible on-screen, choose Window > Show Swatches.)

Now you'll create a pattern swatch.

5 Select the selection tool (▶), and drag the cloud onto the Swatches palette. The new swatch appears in the pattern swatches group.

Select cloud.　　　　*Drag it onto Swatches palette.*　　*Cloud swatch is added to palette.*

6 Click away from the artwork to deselect the cloud.

7 In the Swatches palette, double-click the cloud swatch. Double-clicking the cloud swatch changes the current fill or stroke box to that swatch.

8 Name the swatch **Cloud**, and then click OK.

Now you'll repeat steps 5 through 8 to create a pattern swatch of the sun art.

9 Use the selection tool to drag the sun onto the Swatches palette. The new swatch appears in the pattern swatches group.

10 Click away from the artwork to deselect the sun.

11 In the Swatches palette, double-click the sun swatch.

12 Name the swatch **Sun**, and then click OK.

❓ For more information on creating pattern swatches, see "Creating and working with patterns" in online Help or Chapter 8 in the Adobe Illustrator User Guide.

Creating a Pattern brush from swatches

To create a new Pattern brush, you apply swatches from the Swatches palette to tiles in the Brush Options dialog box. Now you'll apply the Cloud and Sun swatches to tiles for a new Pattern brush.

First you'll open a Brush Options dialog box for a new Pattern brush.

1 Click the Brushes palette tab to view the palette.

2 In the Brushes palette, click the New Brush button.

3 Select New Pattern Brush and click OK.

Create new brush.   *Select brush type.*

You'll apply the Cloud swatch to the Side tile for the new Pattern brush.

4 In the Pattern Brush Options dialog box, select the Side tile box (the far left tile box).

5 In the pattern swatches scroll list, select the Cloud swatch. The Cloud swatch appears in the Side tile box.

Next you'll apply the Sun swatch to the Outer Corner tile and Inner Corner tile for the new Pattern brush.

6 In the Pattern Brush Options dialog box, select the Outer Corner tile box (the second tile box from the left). In the pattern swatches scroll list, select the Sun swatch. The Sun swatch appears in the Outer Corner tile box.

7 In the Brush Options dialog box, select the Inner Corner tile box (the middle tile box). In the pattern swatches scroll list, select the Sun swatch. The Sun swatch appears in the Inner Corner tile box.

You won't create a Start tile or End tile for the new brush. (You'll apply the new brush to a closed path in the artwork later in the lesson, so you won't need Start or End tiles this time. When you want to create a Pattern brush that includes Start and End tiles, you add those tiles the same way you did the Side and Corner tiles.)

8 In the Name text box, name the brush **Clouds and Sun**. Then click OK.

The Clouds and Sun brush appears in the Pattern brush section in the Brushes palette.

Note: When you create a new brush, the brush appears in the Brushes palette of the current artwork only. If you open another file in Illustrator, the Clouds and Sun brush won't appear in that file's Brushes palette.

Painting with the new Pattern brush

So far in this lesson you've used the paintbrush tool to apply brushes to paths. You can also apply brushes to paths created with any drawing tool—including the pen, pencil, ellipse, and rectangle tools—and the other basic shapes tools. In this section, you'll use the rectangle tool to apply the Clouds and Sun brush to a rectangular border around the artwork.

When you use drawing tools to apply brushes to artwork, you first draw the path with the tool and then select the brush in the Brushes palette to apply the brush to the path.

First you'll set the fill color to None.

1 In the toolbox, click the Fill box and click the None box.

2 Use the Navigator palette or the zoom tool ($\mathcal{Q}$) to reduce the view of the artwork.

Now you'll draw a border with the rectangle tool, and apply the brush to the path.

3 Select the rectangle tool (□). Drag to draw a rectangle on the artboard, about one-half inch inside the imageable area on each side, using the guide for placement.

4 In the Brushes palette, click the Clouds and Sun brush.

The rectangle path is painted with the Clouds and Sun brush, with the Cloud tile on the sides and the Sun tile on the corners.

Draw rectangle.   Select Pattern brush.   Brush is applied to
                                                   rectangle path.

5 Ctrl-click (Windows) or Command-click (Mac OS) outside the artwork to deselect it.

Now you'll draw a curved path using the Clouds and Sun brush.

6 In the Brushes palette, double-click the Clouds and Sun Pattern brush to view the Brush Options dialog box for the brush.

You'll change the scale and spacing of the brush for a different look.

7 Under Size, enter **250%** for Scale and **30%** for Spacing. Click OK.

Select Clouds and Sun Pattern brush.   *Change scale and spacing.*

8 In the Brush Change alert window, click Leave Strokes to keep the border brush strokes unchanged.

The Leave Strokes option preserves paths in the artwork that are already painted with the brush. The changes you made to the brush will apply to subsequent uses of the brush. Now you'll use the brush to paint a curved path in the artwork.

9 Select the paintbrush tool ( ) and draw a smooth curve over the tree. Use the guides for placement.

Apply Pattern brush to path with paintbrush.   *Result*

The path is painted with the clouds from the Clouds and Sun brush (the Side tile in the brush). Because the path does not include sharp corners, the Outer Corner tile and Inner Corner tile (the Sun tiles) are not applied to the path.

You've completed the artwork for the lesson. Now you'll remove the guides so you can view the artwork in its finished form.

When working with guides, you can temporarily hide guides by choosing View > Guides > Hide Guides. The guides disappear but are preserved in the artwork. You can display hidden guides by choosing View > Guides > Show Guides. You won't need the guides again in this lesson, so you'll delete them using the Clear Guides command.

10 Choose View > Guides > Clear Guides. The guides are deleted from the artwork.

11 Choose File > Save to save your work. Choose File > Close to close the file.

Exploring on your own

Here are some ideas you can try on your own.

Applying brushes to paths

Practice applying brushes to paths you create with drawing tools (just as you applied the Clouds and Sun Pattern brush to a path drawn with the rectangle tool in the final section of the lesson).

1 In the Brushes palette menu, make sure that Show Scatter Brushes is selected (indicated by a check mark next to the option).

2 Use the drawing tools (the pen or pencil tool, and any of the basic shapes tools) to draw objects. Use the default fill and stroke colors when you draw.

3 With one of the objects selected, click a brush in the Brushes palette to apply the brush to the object's path.

4 Repeat step 3 for each object you drew.

5 Display the Brush Options dialog box for one of the brushes you used in step 3, and change the color, size, or other features of the brush. After you close the dialog box, click Apply To Strokes to apply your changes to the brush in the artwork.

Creating brushes

Use one of the basic shapes tools to create artwork to use as a new Scatter brush.

1 Select a basic shape tool in the toolbox, and draw an object.

2 With the object selected, click the New Brush button at the bottom of the Brushes palette.

Note: You can use more than one object to create the new brush. All selected objects in the artwork will be included in the brush. If you use a brush to create artwork for a new brush, remember to expand the brush strokes before creating the new brush.

3 In the New Brush dialog box, select New Scatter Brush and click OK.

The Brush Options dialog box for the new brush appears, with the selected objects displayed in the brush example. The new brush is named Scatter Brush 1 by default.

4 Enter a name for the brush. Then click OK to accept the settings for the brush.

5 Select the paintbrush tool and draw a path. The new brush is applied to the path.

6 Double-click the new brush to display the Brush Options dialog box. Click Preview and change the brush settings to experiment with different versions of the brush. When you have finished, close the dialog box.

Using a brush library

Try out some of the brushes included in the brush libraries in Illustrator.

1 To open a brush library, choose Window > Brush Libraries.

2 Choose a library from the submenu. Illustrator includes seven brush libraries in addition to the default brush library that appears when you start the program.

▣ You can also create your own brush libraries. See "Using the Brush Libraries" in online Help or Chapter 3 in the Adobe Illustrator User Guide.

Review questions

1 Describe each of the four brush types—Art, Calligraphic, Pattern, and Scatter.

2 What is the difference between applying a brush to artwork using the paintbrush tool and applying a brush to artwork using one of the drawing tools?

3 Describe how to edit paths with the paintbrush tool as you draw. How does the Keep Selected option affect the paintbrush tool?

4 How do you apply the Hue Shift colorization method to an Art, Pattern, or Scatter brush? (Remember you don't use colorization methods with Calligraphic brushes.)

Review answers

1 The following are the four brush types:

• Art brushes stretch artwork evenly along a path. Art brushes include strokes that resemble graphic media (such as the Charcoal brush used to create the tree, or the Marker brush used to create the grass). Art brushes also include objects, such as the Arrow brush.

• Calligraphic brushes are defined by an elliptical shape whose center follows the path. They create strokes that resemble hand-drawn lines made with a flat, angled calligraphic pen tip.

• Pattern brushes paint a pattern made up of separate sections, or tiles, for the sides (middle sections), ends, and corners of the path. When you apply a Pattern brush to artwork, the brush applies different tiles from the pattern to different sections of the path, depending on where the section falls on the path (at an end, in the middle, or at a corner).

• Scatter brushes scatter an object, such as a leaf, along a path. You can adjust the Size, Spacing, Scatter, and Rotation options for a Scatter brush to change the brush's appearance.

2 To apply brushes using the paintbrush tool, you select the tool, choose a brush from the Brushes palette, and draw in the artwork. The brush is applied directly to the paths as you draw. To apply brushes using a drawing tool, you select the tool and draw in the artwork; then you select a path in the artwork and choose a brush in the Brushes palette. The brush is applied to the selected path.

3 To edit a path with the paintbrush tool, simply drag over a selected path to redraw it. The Keep Selected option keeps the last path selected as you draw with the paintbrush tool. Leave the Keep Selected option turned on (the default setting) when you want to easily edit the previous path as you draw. Turn off the Keep Selected option when you want to draw layered paths with the paintbrush without altering previous paths. When the Keep Selected option is turned off, you can use the selection tool to select a path and then edit the path.

4 To apply the Hue Shift colorization method to a brush, double-click the brush in the Brushes palette to view the Brush Options dialog box. Select Hue Shift from the Method pop-up menu in the Colorization section. Click the Key Color eyedropper, and click a color in the brush example to choose the key color, the color that will be shifted. (You can also use the default key color, displayed in the color box.) Click OK to accept the settings and close the Brush Options dialog box. Click Apply to Strokes in the alert box if you want to apply the Hue Shift changes to existing strokes in the artwork.

Existing brush strokes are colorized with the stroke color that was selected when the strokes were applied to the artwork. New brush strokes are colorized with the current stroke color. To change the color of existing strokes after applying the Hue Shift colorization method, select the strokes and select a new stroke color.

Lesson 6

Transforming Objects

You can modify objects in many ways as you create your artwork—letting you quickly and precisely control their size, shape, and orientation. In this lesson, you'll explore the various transform tools, commands, and palettes as you create three pieces of artwork.

In this lesson, you'll learn how to do the following:

• Select individual objects, objects in a group, and parts of an object.

• Move, scale, and rotate objects using a variety of methods.

• Reflect, shear, and distort objects.

• Adjust the perspective of an object.

• Repeat transformations quickly and easily.

Getting started

In this lesson, you'll transform parts of a logo to use in three pieces of artwork to create a letterhead design, an envelope, and business cards. Before you begin, you'll restore the default preferences for Adobe Illustrator and then open a file containing a composite of the finished artwork to see what you'll create.

1 To ensure that the tools and palettes function exactly as described in this lesson, delete or deactivate (by renaming) the Adobe Illustrator 9.0 preferences file. See "Restoring default preferences" on page 3.

2 Start Adobe Illustrator.

3 Choose File > Open, and open the L6comp.ai file in the Lesson06 folder, located inside the Lessons folder within the AICIB folder on your hard drive.

This file contains a composite of the three pieces of finished artwork. The Citrus Bath & Soap logo in the top left corner of the letterhead is the basis for all the modified objects. The logo has been resized for the letterhead, envelope, and business card.

Note: You can also view the individual pieces of finished artwork by opening the files, L6end1.ai, L6end2.ai, and L6end3.ai, in the Lesson06 folder.

4 If you like, choose View > Zoom Out to reduce the view of the finished artwork, adjust the window size, and leave it on your screen as you work. (Use the hand tool ( ) to move the artwork where you want it in the window.) If you don't want to leave the image open, choose File > Close.

 For an illustration of the finished artwork in this lesson, see the color section.

To begin working, you'll open an existing art file set up for the letterhead artwork.

5 Choose File > Open to open the L6start1.ai file in the Lesson06 folder, located inside the Lessons folder within the AICIB folder on your hard drive.

This start file has been saved with the rulers showing, custom swatches added to the Swatches palette, and blue guidelines for scaling the logo and objects on the letterhead.

6 Choose File > Save As, name the file **Letterhd.ai**, and select the Lesson06 folder. Leave the Format option set to Adobe Illustrator® Document, and click Save. In the Illustrator Native Format Options dialog box, select Illustrator 9.0 Compatibility and click OK.

Scaling objects

You scale objects by enlarging or reducing them horizontally (along the *x* axis) and vertically (along the *y* axis) relative to a fixed point of origin that you designate. If you don't designate an origin, the objects are scaled from their center points. You'll use three methods to scale the logo and two objects copied from the logo.

First you'll use the Transform palette to scale down the logo by entering new dimensions and designating the point of origin from which the logo will scale.

1 Using the selection tool ( ) in the toolbox, click the logo to select the group of objects (type, background, lemon, orange slice, lime slice) that make up the logo.

2 Choose Window > Show Transform to display the Transform palette.

The Transform palette contains a small grid of squares or *reference points* that represent points on the selection's bounding box.

3 Click the reference point in the top left corner of the grid (as shown in the illustration) to set the point of origin from which the objects will scale. Type **84** in the W text box, press Tab and type **88.5** in the H text box, and then press Enter or Return to scale down the logo to fit in the blue guideline.

By default, the ruler units of measure are set to points.

Set reference point, width,   Result
and height.

💡 *To scale an object proportionally, enter a value in either the W or the H text box, hold down Ctrl (Windows) or Command (Mac OS), and press Enter or Return to automatically calculate the equivalent value for the other text box.*

Next you'll copy the background object in the logo and scale the new object by dragging its bounding box to fit the background of the letterhead.

4 With the logo still selected, choose Object > Ungroup to ungroup the larger group in the logo. (Smaller subgroups remain grouped.)

Ungrouping the background object from the other objects lets you make copies that are separate from the group.

5 Using the selection tool ( ), click away from the logo to deselect it, and then click below the word *Bath* to select the light-blue background object in the logo. Hold down Alt (Windows) or Option (Mac OS) and drag from the center of the object down to copy the object and move it to the bottom left corner of the page, aligning it with the guides.

Holding down Alt/Option as you drag an object duplicates it.

Next you'll make this background object the background for the page.

6 Shift-drag the top right corner of the new object's bounding box up to the top right side of the blue letterhead guide, to just below the return address.

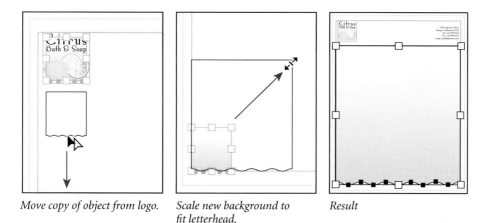

Move copy of object from logo.   *Scale new background to fit letterhead.*   *Result*

You'll use the Swatches palette to paint the background with a lighter gradient that we provided. To learn how to create your own gradients, see Lesson 8, "Blending Shapes and Colors."

7 Click the Swatches tab to bring the palette to the front of its group. With the background selected, hold the pointer over the swatches in the Swatches palette until you see their names. Then click the New Background swatch in the third row to paint the object with a lighter gradient.

8 With the background object still selected, choose Object > Lock to deselect the object and lock it. Locking the background object makes it easier to select other objects you'll add to the artwork.

The lemon is two objects grouped together in the logo. Now you'll copy the lemon and place it in the bottom corner of the letterhead.

9 Select the lemon in the logo, and Alt-drag (Windows) or Option-drag (Mac OS) to copy and move the new lemon to the bottom right corner of the letterhead guide.

You'll use the scale tool to resize the new lemon and designate a fixed point of origin from which to scale.

10 Select the scale tool in the toolbox, hold down Alt (Windows) or Option (Mac OS), and click the bottom right corner point of the letterhead guide.

Clicking the corner point of the guide sets the point of origin from which the lemon will scale. Holding down Alt/Option as you click displays the Scale dialog box.

11 In the Scale dialog box, type **300%** in the Scale text box and click OK to make the lemon three times as large.

Move copy of lemon.　　Set point of origin.　　Scale dialog box

Rotating objects

Objects are rotated by turning them around a designated point of origin. You can rotate objects by displaying their bounding boxes and moving the pointer to one of the outside corners. Once the rotate pointer appears, just click to rotate the object around its center point. You can rotate objects using the Transform palette to designate a point of origin and rotation angle. You can also rotate objects by using the rotate tool and either choosing a rotation angle or dragging to adjust an object visually.

You'll rotate the lemon 30° around its center point using the rotate tool.

1 With the lemon selected, select the rotate tool (⟲) in the toolbox.

Notice that the lemon's point of origin is still at the bottom right corner of the letterhead.

2 Select the lemon and begin dragging it. Notice how the movement is constrained to a circle rotating around the point of origin. Continue dragging until the lemon is in its original position on the letterhead, and then release the mouse button.

3 Now, with the lemon still selected, double-click the rotate tool in the toolbox.

When an object is selected and you double-click the rotate tool in the toolbox, the object is rotated exactly from the center of the object. (This also applies to the scale tool.)

4 In the Rotate dialog box, type **30** in the Angle text box, and click OK to rotate the lemon 30° around its center point.

Rotating around different points of origin

Now you'll select one of the objects within the lemon without ungrouping the lemon so you can paint the lemon with a lighter color.

The group-selection tool lets you select individual objects or subgroups within a group.

5 Select the group-selection tool (▷⁺) from the same group as the direct-selection tool (▷) in the toolbox. Hold down Shift and click the stem's core (not the body of the lemon) to deselect it.

6 With the body of the lemon selected, click a color in the Color palette or a swatch in the Swatches palette to paint it with a lighter gradient. (We used the Pale Yellow gradient swatch.)

7 Choose File > Save.

Distorting objects

Various tools and filters let you distort the original shape of objects in different ways. For example, the wavy line on the bottom of the background object in the logo and on the letterhead was created by applying the Zig Zag distort filter to the straight edge.

Converting straight lines to zigzags

The Zig Zag filter adds anchor points to an existing line and then moves some of the points to the left of (or upward from) the line and some to the right of (or downward from) the line. You can specify the number of anchor points to create and the distance to move them. You can also choose whether to create smooth anchor points for a wavy line effect, or corner anchor points for a jagged line effect.

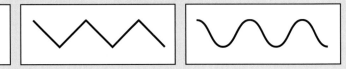

Original line, four corner ridges applied, and four smooth ridges applied

To convert straight lines to zigzags:

1. Do one of the following:

• To apply the distortion permanently, use any selection tool to select the line you want to convert. Then choose Filter > Distort > Zig Zag.

• To apply the distortion as an effect that can be removed, select an object or group, or target a group or layer in the Layers palette. (For more on targeting, see Lesson 10, "Working with Layers.") Then choose Effect > Distort & Transform > Zig Zag.

2. In the Size text box, enter the distance you want to move points on the line, or drag the slider.

3. In the Ridges per Segment text box, enter the number of ridges per segment you want, or drag the slider.

4. Select from the following options:

• Smooth to create smooth points, resulting in a wavy line.

• Corner to create corner points, resulting in a jagged line.

• Relative to move points by a percentage of the size of the object.

• Absolute to move points a specific amount.

5. Click Preview to preview the line.

6. Click OK.

Now you'll create a flower using the twirl tool to twist the shape of a star and the Punk & Bloat distort filter to transform another star in front of it.

To begin, you'll draw a star for part of the flower and use the twirl tool and Info palette to distort it.

1 Select the star tool (☆) from the same group as the ellipse tool (○) in the toolbox, and position the pointer in the artwork next to the lemon. Drag the tool to draw a five-pointed star that's about the same size as the lemon.

The star is painted with the paint attributes of the last selected object (in this case, the lemon).

2 With the star still selected, click a color swatch in the Swatches palette to paint the star with that color. (We selected the Lime Green swatch in the Swatches palette.) Leave the stroke unpainted.

3 Click the Info tab behind the Navigator palette or choose Window > Show Info to display the Info palette.

The Info palette displays information about the size and position of the selected object's bounding box.

4 Select the twirl tool (🌀) from the same group as the rotate tool (○) in the toolbox and select a point on the star (don't release the mouse button). Referring to the Info palette, drag the star's point to the right (in a clockwise direction) until the Info palette displays about 72 degrees.

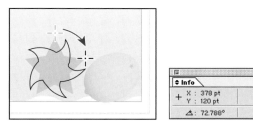

Twirl star using Info palette as guide.

Now you'll draw another star that's centered on top of the first star.

5 With the star selected, click the Attributes tab behind the Color palette or choose Window > Show Attributes to display the Attributes palette. Then click the Show Center button (⊡) to display the star's center point.

Display center point of star.

6 Select the star tool again, hold down Alt (Windows) or Option (Mac OS), and drag from the center point to draw another star over the center of the first one. Before you release the mouse button, drag the star in an arc to rotate it so the points appear between the points of the star behind it.

7 Click the Color tab behind the Attributes palette to bring the Color palette to the front. Click the White color box at the right end of the color bar to paint the star's fill with white. Then click the Stroke box to select the star's stroke, and click a color in the color bar or in the Swatches palette to paint the star's stroke. (We selected the Yellow color swatch.)

Now you'll distort the star using the Punk & Bloat filter. This filter distorts objects inward and outward from their anchor points.

8 With the white star selected, choose Effect > Distort & Transform > Punk & Bloat.

The Punk & Bloat distortion can be applied to objects two ways. Applying it as a filter permanently distorts the object. Applying it as an effect maintains the original shape and lets you remove or edit the effect at any time.

9 In the Punk & Bloat dialog box, select the Preview option, and drag the slider to distort the star (we selected 50%). Click OK.

Draw star shape.

Apply Punk & Bloat effect.

Result

10 Choose Edit > Deselect All to deselect the artwork, and choose File > Save.

Shearing objects

Now you'll complete the flower with an orange center, scale it, and shear it. Shearing an object slants, or skews, the sides of the object along the axis you specify, keeping opposite sides parallel and making the object nonsymmetrical.

1 Click the Appearance tab behind the Info palette to bring the Appearance palette to the front of its group. (If the Appearance palette isn't visible on-screen, choose Window > Show Appearance to display it.)

The Appearance palette displays the fill, stroke, effects, and transparency of the last object created. By default the next shape you create will retain all of these attributes. Since we want the next shape to have different attributes, we will change this default setting.

2 Click the New Art Maintains Appearance button at the bottom of the Appearance palette.

The next shape will maintain only the stroke and fill attributes of the last shape.

3 Select the ellipse tool (○) from the same group as the star tool (☆) in the toolbox, and begin dragging to draw a small oval shape for the flower's center. Before you release the mouse button, press the spacebar to release the ellipse tool, and continue dragging to move the oval shape to the center of the flower. Release the mouse button.

4 Click the Fill box in the toolbox to select the object's fill. In the Swatches palette, click the Orange swatch to paint the oval a light orange color.

5 In the Color palette, drag the None icon, and drop it on the Stroke box to remove the stroke. This action keeps the Fill box selected.

Draw oval shape and paint fill.   *Drag and drop None button over Stroke box.*

Now, you'll shear the flower.

6 Select the selection tool (▶), Shift-click to select the three parts of the flower, and choose Object > Group to group them together.

7 In the Transform palette, type **10** degrees in the Shear text box, and press Enter or Return to apply the shearing effect on the flower.

Enter 10° shear angle.   *Result*

8 Type **.75 in** in the W text box and **.75 in** in the H text box to scale the flower down to three-quarters of an inch.

Although the default unit of measure is set to points, when you type *inches* or *in* in the text boxes, Illustrator calculates the equivalent measurement in points.

💡 *To automatically multiply or divide the size of an object by a number you specify, enter an asterisk (*) or a slash (/) and a number after the value in either the W or the H text box, and press Enter or Return to scale the object. For example, enter /2 after the values in the W and H text boxes to scale the object by 50%.*

9 Using the selection tool, drag the flower next to the lemon in the bottom right corner of the page.

10 Choose Edit > Deselect All to deselect the artwork, and then choose File > Save.

Positioning objects precisely

You can use the Transform palette to move objects to exact coordinates on the X and Y axes of the page and to control the position of objects in relation to the trim edge.

❓ To learn how to produce crop marks for the trim edge, see "Setting crop marks and trim marks" in online Help or Chapter 15 in the Adobe Illustrator User Guide.

First you'll paste a copy of the logo into the envelope artwork, and then you'll specify the exact coordinates on the envelope for the pasted logo to go.

1 Using the selection tool (▸), draw a marquee around the logo so that all of the objects in it are selected.

2 Choose Edit > Copy to copy the logo to the Clipboard.

Now you'll open the start file for the envelope artwork.

3 Choose File > Open to open the L6start2.ai file in the Lesson06 folder, located inside the Lessons folder within the AICIB folder on your hard drive.

4 Choose File > Save As, name the file **Envelope.ai**, and select the Lesson06 folder. Leave the Format option set to Adobe Illustrator® Document, and click Save. In the Illustrator Native Format Options dialog box, select Illustrator 9.0 Compatibility and click OK.

5 Choose Edit > Paste.

Now you'll move the pasted logo to the top left corner of the envelope by specifying the X and Y coordinates in relation to the *ruler origin*. The ruler origin is the point where 0 appears on each ruler. We changed the ruler origin in this file to begin at the top left corner of the envelope and the ruler units to inches.

For more information, see "Defining ruler units" and "Changing the ruler origin" in online Help or Chapter 4 in the Adobe Illustrator User Guide.

6 In the Transform palette, click the top left reference point and then type **.25** in the X text box and **–.25** (a negative coordinate) in the Y text box. Press Enter or Return to apply the last setting you typed.

Copy the logo from the letterhead.

Paste into the envelope.

Select top left reference point and enter X and Y coordinates.

Note: *You can also move selected objects to exact X and Y coordinates by choosing Object > Transform > Move and entering coordinates in the Move dialog box.*

7 With the logo still selected, Shift-drag the bottom right corner of the bounding box to scale the logo and make it fit within the blue square guideline.

Holding down Shift as you drag scales the objects in the logo proportionally.

8 Click away from the artwork to deselect it, and then choose File > Save.

Reflecting objects

Objects are reflected by flipping them across an invisible vertical or horizontal axis. Copying objects while reflecting creates a mirror image of the objects. Similar to scaling and rotating, you designate the point of origin from which an object will reflect or use the object's center point by default.

Now you'll use the reflect tool to make a mirror image of the orange slice in the logo.

1 Use the selection tool ( ) to select the orange slice in the logo.

2 Select the reflect tool ( ) in the toolbox, hold down Alt (Windows) or Option (Mac OS), and click the right edge of the orange slice.

Clicking the edge of the object designates the point of origin. Holding down Alt/Option as you click displays the Reflect dialog box.

3 In the Reflect dialog box, make sure that the Vertical option is selected and **90** degrees is entered in the Angle text box. Then click Copy (don't click OK).

Note: You can also use the Transform palette to reflect selected objects by choosing Flip Horizontal or Flip Vertical from the palette menu.

4 Click the selection tool to select the bounding box of the new orange slice and move the object down below the logo. Then Shift-drag the bounding box to scale the orange slice and make it bigger (as it is in the illustration).

Move reflected copy down and rescale it.

Changing the perspective

Now you'll use the free transform tool to change the perspective of the orange slice.

1 With the orange slice selected, select the free transform tool (⟡) in the toolbox.

2 Position the double-headed arrow pointer over the bottom left corner of the object's bounding box, and select the bottom left corner handle (don't release the mouse button). Hold down Shift+Alt+Ctrl (Windows) or Shift+Option+Command (Mac OS), and slowly drag up to change the perspective of the object.

Holding down Shift as you drag scales the objects proportionally, holding down Alt/Option scales from the center point, and holding down Ctrl/Command as you drag distorts the object from the anchor point or bounding box handle that you're dragging.

3 Select the group-selection tool (⟡⁺) in the toolbox, and click away from the orange slice to deselect it. Then Shift-click to select the segments of the orange slice and its rind. (Don't select the inner white pith of the rind.)

4 In the Swatches palette, select the Pale Orange gradient swatch to paint the selected objects with a lighter gradient.

Change perspective.   *Select colored parts.*   *Paint with lighter gradient.*

5 Choose File > Save.

Using the free transform tool

The free transform tool is a multipurpose tool that, besides letting you change the perspective of an object, combines the functions of scaling, shearing, reflecting, and rotating.

Now you'll use the free transform tool to transform objects copied from the logo into a business card.

1 Choose File > Open, and open the L6start3.ai file in the Lesson06 folder, located inside the Lessons folder within the AICIB folder on your hard drive.

2 Choose File > Save As, name the file **Buscards.ai**, and select the Lesson06 folder. Leave the Format option set to Adobe Illustrator® Document, and click Save. In the Illustrator Native Format Options dialog box, select Illustrator 9.0 Compatibility and click OK.

3 Click the Navigator tab behind the Info palette to bring the Navigator palette to the front of its group. (If the Navigator palette isn't visible on-screen, choose Window > Show Navigator to display it.) In the Navigator palette, click the Zoom In button (⌂) a few times to zoom to 200%, and then move the red view box over the top left corner of the artwork.

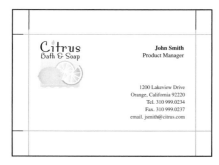

4 Choose the selection tool (⬉), and click to select the lime slice in the logo. Then, Alt-drag (Windows) or Option-drag (Mac OS) to make a copy of the object. Position the new lime slice below and slightly to the right of the logo.

Now you'll use the free transform tool to scale, distort, and rotate the new lime slice.

5 With the lime slice still selected, select the free transform tool (⊞) in the toolbox. Hold down Shift+Alt (Windows) or Shift+Option (Mac OS), and drag the bottom right corner down to scale the object from its center and make the lime slice bigger.

Make copy of lime slice.   *Use free transform tool to scale object.*

Although you can scale objects using the selection tool, scaling with the free transform tool lets you perform other transformations without switching tools.

6 To distort the lime slice using the free transform tool, select the bottom right corner of the object's bounding box—don't release the mouse button—hold down Ctrl (Windows) or Command (Mac OS), and slowly drag toward the opposite corner of the object.

(You can use the free transform tool to shear an object by dragging a side handle rather than a corner handle of the bounding box.)

7 To slightly rotate the lime slice, position the free transform tool just outside of the bottom right corner of the object's bounding box until you see the rotate pointer, and then drag to rotate the object.

Distort object using free transform tool.   *Rotate object using free transform tool.*

8 With the lime slice selected, select the group-selection tool (k⁺) in the toolbox and Shift-click the inner white pith of the rind to deselect it. In the Swatches palette, select the Pale Green gradient swatch to paint the lime slice with a lighter gradient.

9 Select the selection tool (k), click to select the entire lime slice, choose Object > Arrange > Send to Back, and then move the object to tuck it under the logo.

Now you'll explore a slightly different way of distorting objects. Free Distort lets you distort a selection by moving any of its four corner points. It can be used either as a filter to apply a permanent change, or as an effect to apply a change that can be removed.

10 With the lime slice still selected, choose Filter > Distort > Free Distort.

11 Turn on the Preview option and drag one or more of the handles to distort the selection. Click OK.

12 Click outside of the artwork to deselect it, and choose File > Save.

Making multiple transformations

You'll finish the design of the business card and use the Transform commands to multiply it nine times for a print layout.

To finish the design, you'll copy the flower from the letterhead, paste it into the business card, and reflect it using the Transform palette.

1 Choose Window > Letterhd.ai to display the letterhead document (or choose File > Open if you closed the file). Select the flower, and choose Edit > Copy to copy it to the Clipboard.

2 Choose Window > Buscards.ai to display the business card document, and then choose Edit > Paste to paste the copy of the flower into the business card layout. Select the flower and move it next to the lime slice.

Note: You can also copy and paste objects between documents by dragging and dropping them from one window to the other.

3 In the Transform palette, select the center reference point in the small grid that represents the bounding box to designate the point of origin. Then hold down the mouse button on the triangle in the top right corner of the palette to display the palette menu, and choose Flip Horizontal to reflect the selected object.

4 If necessary, use the selection tool to adjust the position of the lime and the flower so that they fit within the boundary of the business card.

Now you'll create multiple copies of the business card in a few easy steps.

5 Double-click the hand tool (🖑) in the toolbox to zoom out and fit the artwork in the window.

6 Choose Edit > Select All to select all of the objects on the business card, and then choose Object > Transform > Transform Each.

The Move options in the Transform Each dialog box let you move objects in a specified or random direction. Now you'll move a copy of the selected objects down 2 inches from the original objects.

7 In the Transform Each dialog box, type **–2** inches in the Move Vertical text box, leave the other settings as they are, and click Copy (don't click OK).

Move object down 2 inches and copy it.

8 Choose Object > Transform > Transform Again to create another copy.

Now you'll use the keyboard shortcut to repeat the transformations.

9 Press Ctrl+D (Windows) or Command+D (Mac OS) twice to transform again two more times, creating a total of five cards in the column.

Note: You can also apply multiple transformations as an effect, including scaling, moving, rotating, and reflecting an object. After selecting the objects, choose Effect > Distort & Transform > Transform. The dialog box looks the same as the Transform Each dialog box. Transforming as an effect has the advantage of letting you change or remove the transformation at any time.

Next you'll use some shortcuts to make a copy of the column.

10 Press Ctrl+A (Windows) or Command+A (Mac OS) to select everything on the five business cards, and right-click (Windows) or Ctrl-click (Mac OS) in the window to display a shortcut menu. Choose Transform > Transform Each from the shortcut menu.

11 This time in the Transform Each dialog box, type **3.5** inches in the Move Horizontal text box and **0** inches in the Move Vertical text box. Leave the other settings as they are, and click Copy (don't click OK).

12 To clear the window so that you can view the finished artwork, press Ctrl (Windows) or Command (Mac OS) and click outside the artwork to deselect it. Then choose View > Hide Guides to hide the blue guidelines, and press Tab to close the toolbox and palettes.

Pressing Tab toggles between hiding and showing the toolbox and all of the palettes. Pressing Shift+Tab hides or shows only the palettes.

13 Choose File > Save. Choose File > Close to close the file.

You've completed the lesson on transforming objects.

For more practice with transforming objects, see Lesson 12, "Drawing Cylinders and Boxes."

Review questions

1 How can you select and manipulate individual objects in a group?

2 How do you resize an object? How do you determine the point from which the object resizes? How do you resize a group of objects proportionally?

3 What transformations can you make using the Transform palette?

4 What does the square diagram indicate in the Transform palette, and how will it affect your transformations?

5 What is an easy way to change perspective? List three other types of transformations you can do with the free transform tool.

Review answers

1 You can use the group-selection tool (k⁺) to select individual objects or subgroups of objects within a group and change them without affecting the rest of the group.

2 You can resize an object by selecting it and dragging handles on its bounding box or by using the scale tool, the Transform palette, or Object > Transform > Scale to specify exact dimensions. You can also scale by choosing Effect > Distort & Transform > Transform.

To determine the point of origin from which the objects scale, select a reference point in the Transform palette, in the Transform Effect or Transform Each dialog box, or click in the artwork with the scale tool. Holding down Alt (Windows) or Option (Mac OS) and dragging the bounding box or double-clicking the scale tool will resize a selected object from its center point.

Shift-dragging a corner handle on the bounding box scales the objects proportionally, as will specifying a uniform scale value in the Scale dialog box or multiples of the dimensions in the Width and Height text boxes in the Transform palette.

3 You use the Transform palette for:

• Moving or strategically placing objects in your artwork (by specifying the X and Y coordinates and the point of origin).

• Scaling (by specifying the width and height of selected objects).

• Rotating (by specifying the angle of rotation).

• Shearing (by specifying the angle of distortion).

• Reflecting (by flipping selected objects vertically or horizontally).

4 The square diagram in the Transform palette indicates the bounding box of the selected objects. Select a reference point in the square to indicate the point of origin from which the objects will move, scale, rotate, shear, or reflect.

5 An easy way to change the perspective of selected objects is to select the free transform tool (⊠), hold down Shift+Alt+Ctrl (Windows) or Shift+Option+Command (Mac OS), and drag a corner handle on the bounding box.

Other types of transformations you can do with the free transform tool are distorting, scaling, shearing, rotating, and reflecting.

1-1: **Toolbox Overview**

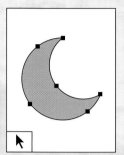

The selection tool (V) *selects entire objects.*

The direct-selection tool (A) *selects points or path segments within objects.*

The group-selection tool (Shift+A) *selects objects and groups within groups.*

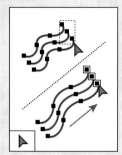

The reshape tool (Shift+S) *smooths or changes a path while retaining the path's overall shape.*

The rotate tool (R) *rotates objects around a fixed point.*

The twirl tool (Shift+R) *twirls objects around a fixed point.*

The scale tool (S) *resizes objects around a fixed point.*

The lasso tool (Y) *selects entire objects.*

The direct select lasso tool (Q) *selects points or path segments within objects.*

The reflect tool (O) *flips objects over a fixed axis.*

The shear tool (Shift+O) *skews objects around a fixed point.*

The pen tool (P) *draws straight and curved lines to create objects.*

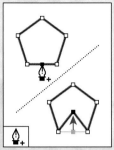

The add-anchor-point tool (+) *adds anchor points to paths.*

The delete-anchor-point tool (-) *deletes anchor points from paths.*

The convert-direction-point tool (Shift+P) *changes smooth points to corner points and vice versa.*

The type tool (T) *creates individual type and type containers and lets you enter and edit type.*

The area type tool (Shift+T) *changes closed paths to type containers and lets you enter and edit type within them.*

The path type tool (Shift+T) *changes paths to type paths and lets you enter and edit type on them.*

The vertical type tool (Shift+T) *creates vertical type and vertical type containers and lets you enter and edit vertical type.*

The vertical area-type tool (Shift+T) *changes closed paths to vertical type containers and lets you enter and edit type within them.*

The vertical path-type tool (Shift+T) *changes paths to vertical type paths and lets you enter and edit type on them.*

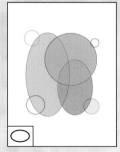

The ellipse tool (L) *draws circles and ovals.*

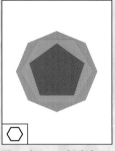

The polygon tool (Shift+L) *draws regular, multisided shapes.*

The star tool (Shift+L) *draws stars.*

The spiral tool (Shift+L) draws clockwise and counterclockwise spirals.

The rectangle tool (M) draws squares and rectangles.

The rounded-rectangle tool (Shift+M) draws squares and rectangles with rounded corners.

The pencil tool (N) draws and edits freehand lines.

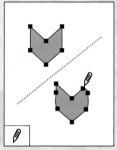

The smooth tool (Shift+N) removes excess anchor points to smooth a path while retaining the overall shape.

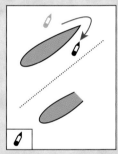

The erase tool (Shift+N) erases paths and anchor points from the artwork.

The paintbrush tool (B) draws freehand and calligraphic lines, as well as art and patterns on paths.

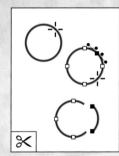

The scissors tool (C) splits paths.

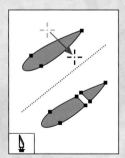

The knife tool (Shift+C) slices objects and paths.

The measure tool (Shift+H) measures the distance between two points.

The eyedropper tool (I) samples paint or type attributes from objects.

Color Palette

The eyedropper tool (I) samples paint or type attributes from objects.

Flower Garden

The paint bucket tool (K) fills objects with the current paint or type attributes.

The gradient mesh tool (U) *creates multicolored objects and applies a mesh for adjusting color shading.*

The gradient tool (G) *adjusts the beginning and ending points of gradients within objects.*

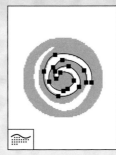

The auto trace tool (Shift+W) *traces the outlines of objects.*

The blend tool (W) *creates a blend between the color and shape of multiple objects.*

The page tool (Shift+H) *adjusts the page grid to control where artwork appears on the printed page.*

The graph tool (J) *positions columns vertically.*

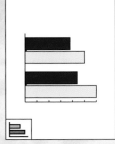

The stacked column graph tool (Shift+J) *stacks columns on top of one another.*

The bar graph tool (Shift+J) *positions columns horizontally.*

The stacked bar graph tool (Shift+J) *stacks columns and positions them horizontally.*

The line graph tool (Shift+J) *shows the trend of one or more subjects over time.*

The area graph tool (Shift+J) *emphasizes totals as well as changes in values.*

The scatter graph tool (Shift+J) *plots data as paired sets of X and Y coordinates.*

1-1: **Toolbox Overview (cont.)**

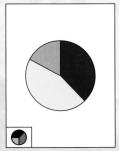

The pie graph tool (Shift+J) creates a circle graph with wedges showing relative percentages of the compared values.

The radar graph tool (Shift+J) uses a circle to compare sets of values at given points in time or in particular categories.

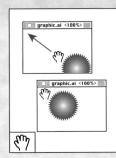

The hand tool (H) moves the Illustrator artboard within the illustration window.

The zoom tool (Z) increases and decreases the magnification in the illustration window.

Illustrator Tour

The free transform tool (E) scales, rotates, or skews a selection.

Lesson 1

Lesson 2

Lesson 3

3-1: **Global and non-global color**

Global process color

Global colors are created by deselecting the Non-Global option in the Swatch Options dialog box and are identified by a white corner icon on the swatch. Tints of global colors are chosen using the Color palette.

When the process mix of a global color is edited in the Swatch Options dialog box, any object in the artwork painted with that color is automatically updated. Individual tints are retained, eliminating the need to select and repaint each object.

Non-global process color

CMYK mix for a non-global process color swatch is edited using the Swatch Options dialog box. Edits made using the Color palette will not update the saved swatch.

When the color is edited using the Swatch Options dialog box, only the swatch and any currently selected artwork are updated— other artwork painted with that color is unaffected.

Lesson 4

Lesson 5

5-1: Colorization methods

None, Tints, Tints and Shades, Hue Shift

 When you choose a colorization method for a brush, the current stroke color is applied to the brush. (To apply a different color to the brush after choosing a colorization method, select the brush and select a new stroke color.)

 None leaves the brush color unchanged.

To apply a colorization method: Select the brush in the Brushes palette, open the Brush Options dialog box, and then select a colorization method from the Method pop-up menu. (The default colorization method varies among different brushes.)

Tints applies a single hue (the stroke color) to the brush. Black areas in the original brush take on the new hue, and lighter areas take on the new hue with white added.

Tints and Shades applies a single hue (the stroke color) to the brush. Darker areas take on the hue with black added; lighter areas take on the hue with white added.

Note: Colorization changes appear when you apply brushes to artwork. Changes do not appear in the Brush Options dialog box or the Brushes palette.

Hue Shift shifts the selected color to the new hue. All other colors in the brush shift in relation to the selected color.

More about Hue Shift

Key color selected in the brush example, and other colors indicated in relation to the key color in the color wheel

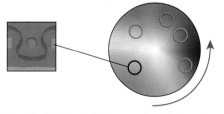

Key color shifted in the brush example, and other colors shifted in relation to the key color in the brush example and the color wheel

To apply Hue Shift colorization: Select Hue Shift from the Method pop-up menu. Then click the Key Color eyedropper, and select a key color in the brush example in the dialog box. The key color is shifted to the current stroke color, and other colors in the brush are shifted around the color wheel, preserving their relationships to the key color.

Lesson 6

Citrus
Bath & Soap

1200 Lakeview Drive
Orange, California 92220
Tel. 310 999.0234
Fax. 310 999.0237
email. jsmith@citrus.com

Citrus
Bath & Soap

Citrus
Bath & Soap

1200 Lakeview Drive
Orange, California 92220

John Smith
Product Manager

1200 Lakeview Drive
Orange, California 92220
Tel. 310 999.0234
Fax. 310 999.0237
email. jsmith@citrus.com

Lesson 7

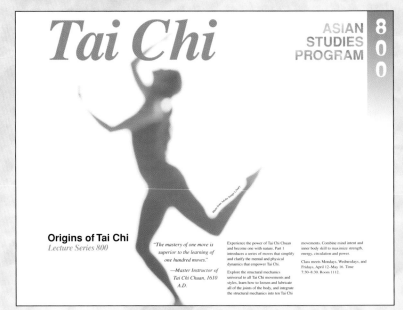

Tai Chi

ASIAN
STUDIES
PROGRAM

800

Origins of Tai Chi
Lecture Series 800

*"The mastery of one move is
superior to the learning of
one hundred moves."*

—*Master Instructor of
Tai Chi Chuan, 1610
A.D.*

Experience the power of Tai Chi Chuan
and become one with nature. Part 1
introduces a series of moves that simplify
and clarify the mental and physical
dynamics that empower Tai Chi.

Explore the structural mechanics
universal to all Tai Chi movements and
styles, learn how to loosen and lubricate
all of the joints of the body, and integrate
the structural mechanics into ten Tai Chi

movements. Combine mind intent and
inner body skill to maximize strength,
energy, circulation and power.

Class meets Mondays, Wednesdays, and
Fridays, April 12–May 16. Time
7:30–8:30. Room 1112.

Lesson 8

8-1: Smooth-color blends

Starting colors

Blends between subtle changes in color require fewer steps.

Starting colors

Blends between distinct changes in color require more steps.

8-2: Modifying blends

Before applying Replace Spine command

After applying Replace Spine command

After applying Reverse Spine command

Lesson 9

Lesson 10

11-1: **Creating gradient mesh objects**

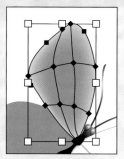

Flat appearance (no highlighting)

To Center highlighting

To Edge highlighting

11-2: **Modifying a gradient mesh**

Gradient mesh applied to object

Mesh points selected before applying color

Moving a mesh point vertically

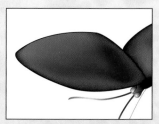

Mesh point added with new color applied

Deleting a mesh line

Result of color blending

11-3: **Changing the opacity of a gradient mesh**

Mesh objects selected

Opacity lowered

12-1: **Pathfinder Gallery**

Unite *creates one shape from overlapping shapes.*

Intersect *creates a new object from shared space.*

Exclude *removes an overlapping area.*

Minus Front *subtracts front object from back.*

Minus Back *subtracts back object from front.*

Divide *creates independent objects from component faces.*

Trim *removes hidden part of filled paths.*

Merge *removes hidden part of filled paths and merges overlapping objects.*

Crop *divides shapes and crops images.*

Outline *creates independent lines divided at each intersection.*

Hard Mix *mixes colors of overlapping areas using the highest value of each color component.*

Soft Mix *makes the top color semitransparent and applies a specified amount of transparency to overlapping colors.*

Lesson 12

Lesson 13

13-1: **Separating colors**

Artwork can consist of spot colors, process colors (global or non-global), registration colors, or a combination. When you separate artwork containing spot colors, a separate plate is created for each spot color. The plate contains only objects of that specific color.

Original

Cyan

Magenta

Yellow

Black

Pantone 185 CVC*

Process plus spot color: *Spot color is printed on separate plate. Options are set in Separation Setup dialog box.*

Process colors: *Spot color is converted to process color equivalent and printed as part of process color plates. Options are set in Separation Setup dialog box.*

* Pantone® 185 CVC is simulated in this example. This book was printed using only the four process colors.

13-2: **Overprint option**

Colors knocked out by default

Overprint option selected for shadow

13-3: **RGB and CMYK color models**

Additive colors (RGB)

Subtractive colors (CMYK)

Lesson 14

ANNUAL DIGITAL CHESS TOURNAMENT
CONVENTION CENTER
WEST WING

14-1: **Color filters**

Adjust filter on placed photo: Original, and after increasing Magenta and Yellow

Saturate filter: Original, and after saturating and desaturating

Adjust filter on artwork: Original, and after increasing and decreasing Magenta

Invert filter: Original, and after inverting

14-2: **Filters Gallery**

Illustrator art

After rasterizing

Dry Brush

Film Grain

Plastic Wrap

Rough Pastels

Smudge Stick

Sponge

Watercolor

Radial Blur

Accented Edges

Angled Strokes

Crosshatch

Ink Outlines

Sprayed Strokes

Sumi-e

Diffuse Glow

Ocean Ripple

Color Halftone

Crystallize

Mezzotint

Pointillize

Bas Relief

Chalk & Charcoal

Chrome

Conté Crayon

Graphic Pen

Halftone Pattern

Note Paper

Photocopy

Reticulation

Torn Edges

Water Paper

Glowing Edges

Mosaic Tiles

Patchwork

Stained Glass

Texturizer

Lesson 15

15-1: Dithering examples

Artwork painted with CMYK colors

Colors dithered in GIF image

Artwork painted with Web palette colors

No color dithering in GIF image

Lesson 7

Working with Type

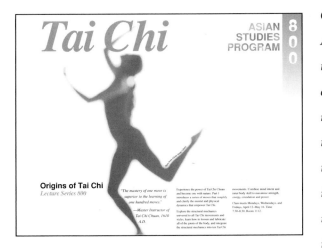

One of the most powerful features of Adobe Illustrator is the ability to use type as a graphic element. Like other objects, type can be painted, scaled, rotated, and so on. You can also wrap type around objects, make it follow along the shape of a path, create type masks, import text files into containers, and modify the shapes of individual letters in a block of type.

In this lesson, you'll learn how to do the following:

• Create type in containers and along paths.

• Import text files into type containers.

• Adjust type attributes and formatting, including the font, leading, and paragraph alignment.

• Wrap type around a graphic.

• Create stylized letterforms with outlined type.

• Create type masks.

• Save a file in PDF format.

Getting started

In this lesson, you'll create a Tai Chi lecture series poster. Before you begin, you'll need to restore the default preferences for Adobe Illustrator and then you'll open the finished art file for this lesson to see an example of what you'll create.

1 To ensure that the tools and palettes function exactly as described in this lesson, delete or deactivate (by renaming) the Adobe Illustrator 9.0 preferences file. See "Restoring default preferences" on page 3.

2 Start Adobe Illustrator.

3 Choose File > Open, and open the L7end.ai file in the Lesson07 folder, located inside the Lessons folder within the AICIB folder on your hard drive.

4 If you like, choose View > Zoom Out to make the finished artwork smaller and leave it on your screen as you work. (Use the hand tool ( ) to move artwork where you want it in the window.) If you don't want to leave the image open, choose File > Close.

For an illustration of the finished artwork in this lesson, see the color section.

Now open the start file to begin the lesson.

5 Choose File > Open, and open the L7start.ai file in the Lesson07 folder, located inside the Lessons folder within the AICIB folder on your hard drive.

6 Choose File > Save As, name the file **TaiChi.ai**, and select the Lesson07 folder. Leave the Format option set to Adobe Illustrator® Document, and click Save. In the Illustrator Native Format Options dialog box, select Illustrator 9.0 Compatibility and click OK.

For now you'll hide the palettes that you don't need yet.

7 Click the close boxes or choose Window > Hide Appearance, Window > Hide Color, and Window > Hide Styles to close these palettes.

8 Bring the Links palette forward by clicking the Links tab behind the Actions palette.

Notice that the Links palette displays two links: the image of the dancing figure, which is linked to the original image file; and the image of the sky to the right of the artboard, which is an embedded image (it was pasted into the document).

9 Click the close box or choose Window > Hide Links to close the Links palette.

For information on using the Links palette, see "Managing linked and embedded images" in online Help or Chapter 2 in the Adobe Illustrator User Guide.

Adding type to a document

Adobe Illustrator lets you add type to a document several different ways. You can type directly in the artwork, copy and paste type from other documents, and import entire text files.

To begin adding type to your artwork, you'll type the Tai Chi title on the poster.

1 Select the type tool (**T**) in the toolbox. Position the pointer so that the I-beam cross hair is in the top left corner of the artwork, using the guides that already exist in the document.

Position type tool at intersection of guides.

The small horizontal line near the bottom of the I-beam—its cross hair—marks the position of the type *baseline*. The baseline is the line on which the type rests.

2 Click to set the type baseline where the guides intersect, and type **Tai Chi**.

By default, the type you create is 12-point Helvetica, filled with black, and stroked with None. The Fill and Stroke boxes in the toolbox display the type's current paint attributes.

Sampling type

Now you'll use the eyedropper tool to pick up, or sample, the attributes of other type in the artwork and apply it to the Tai Chi title.

1 Click the selection tool (▶) in the toolbox to select the words *Tai Chi*.

Clicking the selection tool immediately after typing with the type tool automatically selects the words you typed.

2 Click the eyedropper tool (🖋) in the toolbox, and click anywhere in the line "Lecture Series 800" to sample the type's attributes.

Sample type attributes

Sampled attributes are applied to any selected text (in this case, *Tai Chi*), and the type colors appear in the Fill and Stroke boxes in the toolbox.

Changing the character size

Now you'll use the Character palette to make the title bigger.

1 With the Tai Chi type still selected, choose Type > Character to display the Character palette.

By default, the Character palette displays the selected font and its style, size, kerning, leading, and tracking values. If the type selection contains two or more attributes, the corresponding text boxes are blank. (*Leading* is the amount of space between lines or paragraphs. *Kerning* is the space between two characters. *Tracking* is the spacing in a string of characters.)

A. Font Size *B.* Kerning *C.* Leading
D. Tracking

2 Type **125** in the Font Size text box, and press Enter or Return to increase the font size to 125 points.

Creating columns of type

Another way to add type to your document is to import a text file. You can divide the type container to hold three columns of type for this layout.

You'll create a container that overlaps the bottom leg of the figure so that later you can wrap the text around the leg.

1 Choose File > Place. Select the text file, Text.rtf, located in the Lesson07 folder, and click Place.

2 Select the selection tool (↖) in the toolbox. Move the placed text to the guides at the bottom right of the poster, aligning the top left corner of the text container with the guides that intersect beneath the figure's knee.

Move placed text file to guides at bottom right.

Illustrator supports more than a dozen text formats for Windows and Mac OS, including Microsoft Word®, Rich Text Format, and WordPerfect®. You can also bring text into Illustrator by copying and pasting text from the Clipboard. However, the copied text may lose its type attributes (such as its font and styles) when pasted into the document.

3 Choose View > Guides > Hide Guides.

Next you'll divide this type and its container into a group of three type containers that will each hold a column of type. (You'll use the Rows & Columns command to divide and resize the type block precisely.)

4 Choose Type > Rows & Columns.

The Rows & Columns dialog box is useful for changing the height, width, and gutter size between rows and columns. The Text Flow option lets you control the direction in which text flows (from left to right or up and down).

5 In the Rows section, double-click the amount for Total and enter **120 pt**. Press Tab to enter the amount without closing the dialog box.

6 In the Columns section, double-click the amount for Total and enter **456 pt**. Press Tab to enter the amount.

You have just changed the size of the text container. Next you'll divide it into columns and gutters.

7 In the Columns area, type **3** in the Number text box for three columns, and click OK.

Rows & Columns

Rows
Number: 1
Height: 120 pt
Gutter: 12 pt
Total: 120 pt

Columns
Number: 3
Width: 144 pt
Gutter: 12 pt
Total: 456 pt

OK
Cancel
☑ Preview

Options
Text Flow: ☐ Add Guides

The three type containers are linked so that text flows between containers in the order that the containers are created and grouped—selecting one container selects all three containers. Each container can be moved and resized individually using the direct-selection tool.

8 Before continuing, choose View > Zoom In to magnify your view of the type containers.

9 Click outside of the artwork to deselect the type columns, and choose File > Save.

Text container divided into three columns

Changing character attributes of placed text

Next you'll format the type that you just imported. You'll change the character font of the placed text to match the rest of the poster, and reformat the first two paragraphs, which are a quote and a byline.

1 Select the type tool (**T**), click anywhere in one of the three text columns, and then choose Edit > Select All to select all of the imported text automatically after it is placed.

2 In the Character palette, hold down the mouse button on the Font Menu button (in the top right corner of the palette) and choose a font (we chose Adobe Garamond Regular). Enter sizes for the type and the leading in the Font Size and Leading text boxes. (We specified 8.5 in the Font Size text box and 11 in the Leading text box.) Press Enter or Return to apply the attributes.

Select font from Character palette menu.

Next you'll select the first two paragraphs and format them as a quote and a byline.

3 First, choose Type > Show Hidden Characters to display all of the hidden characters in the text, such as spaces and paragraph breaks.

4 Using the type tool (**T**), triple-click inside the first paragraph to select only that paragraph. (You can also select it by dragging.)

5 In the Character palette, choose a font from the pop-up menu (we selected Adobe Garamond Italic), and enter sizes for the font and leading (we specified 11 points in the Font Size text box and 16 points in the Leading text box). Press Enter or Return to apply the changes.

6 Using the type tool again, triple-click inside the second paragraph to select it, and experiment with different fonts and sizes for the byline. (We used Adobe Garamond Italic, 11 points for font size, and 16 points for leading.)

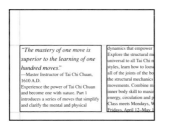

Select and reformat first two paragraphs.

7 Choose Type > Show Hidden Characters to turn off the display of all hidden characters in the text.

8 Choose File > Save.

Changing paragraph attributes

You can set paragraph attributes (such as alignment or indenting) before you enter new type, or reset them to change the appearance of existing, selected type. If you select several type paths and type containers, you can set attributes for all of them at the same time.

Now you'll add more space before all of the paragraphs in the column text.

1 Hold down Ctrl (Windows) or Command (Mac OS) to temporarily convert the type tool to the selection tool, and click the edge of one of the type containers to select it. (Clicking one of the type containers selects all three containers.)

2 Click the Paragraph tab behind the Character palette to display the Paragraph palette.

3 In the Paragraph palette, type **6** in the Space Before Paragraph text box (in the bottom right corner), and press Enter or Return to separate all of the paragraphs by 6 points of spacing. The space before the first paragraph adjusts so that the quote is aligned with the top of the column.

Add space before paragraphs.

4 Choose File > Save.

[?] For information on other features you can use when working with type, such as kerning, tracking, tabs, and searching, see "Using Type" in online Help or Chapter 12 in the *Adobe Illustrator User Guide*.

Adjusting the text flow

You'll shorten the first text column to fit the quote and byline and force the rest of the type to begin in the second column. Because the type containers are linked, adjusting any of the columns affects all of them and the type within them.

1 Choose Edit > Deselect All to deselect the artwork.

2 Select the direct-selection tool (▶) in the toolbox. The direct-selection tool lets you resize one type container without resizing the others.

3 Select the bottom of the left column (don't release the mouse button), and then hold down Shift and drag the bottom of the column up to just below the byline (the second paragraph).

💡 *You can easily locate the edges of type containers in two ways. Choose View > Smart Guides to turn on the Smart Guides and display the outlines, center points, and points of hidden objects whenever the pointer is over them. Or choose View > Outline to see the outlines of all the objects in the artwork without the fills or strokes hiding them.*

Shift-dragging constrains the movement to a straight line. (Shift-clicking the bottom edge of the container with the direct-selection tool alternates between selecting and deselecting the container.)

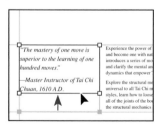

Shift-drag type container to resize.

Notice how the type flows into the second column as you adjust it. Type flows from one object to another based on the type containers' stacking order. In this case, the stacking order is from left to right, in the order in which the columns were created.

4 Click away from the artwork to deselect it, and then choose File > Save.

Wrapping type around a graphic

You can make type wrap around any graphic object in Illustrator. To complete the column layout, you'll wrap the left column of type around the bottom leg of the figure.

In this example, we've added an unpainted object around the leg in the bitmap image so that you can control the way the type will wrap around the figure.

1 Press Ctrl+Y (Windows) or Command+Y (Mac OS) to switch to Outline view.

2 Click the selection tool ( ) in the toolbox, and choose Object > Unlock All to unlock and select the object that overlaps the left side of the type containers. (The object was locked so that it wouldn't interfere with drawing the containers.)

Objects that you use for wrapping type around must be in front of the type container.

3 Choose Object > Arrange > Bring to Front, and then Shift-click the border of the left column to select the type containers too.

Because the containers are linked together, Shift-clicking one of the type containers selects all three containers.

4 Choose Type > Wrap > Make to wrap the type around the object, and then choose View > Preview.

Bring object border to the front.   Select type and object to be wrapped.   Result

The type is wrapped around the object, and the type containers are now grouped with it. You can use the direct-selection tool to select parts of the group and make changes.

5 Press Ctrl+Y (Windows) or Command+Y (Mac OS) to toggle between Preview view and Artwork view as you work. Artwork view lets you see the unpainted object over the leg.

6 Click away from the artwork to deselect it, and then select the direct-selection tool ( ) in the toolbox.

7 Select the object over the leg and drag segments of the object's path outward, or select an anchor point and drag the direction lines to change the shape of the object and, consequently, the shape of the wrapped type.

8 If necessary, use the direct-selection tool to select the bottom of the left column (don't release the mouse button), and drag it down to adjust the last line of the byline.

You can use the type tool to click anywhere in the columns of placed text and make changes as you wish, such as typing some new words or correcting the spelling.

9 When you are satisfied with how the type wraps, choose Edit > Deselect All to deselect the artwork.

10 Choose File > Save.

Typing along a path

Another way to create type in Illustrator is to enter type along a path. Now you'll add a credit line to the image of the dancing figure.

1 If necessary, press Ctrl+Y (Windows) or Command+Y (Mac OS) to switch to Preview view.

The current fill and stroke settings were both set to None when you selected the path along the bottom leg. You'll change the paint settings so you can see a path as you draw it along the upper leg in Preview view.

2 With the artwork deselected, set the paint attributes in the toolbox to a fill of none and a black stroke (by clicking the Fill box and the None button, and then clicking the Stroke box and the Color button).

3 Select the pencil tool (𝒫) in the toolbox, and drag it to draw a line along the back of the figure's raised leg. The line remains selected after you draw it.

4 Select the path-type tool (✢) from the same group as the type tool in the toolbox, and click at the beginning of the line.

Clicking a line with the path-type tool converts the line to an invisible path (without any fill or stroke color), and a blinking insertion point appears.

5 Click the Character tab behind the Paragraph palette to display the Character palette, choose a font from the pop-up menu (we selected Adobe Garamond Regular), type **6** points in the Font Size text box, and press Enter or Return to set the new attributes.

6 Type the credit for the figure: **Photo from Adobe Image Library**.

Draw a line.

Convert line to type path.

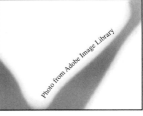
Type words along path.

When you turn a path or object into a type path, the path becomes unstroked and unfilled, even if the path was originally stroked or filled. After the type is selected, any changes to the paint settings affect only the type, not the path.

7 To move the type path, use the selection tool ( ) to select the block of type, and drag it to the new position.

8 To adjust the starting position of the type along the path, select the path-type tool, and then click before the word *Photo*. Press the spacebar to move the type further along the path.

9 Choose File > Save.

Creating type outlines

You can modify the shapes of individual letters in a block of type by converting the block to type outlines or *letterforms*. When you create type outlines, each character becomes a separate object with compound paths outlining the character.

Now you'll convert the number *800* into outlines and change the shape of the letterforms to create a special effect.

1 Choose View > Outline, and then choose Window > Show Navigator to display a thumbprint of the artboard in the Navigator palette. Click in the top right corner of the thumbprint image to move the red box over the number *800*.

2 Use the selection tool ( ) to select the type *800* in the top right corner of the artwork, and then choose Type > Create Outlines.

The type is converted to a set of compound paths around each number that can be edited and manipulated like any other object.

3 Click away from the artwork to deselect the numbers, and then select the group-selection tool ( ) from the same group as the direct-selection tool in the toolbox.

The group-selection tool lets you select individual outlines in a compound path.

4 Shift-click to select the outer paths of all three numbers, and press the Up Arrow key a few times to move the paths up, leaving the inner paths of all three in their original position.

  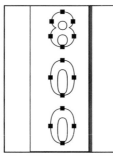

Create outlines.   *Select the outer lines.*   *Press the Up Arrow key.*

You can also change the shape of letterforms by using the direct-selection tool to select path segments or anchor points in the outlines and dragging the direction lines in new directions.

5 Click away from the artwork to deselect it, and press Ctrl+Y (Windows) or Command+Y (Mac OS) to switch back to Preview view.

Creating type masks

Masks crop part of an image so that only a portion of it is revealed through the shape or shapes that you create. You can use type as a mask without having to convert the type to outlines first. After creating a mask using type, you can still edit it—for example, by adjusting the font or size and even by typing in new text.

In this example, you'll create a mask using type and an embedded bitmap image. We pasted an image of a cloudy sky into the document to use as the background of the mask.

For information on embedding and linking image files in your artwork, see "Setting Up Artwork in Illustrator" in online Help or Chapter 2 in the Adobe Illustrator User Guide.

Now you'll add the heading "ASIAN STUDIES PROGRAM" in the top right corner of the poster and convert it to a type mask over the cloudy sky image.

1 Click the selection tool ( ) in the toolbox, and move the image of the sky from the area outside of the artboard to the top right corner of the artwork next to the 800 rectangle.

2 Select the type tool (T) from the same group as the path-type tool ( ) in the toolbox, and click in the sky next to the number *8*.

Move the sky image.   Select the type tool and click.

3 In the Character palette, choose a font from the pop-up menu (we chose Myriad Bold), enter sizes for the font and the leading (we specified 28 points in the Font Size text box and 28 points in the Leading text box), and press Enter or Return to apply the settings.

4 Click the Paragraph tab to display the Paragraph palette, and click the Align Right button.

A. Align left B. Align center
C. Align right D. Justify full lines
E. Justify all lines

5 Press the Caps Lock key to type in all uppercase letters. Type **ASIAN**, and then press Enter or Return to move the insertion point to the next line. Type **STUDIES**, press Enter or Return, and then type **PROGRAM**.

6 Click the selection tool to select the entire block of type, and Shift-click to select the sky image behind it.

The object that will be the mask can be a single shape, multiple shapes, or type. The masking object (in this case, the type) must be on top of the artwork you want to mask.

7 Choose Object > Clipping Mask > Make to convert the front object into a mask and see through to the image.

Select type and sky image.   *Apply clipping mask.*

The type mask loses its paint attributes and is assigned a fill and stroke of None. Thus, if you moved the type away from the background image, you would no longer see the type mask in Preview view unless you select it or assign it new paint attributes.

Once you have created a mask, you can still adjust the artwork and the type (the mask) independently. For example, you can resize either the artwork (here an embedded photo) or the type, as well as rotate, skew, and reflect them.

8 Double-click the hand tool (🖐) in the toolbox to fit the artwork in the window.

9 Choose File > Save.

You've completed the artwork for the Tai Chi poster using a variety of options for working with type.

Saving your file for electronic distribution

Now you'll save a copy of the poster in Portable Document Format (PDF) so you can distribute it electronically, or link it to your Web site. When you save your artwork in PDF format, Illustrator creates an exact snapshot of the page that lets you view it online without the fonts, linked images, or software used to create it.

1 Choose File > Save a Copy. In the dialog box, choose Adobe PDF (PDF) from the Save as Type (Windows) or Format (Mac OS) pop-up menu, name the file **TaiChi.pdf**, and click Save.

2 In the Adobe PDF Format Options dialog box, choose Screen Optimized from the Options Set pop-up menu to display a set of options for the Web. (Notice that the document's color mode will automatically be converted to RGB for optimal screen viewing.) Leave the other settings as they are and click OK.

3 In the warning dialog box on "Preserve Illustrator Editing Capabilities" not being checked, click OK to save the file.

Note: Select the Preserve Illustrator Editing Capabilities when exporting a file only if you want to be able to reopen and edit the file in Adobe Illustrator. If you are posting the file on a Web site, you probably don't want it to be editable.

Illustrator saves the copy of the poster as a Web-ready PDF file that can be viewed electronically in Adobe Acrobat Reader® and linked to your Web pages to be viewed in a browser. Acrobat Reader—electronic publishing software for Windows, DOS, UNIX®, and Macintosh®—is provided on the Adobe Illustrator CD and is available on the Adobe Web site (http://www.adobe.com) for free distribution.

For information on saving Illustrator files in different formats, see "Saving and Exporting Artwork" in online Help or Chapter 14 in the Adobe Illustrator User Guide.

For information on converting artwork to GIF and JPEG images for your Web pages, see Lesson 15, "Preparing Graphics for Web Publication."

To learn about printing your poster, see Lesson 13, "Printing Artwork and Producing Color Separations."

Review questions

1 Describe three ways to enter text into the artwork.

2 How do you change the leading between lines in a paragraph? How do you change the leading between paragraphs?

3 How can you divide a type container into smaller containers?

4 How do you create type that follows the shape of a path or an object?

5 What is a reason for converting type to outlines?

6 How do you create a type mask?

Review answers

1 To enter text in the artwork, do any of the following:

• Select the type tool (T) and start typing.

• Import text from another file by choosing File > Place.

• Select the path-type tool, click on any path, and start typing.

2 To change the leading between lines in a paragraph, select the paragraph and then enter a new leading value in the Character palette. (Choose Type > Character to display the Character palette.) To change the leading (or space) between paragraphs, select the block of type and then enter a new leading value in the Space Before Paragraph text box in the Paragraph palette. (Choose Type > Paragraph to display the Paragraph palette.)

3 To divide a type container into smaller containers, select the container and choose Type > Rows & Columns. In the Rows & Columns dialog box, enter the number of horizontal or vertical containers, or both, into which you'll divide the container, their size, and the space between each container.

4 You can use the path-type tool (⤳) to type words along an existing path. You can also wrap a block of type around an object by selecting the type and the object and choosing Type > Wrap > Make. (The object must be in front of the type.)

5 Convert type to outlines when you want to transform (scale, reshape, and so on) letters individually in the word or block of type. Outlines are also useful for filling type with a gradient fill.

6 One way to create a type mask is to select the type that you want to be the mask, and select the object, bitmap image, or type that you want to show through the mask. (The masking type must be in front of any other objects.) Then choose Object > Clipping Mask > Make to create the type mask.

Blending Shapes and Colors

Gradient fills are graduated blends of two or more colors. You use the Gradient palette to create or modify a gradient fill. The blend tool blends the shapes and colors of objects together into a new blended object or a series of intermediate shapes.

In this lesson, you'll learn how to do the following:

• Create and save gradients.

• Add colors to a gradient.

• Adjust the direction of a gradient blend.

• Create smooth-color blends between objects.

• Blend the shapes of objects in intermediate steps.

• Modify a blend, including adjusting its path and changing the shape or color of the original objects.

Getting started

You'll explore various ways to create your own color gradients and blend colors and shapes together using the Gradient palette and the blend tool.

Before you begin, you'll restore the default preferences for Adobe Illustrator. Then you'll open the finished art file for this lesson to see what you'll create.

1 To ensure that the tools and palettes function exactly as described in this lesson, delete or deactivate (by renaming) the Adobe Illustrator 9.0 preferences file. See "Restoring default preferences" on page 3.

2 Start Adobe Illustrator.

3 Choose File > Open, and open the L8end.ai file in the Lesson08 folder, located inside the Lessons folder within the AICIB folder on your hard drive.

The chili peppers, *CHILES* type, and wavy lines are all filled with gradients. The objects that make up the inside of the bowl, the objects on the outside of the bowl, and the top and bottom wavy lines on the blanket have all been blended to create new objects.

4 If you like, choose View > Zoom Out to make the finished artwork smaller, adjust the window size, and leave it on your screen as you work. (Use the hand tool (₹^m) to move the artwork where you want it in the window.) If you don't want to leave the image open, choose File > Close.

 For an illustration of the finished artwork in this lesson, see the color section.

To begin working, you'll open an existing art file.

5 Choose File > Open, and open the L8start.ai file in the Lesson08 folder, located inside the Lessons folder within the AICIB folder on your hard drive.

6 Choose File > Save As, name the file **Chiles.ai,** and select the Lesson08 folder. Leave the Format option set to Adobe Illustrator® Document, and click Save. In the Illustrator Native Format Options dialog box, select Illustrator 9.0 Compatibility and click OK.

7 Click the close box or choose Window > Hide Layers to close the Layers palette group. You won't need these palettes for this lesson.

Creating a gradient fill

Gradients can be used very much like colors to fill objects that you create. A *gradient fill* is a graduated blend between two or more colors. You can easily create your own gradients. Or you can use the gradients provided with Adobe Illustrator and edit them for the desired effect.

To begin the lesson, you'll create a gradient fill for one of the chili peppers.

1 Using the selection tool ( ), click to select the chili pepper in the back.

The pepper is painted with a solid color fill and no stroke, as indicated in the Fill and Stroke boxes in the toolbox. The Gradient button below the Fill and Stroke boxes indicates the current gradient fill (which is by default a black-and-white gradient until you select a gradient-filled object or a gradient swatch in the Swatches palette).

2 Click the Gradient button in the toolbox.

The default, black-and-white gradient appears in the Fill box in the toolbox and is applied to the selected chili pepper.

Click gradient button to paint selected object with default or current gradient fill.

When you click the Gradient button in the toolbox, the Gradient palette appears from behind the Stroke palette. You use the Gradient palette to create your own gradients and to modify the colors of existing gradients.

3 In the Gradient palette, position the pointer on the triangle in the upper right corner of the palette, press the mouse button, and choose Show Options from the palette's menu. (Use the same technique for choosing options from other palette menus.)

4 Now select the Gradient tab on the palette and drag it to move the palette to another area on your screen. This action separates, or undocks, the Gradient palette from the Stroke palette.

A. *Starting gradient stop*
B. *Midpoint between blended colors*
C. *Ending gradient stop*

In the Gradient palette, the left gradient square, or stop, under the gradient bar marks the gradient's starting color; the right gradient stop marks the ending color. A *gradient stop* is the point at which a gradient changes from one color to the next. A diamond above the bar marks the midpoint where two colors blend equally.

5 Click the left gradient stop to select the starting color of the gradient. The tip of the gradient stop appears darker to indicate that it's selected.

In the Color palette, a gradient stop appears beneath the Fill box, indicating which color in the gradient is currently selected. Now you'll paint the selected color in the gradient with a new color.

6 In the Color palette, position the pointer on the triangle in the upper right corner of the palette, press the mouse button, and choose CMYK to switch from the Grayscale palette to the CMYK palette.

7 With the gradient stop selected, position the eyedropper pointer in the color bar at the bottom of the Color palette, and drag or click to select a new color. Notice the change to the gradient fill in the selected chili pepper.

Gradient stop selected   Result

You can also drag the Color palette sliders or type in values in the percent text boxes to select a color. The selected gradient stop changes to reflect your choice.

8 With the left gradient stop still selected, type in these CMYK values in the Color palette: C=**20**, M=**100**, Y=**80**, and K=**0**. (To quickly select each text box before typing, press Tab.) Press Enter or Return to apply the last value typed.

9 In the Gradient palette, select the ending gradient stop on the right.

10 In the Color palette, choose CMYK from the palette menu to switch to the CMYK palette from the Grayscale palette.

11 Change the ending color by entering these values in the Color palette: C=**100**, M=**30**, Y=**100**, and K=**0**. (Press Tab to select each text box.) Press Enter or Return to apply the last value typed.

Now you'll save the new gradient in the Swatches palette.

12 Click the Swatches tab to bring the palette to the front of its group. (If the Swatches palette isn't visible on-screen, choose Window > Show Swatches to display it.)

13 To save the gradient, drag it from the Fill box in the toolbox or the Gradient palette and drop it on the Swatches palette, or select it and click the New Swatch button at the bottom of the Swatches palette.

14 In the Swatches palette, double-click the new gradient swatch to open the Swatch Options dialog box. Type **Pepper2** in the Swatch Name text box, and click OK.

15 To display only gradient swatches in the Swatches palette, click the Show Gradient Swatches button at the bottom of the Swatches palette.

16 Try out some of the different gradients in the selected chili pepper.

Notice that some of the gradients have several colors. You'll learn how to make a gradient with multiple colors later in this lesson.

17 Deselect the artwork by choosing Edit > Deselect All, and then choose File > Save.

Adjusting the direction of the gradient blend

Once you have painted an object with a gradient fill, you can adjust the direction that the gradient colors blend in the object. Now you'll adjust the gradient fill in the other chili pepper.

1 Use the selection tool (▶) to select the chili pepper in front. Notice that it's painted with a radial-type gradient (as indicated in the Gradient palette).

You can create linear or radial gradients. Both types of gradient have a starting and an ending color of the fill. With a radial gradient, the starting color of the gradient defines the center point of the fill, which radiates outward to the ending color.

2 Select the gradient tool (▨) in the toolbox.

The gradient tool works only on selected objects that are filled with a gradient.

3 Click or drag the gradient tool across the selected chili pepper to change the position and direction of the gradient's starting and ending colors.

Drag gradient tool at an angle.   *Result*

For example, drag within the pepper to create a short gradient with distinct color blends; drag a longer distance outside the pepper to create a longer gradient with more subtle color blends. You can also drag from the ending color to the starting color and vice versa to transpose the colors and reverse the direction of the blend.

4 Deselect the artwork by choosing Edit > Deselect All, and then choose File > Save.

Adding colors to a gradient

Every gradient in Adobe Illustrator has at least two gradient stops. By editing the color mix of each stop and by adding gradient stops in the Gradient palette, you can create your own custom gradients.

Now you'll paint some type that has been converted to path outlines with a linear gradient fill, and edit the colors in it.

1 Select the selection tool ( ), and Shift-click to select each letter in the type *CHILES*.

The *CHILES* type has already been converted to path outlines so you can fill it with a gradient. (To convert type to path outlines, select it and choose Type > Create Outlines. See Lesson 7, "Working with Type," for more information.)

2 Choose Object > Group to group the letters.

Select letter outlines.   *Group type.*

By grouping the letters, you'll fill each individual letter with the same gradient at once. Grouping them also makes it easier to edit the gradient fill globally.

3 In the toolbox, click the Gradient button (below the Fill and Stroke boxes) to paint the type outlines with the current gradient fill—in this case, with the radial gradient that was last selected in the chili pepper.

Paint selected type with last-selected gradient fill.

To edit the colors in a gradient, you click their gradient stops below the gradient bar.

4 In the Gradient palette, for Type choose Linear to change the fill to a linear gradient, and then click the left gradient stop to select it so that you can adjust the starting color of the gradient.

The Color palette displays the color of the currently selected gradient stop in the Fill box.

Now, you'll change the display of the Swatches palette so that you can choose any color from it.

5 At the bottom of the Swatches palette, click the Show All Swatches button to display all of the color, gradient, and pattern swatches in the Swatches palette.

6 With the left gradient stop selected in the Gradient palette, hold down Alt (Windows) or Option (Mac OS) and click a color swatch in the Swatches palette to assign the color to the gradient. (We selected the Lime color swatch.)

Holding down Alt/Option as you click a color swatch applies the color to the selected gradient stop in the gradient rather than to the selected objects in the artwork.

Colors in gradients can be assigned as CMYK process colors, RGB process colors, Web Safe RGB colors, or spot colors. When a gradient is printed or separated, mixed-mode gradient colors are all converted to CMYK process color.

Now you'll add intermediate colors to the gradient to create a fill with multiple blends between colors.

7 In the Gradient palette, click anywhere below the gradient bar to add a stop between the other gradient stops.

You add a color to a gradient by adding a gradient stop. When you add a new gradient stop, a diamond appears above the gradient bar to mark the colors' new midpoint.

8 With the new gradient stop selected, hold down Alt (Windows) or Option (Mac OS) and click a color swatch in the Swatches palette to assign it to the gradient. (We selected the Yellow color swatch.)

Observe how the new color looks in the *CHILES* type.

Select gradient stop and change   Result
middle color of gradient.

9 To adjust the midpoint between two colors, drag the diamond above the gradient bar
to the right or left.

Drag diamond to adjust color
midpoint.

Note: *You can delete a color in a gradient by dragging its gradient stop downward and out of
the Gradient palette.*

Another way to apply a color to the gradient is to sample the color from the artwork using
the eyedropper tool.

10 Select the right gradient stop in the Gradient palette. Select the eyedropper tool ( )
in the toolbox. Then hold down Shift and click a color in the artwork. (We sampled the
light red color in the front chili pepper.)

Holding down Shift as you click with the eyedropper tool applies the color sample to the selected gradient stop in the gradient rather than replacing the entire gradient with the color in the selected *CHILES* type.

Shift-click to apply sample to selected color in gradient.

Now you'll save the new gradient.

11 In the Swatches palette, choose New Swatch from the palette menu, type a name for the gradient in the Swatch Name text box (we named it "Chiles type"), and click OK to save the new gradient.

12 Deselect the artwork by choosing Edit > Deselect All, and then choose File > Save.

Creating smooth-color blends

You can choose several options for blending the shapes and colors of objects to create a new object. When you choose the smooth-color blend option, Illustrator combines the shapes and colors of the objects into many intermediate steps, creating a smooth graduated blend between the original objects.

For an example of smooth-color blends, see figure 8-1 in the color section.

Now you'll combine the two inner shapes of the bowl into a smooth-color blend.

1 Select the selection tool ( ), click the smallest shape inside the bowl to select it, and then Shift-click to select the second shape inside the bowl.

Both objects are filled with a solid color and have no stroke. Objects that have painted strokes blend differently than those that have no stroke.

2 Choose Object > Blend > Blend Options.

3 In the Blend Options dialog box, for Spacing choose Smooth Color (selected by default), and click OK.

This action sets up the blend options, which remain set until you change them. Now you'll apply the blend.

4 Choose Object > Blend > Make.

When you make a smooth-color blend between objects, Illustrator automatically calculates the number of intermediate steps necessary to create a smooth transition between the objects.

Note: *To release a blend and revert to the original objects, select the blend and choose Object > Blend > Release.*

Blending intermediate steps

Now you'll create a series of blended shapes between three different-colored shapes on the outside of the bowl by specifying the number of steps in the blend and using the blend tool to create the blend.

1 Click away from the artwork to deselect it, and then double-click the blend tool ( ) to open the Blend Options dialog box.

2 For Spacing, choose Specified Steps, type **6** for the number of steps, and click OK.

3 Using the blend tool, click the red diamond with the tool's upper hollow square, and then click the green diamond to make a blend between them.

A new object is created that blends the shapes of the diamonds and their colors together in six steps.

4 Now click the blue circle to complete the blended path.

Click objects with blend tool to create a blend.   *Result*

Note: *To end the current path and continue blending other objects on a separate path, click the blend tool in the toolbox first and then click the other objects.*

Modifying the blend

Now you'll modify the shape of the path or *spine* of the blend using the convert-anchor-point tool.

1 Select the convert-anchor-point tool (⌐) from the same group as the pen tool (✒) in the toolbox.

2 Select the endpoint of the spine at the center of the blue circle (don't release the mouse button). Drag slowly down until you see two direction lines, and continue dragging down and a little to the left until the path runs parallel to the bottom edge of the bowl.

3 Repeat step 2 with the endpoint of the spine at the center of the red diamond, but drag *up* instead of down.

Now you'll adjust the spacing between the center shapes on the blend.

4 Using the convert-anchor-point tool, select the middle anchor point of the spine (at the center of the green diamond)—don't release the mouse button—and drag to the left to lengthen the direction line and stretch out the spacing between the blend steps.

Select end and middle anchor points and drag direction handles to reshape blend path.

💡 *A quick way to reshape the blend's path is to wrap it around another path or object. Select the blend, select the other object or path, and then choose Object > Blend > Replace Spine.*

You can modify the blend instantly by changing the shape or color of the original objects. Now you'll delete an anchor point on an object and reshape the object to modify the blend.

5 Zoom in closer on the red diamond by using the zoom tool (🔍) or the Navigator palette.

6 Hold down Ctrl (Windows) or Command (Mac OS), and click the red diamond to select it.

7 Select the delete-anchor-point tool ( ) from the same group as the convert-direction-point tool in the toolbox and click a corner point on the red diamond to delete it.

Notice how changing the shape of the diamond affects the shape of the intermediate steps in the blend.

8 Select the direct-selection tool ( ) in the toolbox and drag another anchor point on the diamond out to extend the shape of the corner.

Delete anchor point on
original object.

Drag anchor point to
reshape object.

Result

You can switch the starting and ending objects in the blend without affecting the shape of the spine by selecting the blend and choosing Object > Blend > Reverse Spine.

9 Choose File > Save.

For an example of modified blends, see figure 8-2 in the color section.

Combining blends with gradients

You can blend objects that are filled with gradients to create different effects of color blending. The two zigzag lines in the artwork are filled with gradients. (See "Exploring on your own" on page 248 to learn how to create them.)

Now you'll blend the gradient-filled lines to create a multicolored blanket in the artwork.

1 Double-click the hand tool (✋) in the toolbox to fit the artwork in the window.

Click top line to select first object for blend.   *Click corresponding point on bottom line.*   *Result*

2 Select the blend tool (◧) in the toolbox and click the top zigzag line to select the first object for the blend. Then click the corresponding point on the bottom zigzag line to create the blend. (If you don't click the corresponding point, you'll get a distorted result.)

The current blend settings for six specified steps are applied to the blend. You can change these settings for an existing blend.

3 Click the selection tool (▸) to select the bounding box of the new blend, and choose Object > Blend > Blend Options.

4 In the Blend Options dialog box, select Preview, type a number in the text box (we specified 4 steps), and press Tab to see the effect in the artwork. Click OK.

Change number of steps in the blend.   *Result*

5 Click away from the artwork to deselect it.

Now you'll adjust the blend by changing a gradient color in one of the original objects.

6 Select the direct-selection tool ( ), and select one of the original zigzag lines. (We selected the bottom zigzag line.)

Select original object.

7 In the Gradient palette, click a gradient stop to select a color in the gradient fill. (We selected the right gradient stop to select the ending color of the gradient.)

8 Hold down Alt (Windows) or Option (Mac OS), and click a color in the Swatches palette to apply it to the selected gradient stop. (We selected the Teal color swatch.)

Holding down Alt/Option as you click allows you to apply the color swatch to the selected gradient stop rather than to the selected zigzag line.

♀ *You can paint the individual steps in the blend with separate gradients or colors by expanding the blend. Select the blend and choose Object > Blend > Expand.*

9 To view your final artwork, press Tab to hide the toolbox and all of the open palettes.

Pressing Tab toggles between hiding and showing the toolbox and palettes. Pressing Shift+Tab toggles between hiding and showing just the palettes (and not the toolbox).

10 Deselect the artwork.

11 Choose File > Save. Choose File > Close to close the file.

This completes the lesson. To learn how to use the gradient mesh tool to make colors in an object blend in multiple directions, see Lesson 11, "Creating Airbrush Effects." To learn how to use the color modes or transparency to blend colors together, see Lesson 9, "Using Appearance Attributes, Styles, and Effects."

Exploring on your own

The two wavy lines in the artwork were created by applying the Zig Zag distort filter to two straight lines, and then they were converted to path outlines so they could be filled with gradients.

To create a gradient-filled zigzag line like those in the artwork, do the following:

1 Draw a straight line using the pen tool.

2 Select the line, remove the fill, paint the stroke with a color, and increase the stroke weight to 10 points.

3 With the line selected, choose Filter > Distort > Zig Zag.

4 In the Zig Zag dialog box, enter **.15 in** in the Size text box and **11** in the Ridges per segment text box. Click OK.

5 Choose Object > Path > Outline Stroke.

Notice that the stroke color has switched with the fill of None, so now you can fill the object with a gradient.

Review questions

1 What is a gradient fill?

2 Name two ways to fill a selected object with a gradient.

3 What is the difference between a gradient fill and a blend?

4 How do you adjust the blend between colors in a gradient?

5 How do you add colors to a gradient?

6 How do you adjust the direction of a gradient?

7 Describe two ways to blend the shapes and colors of objects together.

8 What is the difference between the Smooth Color blend option and specifying the number of steps in a blend?

9 How do you adjust the shapes or colors in the blend? How do you adjust the path of the blend?

Review answers

1 A gradient fill is a graduated blend between two or more colors or tints of the same color.

2 Select an object and do one of the following:

• Click the Gradient button in the toolbox to fill an object with the default white-to-black gradient or with the last selected gradient.

• Click a gradient swatch in the Swatches palette.

• Make a new gradient by clicking a gradient swatch in the Swatches palette and mixing your own in the Gradient palette.

• Use the eyedropper tool to sample a gradient from an object in your artwork, and then apply it to the selected object.

3 The difference between a gradient fill and a blend is the way that colors combine together—colors blend together within a gradient fill and between objects in a blend.

4 You drag one of the gradient's stops in the Gradient palette.

5 In the Gradient palette, click beneath the gradient bar to add a gradient stop to the gradient. Then use the Color palette to mix a new color, or in the Swatches palette, Alt-click (Windows) or Option-click (Mac OS) a color swatch.

6 You click or drag with the gradient tool to adjust the direction of a gradient. Dragging a long distance changes colors gradually; dragging a short distance makes the color change more abrupt.

7 You can blend the shapes and colors of objects together by doing one of the following:

• Clicking each object with the blend tool to create a blend of intermediate steps between the objects according to preset blend options.

• Selecting the objects and choosing Object > Blend > Blend Options to set up the number of intermediate steps, and then choosing Object > Blend > Make to create the blend.

Objects that have painted strokes blend differently than those with no strokes.

8 With the Smooth Color blend option selected, Illustrator automatically calculates the number of intermediate steps necessary to create a seamlessly smooth blend between the selected objects. Specifying the number of steps lets you determine how many intermediate steps are visible in the blend. You can also specify the distance between intermediate steps in the blend.

9 You use the direct-selection tool ( ) to select and adjust the shape of an original object, thus changing the shape of the blend. You can change the colors of the original objects to adjust the intermediate colors in the blend. You use the convert-anchor-point tool ( ) to change the shape of the path, or spine, of the blend by dragging anchor points or direction handles on the spine.

Lesson 9

Using Appearance Attributes, Styles, and Effects

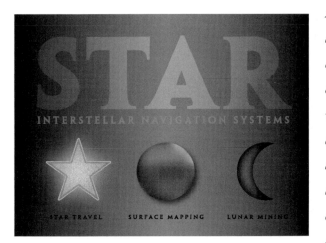

Appearance attributes are properties of an object—such as fills, strokes, transparency, effects, blending modes, or any combination of these—that affect its look without changing its structure. You can alter or remove appearance attributes at any time. You can also save them as styles and apply them to other objects. You can edit an object that has a style applied to it at any time, plus edit the style—an enormous time-saver.

In this lesson, you'll learn how to do the following:

- Create an appearance attribute.
- Add an effect to an appearance.
- Save an appearance as a style.
- Apply a style to a layer.

Getting started

In this lesson, you'll enhance the basic design for a Web page by applying appearance attributes and styles to the page's type, background, and three buttons. Before you begin, you'll need to restore the default preferences for Adobe Illustrator and then you'll open the finished art file for this lesson to see what you'll be creating.

1 To ensure that the tools and palettes function exactly as described in this lesson, delete or deactivate (by renaming) the Adobe Illustrator 9.0 preferences file. See "Restoring default preferences" on page 3.

2 Start Adobe Illustrator.

3 Choose File > Open, and open the L09end.ai file located in the Lesson09 folder inside the Lessons folder within the AICIB folder on your hard drive.

The artwork in this file is a design mock-up of a Web home page. The design for the completed page includes several styles and effects, including overlapping gradients, transparent type, drop shadows, and texturized and shaded graphics.

4 If you like, choose View > Zoom Out to make the design mock-up smaller, adjust the window size, and leave it on-screen as you work. (Use the hand tool (✋) to move the artwork where you want it in the window.) If you don't want to leave the artwork open, choose File > Close.

For an illustration of the finished artwork in this lesson, see the color section.

Using appearance attributes

You can apply appearance attributes to any object, group, or layer by using effects and the Appearance and Styles palettes. An appearance attribute is a property—such as a fill, stroke, transparency, or effect—that affects the look of an object, but that can be changed or removed at any time without changing the object's basic structure.

The advantage to using the Appearance palette to add effects or other attributes is that they can be selected and edited at any time.

For example, if you apply a drop shadow effect to an object, at any time you can change the drop shadow distance, blur, or color. You can also copy that effect, and apply it to other shapes, groups, or layers. You can even save it as a style and use it for other objects or other files. In contrast, if you apply the Drop Shadow filter to an object, you cannot edit the filter results, copy the filter effect, or apply it to other objects globally.

The types of editable attributes found in the Appearance palette are:

• Fill lists all fill attributes (fill type, color, transparency, and effects).

• Stroke lists some stroke attributes (stroke type, brush, color transparency, and effects). All other stroke attributes are displayed in the Strokes palette.

• Transparency lists opacity and blending mode.

• Effects lists commands in the Effect menu.

A. *Stroke color and paintbrush name*
B. *Stroke opacity and blending mode*
C. *Second stroke color and weight*
D. *Second stroke effects*
E. *Fill color, opacity, and blending mode*
F. *New Art Maintains Appearance*
G. *Clear Appearance*
H. *Reduce to Basic Appearance*
I. *Duplicate Selected Item*

Adding an appearance attribute

You'll start by selecting the star shape and adding to its basic appearance using the Appearance palette.

1 Choose File > Open, and open the L09start.ai, located in the Lesson09 folder inside the Lessons folder within the AICIB folder on your hard drive.

2 Choose File > Save As, name the file **StarArt.ai**, and select the Lesson09 folder. Leave the Format option set to Adobe Illustrator® Document, and click Save. In the Illustrator Native Format Options dialog box, select Illustrator 9.0 Compatibility and click OK.

3 Using the selection tool (▶), select the star shape.

4 In the Layers palette, expand the Star Button layer so that you can see its contents. Notice that the star shape is selected and its path is targeted, as indicated by the double-circle (target) icon to the right of the path name.

5 Notice the fill and stroke attributes of the star shape listed in the Appearance palette. (If the palette isn't visible on-screen, choose Window > Show Appearance to display it.)

Star selected

Expanded Star button layer

Fill and stroke attributes

Targeting layers, groups, and objects to apply appearance attributes

Using the Layers palette, you can apply appearance attributes—such as styles, effects, and transparency—to layers, groups, and objects. When an appearance attribute is applied to a layer or group in the Layers palette, any artwork created on or moved to that layer or group takes on that appearance.

For example, if you apply a style that has a drop shadow to Layer 2 in your artwork, anything you create on Layer 2 will have a drop shadow. If you move an object from Layer 2 to another layer, that object will no longer have the drop shadow.

--From the Adobe Illustrator User Guide, Chapter 9

6 In the Appearance palette, click the Stroke attribute to select it.

You can expand and collapse attributes in the Appearance palette by clicking the triangle (▷) to the left of the attribute in the palette list.

7 In the Transparency palette, choose Multiply from the blending modes pop-up menu.

8 Using the keyboard shortcut, press Ctrl+spacebar (Windows) or Command+spacebar and click the star shape to zoom in on it without deselecting the star shape or selection tool. Inspect the stroke around the star to see how it has changed. The effect of the Multiply blending mode is similar to drawing on a page with transparent marker pens.

Strokes are centered on a path outline—half of the stroke color overlaps the filled star shape and half of the stroke color overlaps the background gradient.

Star shape with Multiply blending mode applied

For a color illustration of the Multiply blending mode, see figure 9-1 in the color section.

Reordering appearance attributes

Now you'll change the appearance of the Multiply blending mode by rearranging the attributes in the Appearance palette.

1 Resize the Appearance palette so that you can view all of its contents. Click the Fill attribute and drag it above the Stroke attribute. (This technique is similar to dragging layers in the Layers palettes to adjust their stacking order.)

Moving the Fill attribute above the Stroke attribute changes the look of the Multiply blending modes on the stroke. Half of the stroke has been covered up. Blending modes work only on objects that are beneath them in the stacking order.

You'll add another stroke to the object using the Appearance palette.

2 With the star shape still selected, choose Add New Stroke from the Appearance palette menu. A stroke is added to the top of the appearance list. It has the same color and stroke weight as the first stroke.

3 Select the new stroke in the Appearance palette.

4 In the Color palette, choose RGB from the palette menu, and then use the sliders or text boxes to change the color to a dark orange. (We used a color mix of R=255, G=73, and B=0.)

5 Click the Stroke palette tab to bring it to the front of its group. Then change the Stroke weight to **2** points. Press Enter or Return.

You'll rearrange the order of the appearance attributes to prepare for adding live effects in the next part of the lesson.

6 In the Appearance palette, select the 4-point Stroke attribute and drag it to the very top of the Appearance attributes list. (It should be directly above the 2-point stroke.)

7 Choose File > Save to save the artwork.

Using live effects

The Effect menu commands alter the appearance of an object without changing the underlying object. Many Effect commands also appear in the Filter menu, but only the Effect commands are fully editable. Applying an effect to an object automatically adds the effect to the object's appearance attribute. You can select and edit the effect at any time using the Appearance palette.

You can apply more than one effect to an object. In this part of the lesson, you'll apply two effects to the star shape—an outer glow to make the star appear to glow and a texture using a Photoshop effect called Grain.

1 With the star shape still selected, choose Effect > Stylize > Outer Glow.

Note: Choose the top Stylize command in the Effect menu.

2 Click the Preview option and try different Opacity and Blur amounts until you are satisfied with the result. Leave the blend mode set to screen. (We used 86% opacity and a 19-point blur.)

3 Click the color square next to the Mode menu to change the glow color. (We used a color mix of R=255, G=255, and B=51 to get a richer, brighter yellow.) Click OK to exit the Color Picker, and click OK again to apply the effect.

Now you'll add a second effect to the star shape.

4 Choose Effect > Texture > Grain.

5 Adjust the settings until you are satisfied with the preview in the Grain dialog box. (We used an Intensity of 30, Contrast of 100, and Regular type.)

6 Click OK to see the result. Notice that Grain has been added to the list of attributes in the Appearance palette.

7 Choose File > Save to save your changes.

Editing an effect

Effects can be edited at any time. To edit an effect, you simply double-click its name in the Appearance palette to display that effect's dialog box. Changes you make update the artwork.

You'll change the texture you applied to the star in the last section.

1 Make sure that the star is still selected.

2 If necessary, resize the Appearance palette to view all of its contents. Then double-click the Grain attribute.

3 In the Grain dialog box, change the Type to Soft and click OK.

Now you'll adjust the blending mode of the star's fill to make it glow more.

4 With the star shape still selected, click the Fill attribute in the Appearance palette.

5 In the Transparency palette, choose Luminosity from the blending mode menu.

6 Choose File > Save to save the artwork.

Now you're ready to save the star's appearance as a style.

Using styles

A style is a named set of appearance attributes. By applying different styles, you can quickly and globally change the entire appearance of an object.

For example, you may have a symbol on a map that represents a city, with a style applied that paints the symbol green with a drop shadow. You can use that style to paint all of the cities' symbols on the map. If you change your mind, you can change the fill color of the style to blue. All the symbols painted with that style will be automatically updated.

The Styles palette lets you create, name, save, and apply styles to objects, layers, or groups. Just like attributes and effects, styles are completely reversible. For example, you could apply a style to a circle that contains the ZigZag effect, turning the circle into a starburst. You can revert the object to its original appearance with the Appearance palette or you can break the link with that style and edit one of its attributes without affecting other objects that are painted with the same style.

Creating and saving a style

Now you'll save and name a new style using the appearance attributes you just created for the star button.

1 Click the Styles tab to bring the palette to the front of its group. (If the Styles palette isn't visible on-screen, choose Window > Show Styles.)

2 Position the Styles palette and the Appearance palette so that you can see both of them at the same time.

3 Make sure that the star shape is still selected so that its appearance attributes are displayed in the Appearance palette.

The appearance attributes are stored in the appearance thumbnail, named "Object" in the Appearance palette.

4 In the Appearance palette, drag the appearance thumbnail onto the Styles palette.

5 Release the mouse button when a thick black border appears on the inside of the palette. The border indicates that you are adding a new style to the palette.

Drag object's appearance thumbnail onto Styles palette to save appearance attributes as new style.

6 In the Styles palette, double-click the new thumbnail and name the new style **Grainy Glow.** Click OK.

7 Choose Edit > Deselect All to deselect the star shape, and then choose File > Save.

Applying a style to a layer

Once a style is applied to a layer, everything added to that layer also will have that style applied to it. Now you'll create a new style and apply it to a layer. Then you'll create a few new shapes on that layer to see the effect of the style.

1 In the Appearance palette, click the Clear Appearance button at the bottom of the palette. Then select the appearance name or thumbnail.

2 Choose Effect > Stylize > Drop Shadow.

3 Use the default settings. If desired, click the color swatch in the Drop Shadow dialog box to change the shadow color. (We used a color setting of R=215, G=65, and B=4.) Click OK to exit the Color Picker, and click OK again to apply the effect.

Note: *Because the Drop Shadow appearance has no stroke or fill, its thumbnail will be blank. But once applied to a shape, the drop shadow will appear.*

Clear appearances.   *Choose Drop Shadow effect.*   *Result*

When creating a new style, the Style palette automatically uses the current appearance attributes displayed in the Appearance palette.

4 In the Styles palette, Alt-click (Windows) or Option-click (Mac OS) the New Style button at the bottom of the palette, and type **Drop Shadow** as the name of the new style. Click OK.

Now you'll target the Planet Button layer, to apply a drop shadow to all the shapes on that layer.

5 In the Layers palette, click the target icon to the right of the Planet Button layer. (Be careful not to target the mesh-filled path (the Planet button sublayer). If you target the path, only the planet shape will have a drop shadow.

6 In the Styles palette, click the Drop Shadow style to apply the style to the layer.

7 Choose Edit > Deselect All to deselect the planet shape.

Now you'll test the layer effect by adding some shapes to the Planet Button layer.

8 Select the star tool (☆) in the same group as the ellipse tool (○) in the toolbox.

9 In the Color palette, choose a fill color (we used R=129, G=23, B=136) and a stroke of None.

(Click the Color tab to bring the palette to the front of its group. If the Color palette isn't visible on-screen, choose Window > Show Color to display it.)

10 With the Planet Button layer still selected, in the artwork draw one or two small stars around the planet shape.

Because the Drop Shadow style contains only an effect and no stroke or fill, the objects retain their original stroke and fill attributes.

Layer targeted   *Style applied to layer*   *Artwork added to layer*

11 Notice the following icons on the right side of a layers in the Layers palette, indicating whether any appearance attributes are applied to the layer or whether it is targeted:

• (○) indicates that the layer, group, or object is not targeted and has no appearance attributes applied to it.

• (◉) indicates that the layer, group, or object is not targeted but has appearance attributes applied to it.

• (◎) indicates that the group is targeted and has appearance attributes applied to it. This icon also designates any targeted object that has appearance attributes more complex than a single fill and stroke applied to it.

12 Choose File > Save to save the artwork.

Applying existing styles

Adobe Illustrator comes with a palette of premade styles that you can apply to your artwork. Now you'll finish the button designs by adding an existing style to the Moon Button layer.

It's a good habit to use the Layers palette to select objects or layers to which you'll apply styles. An effect or style varies, depending on whether you're targeting a layer, or an object or group within a layer. Now you'll select the Moon button shape, not the layer.

1 In the Layers palette, click the triangle (▶) to expand the Moon Button layer. Then click the target icon to the right of the <path> sublayer.

2 Click the Swatches tab to bring the palette to the front of its group. In the Swatches palette, select the Moon gradient to fill the selected path.

Select path in Layers palette.   *Change fill color to Moon gradient.*   *Icon indicates targeted layer.*

Now you'll apply a style to the Moon Button layer. The style contains a color, which you'll apply to the layer in place of the moon's existing color.

3 In the Appearance palette menu, make sure that the Layer/Group Overrides Color option is selected (indicated by a check mark). This option replaces the color of objects on a layer with the color of the style or appearance.

You can retain the fill and stroke color of objects on a targeted layer by deselecting the Layer/Group Overrides Color option.

4 In the Layers palette, click the target icon for the Moon Button layer.

5 Click the Styles tab to bring the palette to the front of its group. In the Styles palette, click the Green relief style (fourth row, leftmost swatch) to apply it to the layer.

6 Choose File > Save to save the artwork.

Path selected   *Style applied*   *Result*

Applying an appearance to a layer

You can also apply simple appearance attributes to layers. For example, to make every-thing on a layer 50% opaque, simply target that layer and change the opacity in the Transparency palette.

Next you'll target a layer and change its blending mode to soften the effect of the type.

1 In the Layers palette, click the target icon for the Star Type layer. This action selects everything on the layer and targets all of its objects.

2 In the Transparency palette, choose Soft Light from the blending mode menu.

3 Choose File > Save to save the artwork.

Star Type layer targeted; Soft Light mode applied; result

Copying, applying, and removing styles and appearances

Once you've created several styles and appearances, you may want to use them on other objects in your artwork. You can use the Styles palette, the Appearance palette, the eyedropper tool, or paintbucket tool to apply and copy appearance attributes.

Next you'll apply a style to one of the objects using the Appearance palette.

1 Choose Edit > Deselect All.

2 Select the selection tool ( ) in the toolbox, and click the star shape to select it.

3 In the Appearance palette, drag the appearance thumbnail (labeled "Object: Grainy glow") onto the moon shape to apply those attributes to it.

You can apply styles or attributes by dragging them from the Styles palette or the Appearance palette onto any object. The object doesn't have to be selected.

Star shape attributes   *Drag thumbnail onto new object to apply the same attributes.*

4 Ctrl-click (Windows) or Command-click (Mac OS) away from the artwork to deselect it.

Next you'll apply a style by dragging it directly from the Styles palette onto an object.

5 In the Styles palette, drag the Green relief style thumbnail onto the moon shape in the artwork.

6 Release the mouse button to apply the style to the shape.

Drag style thumbnail onto object (selected or not) to apply the style.

7 Ctrl-click (Windows) or Command-click (Mac OS) away from the artwork to deselect it.

Now you'll use the Layers palette to copy an attribute from one layer to another.

8 In the Layers palette, Alt-drag (Windows) or Option-drag (Mac OS) the appearance indicator from the Planet Button layer onto the appearance indicator of the Button Type layer.

Using Alt or Option copies one layer effect onto another, as indicated by the hand pointer with the plus sign. To simply move an appearance or style from one layer or object to another, just drag the appearance indicator.

Now you'll remove an appearance from a layer using the Layers palette.

9 In the Layers palette, click the target indicator to the right of the Button Type layer.

10 Drag the appearance indicator to the Trash button at the bottom of the Layers palette to remove the appearance.

Another way to remove attributes of a selected object or layer is by using the Appearance palette. You select the object and then click the Reduce to Basic Appearance button at the bottom of the palette to return the object to its original state before the appearance attribute or style was applied.

Drag appearance indicator to Trash button to remove attributes.

11 Ctrl-click (Windows) or Command-click (Mac OS) away from the artwork to deselect it, and then choose File > Save.

Printing and saving files with transparency effects

Once you've created a document with transparency, blending modes, feathering, or other effects that produce artwork with transparency effects, you must set up the document for printing or exporting. The best way to preserve transparency effects is to export the document to the Photoshop (PSD) file format. Exporting to the Photoshop file format retains the transparency masks and links created in the Transparency palette, and layers as they were created in Illustrator. However, only top-level layers are preserved; any nested layers in Illustrator are flattened into the top-level layer.

To preserve as much of the vector art in your document as possible, use the Quality/Speed slider in the Document Setup dialog box. Illustrator uses these settings to determine the quality, printing speed, or both, for your artwork. Using these settings, you can vary the percentage of vector artwork to rasterized artwork when flattening transparent artwork, or you can change the output resolution for rasterized artwork. Each setting has trade-offs. Rasterizing everything in a file degrades some of vector graphics' crisp edges. But maintaining too much of the vector artwork may make a file difficult to print due to your printer's memory limitations.

Specifying rasterization settings with the Quality/Speed slider

Even though the image created in this lesson is meant for a Web page, not for print, you can still experiment with the settings to use for exporting or printing the file.

Now you will specify the degree of rasterization of flattened artwork using the Quality/Speed slider in the Document Setup dialog box. You will also set the resolution for objects that will be rasterized (drop shadows and gradient mesh objects).

1 Choose File > Document Setup.

2 Select Transparency from the pop-up menu in the Document Setup dialog box.

You can select one of five slider settings to determine the percentage of rasterized artwork to vector artwork. (For more information, see "Vector versus bitmap graphics" on page 388.)

3 Drag the Quality/Speed slider to determine the percentage of rasterization. Beneath the slider appears an explanation for each selected setting. The settings from left to right are as follows:

• Position 1 (leftmost setting) rasterizes all objects in the artwork. Use this setting when printing or exporting very complex artwork with many transparent objects.

• Position 2 (second from left) maintains simple vector objects but rasterizes most complex areas. This setting is ideal for objects containing only a few transparent objects.

• Position 3 (the middle, default setting) maintains most objects as vectors but rasterizes the most complex transparent areas. This setting provides the best results for most artwork.

• Position 4 (second from the right) maintains most of the artwork in vector form and rasterizes very complex artwork. This setting can increase processing time when the artwork contains much transparent artwork.

• Position 5 (rightmost) maintains as much of the artwork as possible in vector form. However, very complex artwork may still be rasterized. This setting is both time and memory intensive, but usually produces the highest-quality resolution.

Using the Quality/Speed slider to specify rasterization at setting 3

4 When you have selected a Quality/Speed setting, click OK.

5 Choose File > Save to save the artwork.

Specifying the resolution of rasterized objects

If you know that all or part of your file will be rasterized, you must determine the resolution for the rasterization, based on your desired end result. If your file ultimately will be separated and printed on a high-quality, four-color press, you'll want to choose a higher resolution than if it will appear in a black-and-white, laser-printed newsletter.

The StarArt file contains gradient meshes. To change the output resolution of all objects and gradient mesh objects do the following:

1 Choose File > Document Setup.

2 Choose Printing & Export from the pop-up menu.

3 Set the rasterization resolution of all objects or gradient mesh objects:

• Enter a value in the Rasterization Resolution text box to set a resolution for all objects except gradient mesh objects to be rasterized.

• Enter a value in the Mesh text box to set an output resolution for gradient mesh objects.

4 Click OK.

Specifying the resolution of filters and live effects

Some filter effects and live effects, such as drop shadows and bevels, use settings in the Rasterize Effects Settings dialog box. Now you'll change the resolution in the Rasterize Effects Settings and see the effect on your artwork.

1 Select the zoom tool (🔍) in the toolbox. Position the zoom tool over the star shape in the artwork and click. Continue clicking the center of the star until you have zoomed in to 200%. You should be able to see the pixelated texture of the star button.

Notice the edges of the star shape, with stair-stepping on the angled edges. This is due to the resolution setting for the raster effects. The default setting is 72 ppi.

You will change that setting to improve the edge quality of the star shape.

2 Choose Effect > Rasterize > Raster Effects Settings.

3 Change the Resolution setting to Medium (150 ppi).

4 Leave the other settings as they are, and click OK.

5 Notice that the grain texture has become finer and the edge quality smoother.

Now you'll see how the star looks at a higher resolution.

6 To see detail more easily, use the zoom tool to zoom in closer on the artwork.

7 Choose Effect > Rasterize > Raster Effects Settings.

8 Change the Resolution setting to High (300 ppi), and click OK.

9 If you prefer the texture that the medium resolution gives, choose Edit > Undo.

You can switch between Edit > Undo and Edit > Redo to compare the resolution settings.

Raster Effects resolution: 72 ppi   *150 ppi*   *300 ppi*

10 Choose File > Save to save the artwork. Choose File > Close to close the file.

This completes the lesson. Now you're ready to create your own styles and effect combinations. To learn more about styles, effects, and appearance attributes, see "Using Appearance Attributes, Styles, and Effects" in online Help or Chapter 10 of the Adobe Illustrator User Guide.

Exploring on your own

Now that you've learned the basic steps about creating and using effects and styles, experiment with different combinations of appearance attributes to create interesting special effects. Try combining different styles to create new ones.

For example, here's how to merge two existing styles to create a brand new style.

1 Choose File > New to open a new file.

2 If the Styles palette isn't visible on-screen, choose Window > Show Styles to display it.

3 In the Styles palette, select the Rustic Pen style (second row, second style from the right).

4 Add the Rainbow Plaid style to the selection by Ctrl-clicking (Windows) or Command-clicking (Mac OS) the leftmost style in the second row of the Styles palette.

5 Choose Merge Styles from the Styles palette menu.

6 Name the Style in the Style options dialog box, and click OK.

7 In the artwork, draw a shape and apply the new style.

If you want to edit the style and save it again, do the following:

8 Deselect the artwork.

9 In the Appearance palette, drag the 6-point stroke to the top, above the two fills.

10 Create a new shape or drag the appearance thumbnail onto the existing shape to view the results.

If you like the new effect, you can replace the first merged style with it.

11 To replace a style, Alt-drag (Windows) or Option-drag (Mac OS) the appearance thumbnail onto the style you are replacing in the Styles palette. The style being replaced displays a thick black border when you position the pointer over it.

12 Release the mouse button, and save the file.

Select appearance thumbnail.   *Drag onto style in Styles palette.*   *Result*

Review questions

1 Name two types of Appearance attributes.

2 How do you add a second stroke to an object?

3 What's the difference between a filter and an effect?

4 How do you edit an effect that's part of an object's appearance attributes?

5 What's the difference between applying a style to a layer versus an object?

6 How do you remove an appearance using the Layers palette?

7 How do you set the resolution for a file that contains filter effects?

Review answers

1 The types of editable attributes found in the Appearance palette are:

• Fill attributes (fill type, color, transparency, and effects).

• Stroke attributes (stroke type, brush, color transparency, and effects).

• Transparency attributes (opacity and blending mode).

• Effects commands from the Effect menu.

2 From the Appearance palette menu choose Add New Stroke. A stroke is added to the top of the appearance list. It has the same color and stroke weight as the first stroke.

3 Many commands in the Effect menu also appear in the Filter menu, but only the Effect menu commands are fully editable.

4 To edit an effect you simply double-click its name in the Appearance palette to display that effect's dialog box. You can then make changes, and click OK to update them in the artwork.

5 Once a style is applied to a layer, everything you add to that layer will have that style applied to it. For example, if you create a circle on Layer 1 and then move it to Layer 2, which has a drop shadow effect applied, the circle would adopt that effect. When a style is applied to an object, nothing else on that object's layer is affected by the object's style. For example, if a triangle has a Roughen effect applied to its path, and you move it to another layer, it will still retain the Roughen effect.

6 In the Layers palette, click the target indicator of a layer. Drag the appearance indicator down to the Trash icon in the Layers palette to remove the appearance. You can also remove the appearance of a selected object or layer by using the Appearance palette. Select the object and click the Reduce to Basic Appearance button to return the object to its original state before the appearance attribute or style was applied.

7 You change the resolution in the Rasterize Effects Settings. Choose Effect > Rasterize > Raster Effects Setting. Change the Resolution setting to Low (72 ppi), Medium (150 ppi), High (300 ppi), or Other. Click OK.

Lesson 10

Working with Layers

Layers let you organize your work into distinctive levels that can be edited and viewed as individual units. Every Adobe Illustrator document contains at least one layer. Creating multiple layers in your artwork lets you easily control how artwork is printed, displayed, and edited.

In this lesson, you'll learn how to do the following:

- Work with the Layers palette.
- Create, rearrange, and lock layers, nested layers, and groups.
- Move objects between layers.
- Paste layers of objects from one file to another.
- Merge layers into a single layer.
- Apply a drop shadow to a layer.
- Make a layer clipping mask.

Getting started

In this lesson, you'll finish the artwork of a wall clock as you explore the various ways to use the Layers palette. Before you begin, you'll need to restore the default preferences for Adobe Illustrator and then you'll open the finished art file for this lesson to see what you'll be creating.

1 To ensure that the tools and palettes function exactly as described in this lesson, delete or deactivate (by renaming) the Adobe Illustrator 9.0 preferences file. See "Restoring default preferences" on page 3.

2 Start Adobe Illustrator.

3 Choose File > Open, and open the L10end.ai file in the Lesson10 folder, located inside the Lessons folder within the AICIB folder on your hard drive.

Separate layers are used for the objects that make up the clock's frame, striped clock face, hands, and numbers—as indicated by their layer names in the Layers palette.

A. *Eye icon (Hide/Show)*
B. *Current layer indicator*
C. *Layers palette menu*
D. *Selection indicator*
E. *Target and appearance indicator*
F. *Template layer icon*
G. *Edit column (Lock/Unlock)*
H. *Expand/Collapse triangle*
I. *Make/Release layer clipping mask*
J. *Create New Sublayer button*
K. *Create New Layer button*
L. *Delete button*

4 If you like, choose View > Zoom Out to make the finished artwork smaller, adjust the window size, and leave it on your screen as you work. (Use the hand tool (🖑) to move the artwork where you want it in the window.) If you don't want to leave the image open, choose File > Close.

For an illustration of the finished artwork in this lesson, see the color section.

To begin working, you'll open an existing art file.

5 Choose File > Open, and open the L10start.ai file in the Lesson10 folder, located inside the Lessons folder within the AICIB folder on your hard drive.

The artwork contains some of the basic objects for the clock illustration.

6 Choose File > Save As, name the file **Clock.ai**, and select the Lesson10 folder. Leave the Format option set to Adobe Illustrator® Document, and click Save. In the Illustrator Native Format Options dialog box, select Illustrator 9.0 Compatibility and click OK.

Using layers

Using the Layers palette, you can create multiple levels of artwork that reside on separate, overlapping layers, sublayers, and groups in the same file. Layers act like individual, clear sheets containing one or more objects. Where no filled (or nontransparent) objects overlap, you can see through any layer to the layer below.

You can create and edit objects on any layer without affecting the artwork on any other layer. You can also display, print, lock, and reorder layers as distinct units.

Example of composite art and how layers break out individually

Creating layers

Every document in Illustrator contains one layer by default. You can rename the layer and add more layers at any time as you create the artwork. Placing objects on separate layers lets you easily select and edit them by their organization. For example, by placing type on a separate layer, you can change the type all at once without affecting the rest of the artwork.

You'll change the layer name to "Clock," and then you'll create another layer.

1 If the Layers palette isn't visible on-screen, choose Window > Show Layers to display it.

Layer 1 (the default name for the first layer) is highlighted, indicating that it is selected. The layer also has a triangle (▾), indicating that it's active and that objects on the layer can be edited when you use the tools.

2 In the Layers palette, double-click the layer name to open the Layer Options dialog box. Type **Clock** in the Name text box, and then click OK.

Double-click layer name.   *Change layer name to Clock.*

Now you'll create a sublayer for the clock numbers.

3 Alt-click (Windows) or Option-click (Mac OS) the Create New Sublayer button at the bottom of the Layers palette to create a new sublayer and display the Layer Options dialog box.

(If you simply want to create a new sublayer without setting any options or naming the layer, you can click the Create New Sublayer button. New sublayers created this way are numbered in sequence, for example, Layer 2.)

4 In the Layer Options dialog box, type **Numbers** in the Name text box, and click OK. The new sublayer appears directly beneath its main layer name (Clock) and is selected.

Create sublayer named Numbers.

Moving objects and layers

By rearranging the layers in the Layers palette, you can reorder layered objects in your artwork. You can also move selected objects from one layer or sublayer to another.

First you'll move the clock numbers onto their own sublayer.

1 In the Layers palette, grab the thumbnail for the 11 and drag it onto the thumbnail for the Numbers layer. Release the mouse button when you see the large black triangles at either end of the Numbers layer in the palette. (The large triangles indicate that you are adding something to that layer.)

Grab thumbnail and move it onto sublayer thumbnail.

2 Repeat step 1 for each of the twelve numbers in the Layers palette.

3 Choose File > Save.

Now you'll move the face of the clock to a new layer to use later when you add the stripes, hands, and brand name of the clock, and you'll rename the Clock layer to reflect the new organization of the artwork.

4 In the artwork, click behind the numbers to select the clock face. In the Layers palette, the Clock layer becomes active (as indicated by the small triangle (▾).

5 Alt-click (Windows) or Option-click (Mac OS) the Create New Layer button at the bottom of the Layers palette, or choose New Layer from the Layers palette menu.

6 In the Layer Options dialog box, enter **Face** in the Name text box, choose a different layer color from the pop-up menu (such as Orange), and click OK.

The new Face layer is added above the Clock layer and becomes active.

7 In the Layers palette, select the small square icon on the Clock layer, and drag it directly up to the right of the target indicator on the new Face layer.

Drag selection indicator up to move object to another layer.

This action moves the selected object to the new layer. Notice the color of the selection lines in the artwork changes to the color of the new Face layer (such as Orange).

Now that the Face layer is on top of the Clock layer, as well as the Numbers layer, the clock numbers are covered up. You'll move the Numbers sublayer onto a different layer and rename the Clock layer to reflect the new organization of the artwork.

8 In the Layers palette, drag the Numbers sublayer thumbnail onto the Face layer thumbnail. Release the mouse button when you see the indicator bar with large black triangles at either end of the Face layer in the palette.

Now you can see the numbers again.

9 Double-click the Clock layer to display the Layer Options dialog box, and change the layer name to **Frame**. Then click OK.

Drag sublayer thumbnail   *Change layer name.*
to move it to another layer.

10 Choose Edit > Deselect All, and then choose File > Save.

Locking layers

As you edit objects on a layer, you can use the Layers palette to lock other layers and prevent selecting or changing the rest of the artwork.

Now you'll lock all the layers except the Numbers sublayer so that you can easily edit the clock numbers without affecting objects on other layers. Locked layers cannot be selected or edited in any way.

1 To simplify your work, click the triangle to the left of the Frame layer to collapse the layer view.

2 Click the edit column to the right of the eye icon on the Frame layer to lock the layer.

3 Click the edit column to the right of the eye icon on the <path> layer below the Numbers layer.

The padlock icon (🔒) indicates that a layer is locked.

4 Click the Numbers sublayer in the Layers palette to select the layer.

Click the edit column to lock layer.

You can unlock individual layers by clicking the padlock icon in the edit column to make it disappear. Clicking again in the edit column locks the layer. Holding down Alt (Windows) or Option (Mac OS) as you click in the edit column alternately locks and unlocks all other layers.

Now you'll change the type size and font of the numbers.

5 In the Layers palette to the right of the Numbers layer, click the selection column to select all objects on that layer.

As a shortcut for choosing Edit > Select All to select all of the type on the layer, you can click the selection column—the blank area to the right of the target icons—in the Layers palette.

The Numbers layer now has a large red square, indicating that everything on the layer is selected.

6 Choose Type > Character to display the Character palette.

7 In the Character palette, select another font or size for the group of numbers. (We used Myriad Bold, size 28 points.)

Click the selection column.   *All type selected.*   *Font changed globally*

8 If you wish, use the Color palette or Swatches palette to change the color of the selected numbers.

9 In the Layers palette, choose Unlock All Layers from the palette menu, and then choose File > Save to save the changes.

Viewing layers

The Layers palette lets you hide layers, sublayers, or individual objects from view. When a layer is hidden, objects on the layer are also locked and cannot be selected or printed. You can also use the Layers palette to display layers or objects in either Preview or Artwork view independently from other layers in the artwork.

Now you'll edit the frame on the clock, using a painting technique to create a three-dimensional effect on the frame.

1 In the Layers palette, click the Frame layer to select it, and then Alt-click (Windows) or Option-click (Mac OS) the eye icon next to the Frame layer name to hide the other layers.

Alt/Option-clicking the layer eye icon alternately hides and shows a layer. Hiding layers also locks them.

Alt/Option-click eye icon.   *Only objects on Frame layer appear.*   *Only Frame layer is showing and unlocked.*

2 Using the selection tool (⬉), click the inside circle of the frame to select it. Then Shift-click to select the next largest circle.

3 With the two inner circles selected, make sure that the Fill box is selected in the toolbox, and then click the Clock.frame swatch in the Swatches palette to paint the circles with a custom gradient.

Select two inner circles.   *Paint with gradient fill.*

4 Shift-click the second largest circle to deselect it and keep the inside circle selected.

5 Select the gradient tool (▦) in the toolbox. Drag the tool in a vertical line from the top of the circle straight down to the bottom to change the direction of the gradient.

The gradient tool works only on selected objects that are filled with gradients. To learn more about using the gradient tool, see Lesson 8, "Blending Shapes and Colors."

*Select
gradient
tool.*

Drag over selected object.

6 Choose Edit > Deselect All to deselect the artwork, and then choose File > Save.

7 In the Layers palette, choose Show All Layers from the palette menu.

As you edit objects in layered artwork, you can display individual layers in Artwork view, keeping the other layers in Preview view.

8 Ctrl-click (Windows) or Command-click (Mac OS) the eye icon next to the Face layer to switch to Artwork view for that layer.

This action lets you see the gradient-filled circle behind the clock face. Displaying a layer in Artwork view also is useful for viewing the anchor points or center points on objects without selecting them.

*White fill in eye icon
indicates Artwork view.*

*Preview view of other layers
shows through Face layer.*

9 Ctrl/Command-click the eye icon next to the Face layer again to return to Preview view for that layer.

Pasting layers

To complete the clock, you'll copy and paste the finishing parts of artwork from another file. You can paste layered files into another file and keep all the layers intact.

1 Choose File > Open, and open the Details.ai file, located in the Lesson10 folder, inside the Lessons folder within the AICIB folder on your hard drive.

Clock.ai file   *Details.ai file*   *Layers palette for Details.ai file*

2 If you want to see how the objects are organized on the layers, Alt/Option-click the eye icons in the Layers palette to alternately display each layer and hide the others. You can also click the triangles (▶) to the left of the layer names to expand and collapse the layers for further inspection. When you've finished, make sure that all the layers are showing and that they are fully collapsed.

Hiding layers also locks them, thus preventing objects on hidden layers from being selected and copied.

3 Choose Edit > Select All and then Edit > Copy to select and copy the clock details to the Clipboard.

4 Choose File > Close and click Don't Save to close the Details.ai file without saving any changes.

5 In the Clock.ai file, choose Paste Remembers Layers from the Layers palette menu to select the option. (A check mark next to the option indicates that it's selected.)

Selecting the Paste Remembers Layers option indicates that when layers from another file are pasted into the artwork, they're added separately to the Layers palette. If the option is not selected, all objects are pasted into the active layer.

6 Choose Edit > Paste In Front to paste the details into the clock.

The Paste In Front command pastes the objects from the Clipboard to a position relative to the original position in the Details.ai file. The Paste Remembers Layers option causes the Details.ai layers to be pasted as four separate layers (Highlight, Hands, Brand, Stripes) at the bottom of the Layers palette.

7 Drag the Layers palette by its lower right corner to resize it and display all of the layers in the palette. As you can see, some of the layers need to be repositioned.

Paste artwork from
Details.ai file.

Layers are added from
Details.ai file.

Now you'll move the brand and hands into the Face layer and the highlight in front of the Frame layer.

8 Select the selection tool ( ), and click away from the artwork to deselect it.

9 In the Layers palette, select the Highlight layer, and drag it up between the <path> and Frame layers.

Move Highlight layer up above Frame layer.

10 Shift-click the Hands and Brand layers in the Layers palette.

11 Drag the selected layers up between the Numbers and <path> sublayers; when the insertion bar appears between those sublayers, release the mouse button to make the Hands and Brand layers sublayers of the Face layer.

Drag Hands and Brand layers up into Face layer.

12 Choose File > Save to save the changes.

Creating clipping masks

The Layers palette lets you create clipping masks to control how artwork on a layer (or in a group) is hidden or revealed. A *clipping mask* is an object or group of objects whose shape masks artwork below it so that only artwork within the shape is visible.

Now you'll create a clipping mask with the circle shape in the Face layer. You'll group it with the Stripes sublayer so that only the stripes show through the circle shape.

1 In the Layers palette, drag the Stripes layer up until the insertion bar's double lines are highlighted above the <path> layer within the Face layer. Release the mouse button when the indicator bar appears.

Drag Stripes layer up above <path> sublayer within Face layer.

In order for the clipping mask to mask only the stripes, you must move it into the Stripes sublayer. You'll move the <path> into the Stripes sublayer and then create the clipping mask.

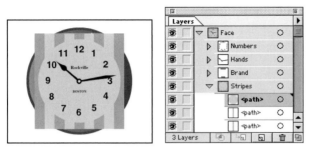

Drag circle named <path> into Stripes layer.

2 In the Layers palette, make sure that the <path> with the circle color fill is the topmost layer in the Stripes layer, moving it if necessary. (Clipping masks are always the first object in a layer or group.) Then select the Stripes layer.

3 Click the Make Clipping Mask button at the bottom of the Layers palette. Notice that all the layer's dividing lines are now dotted and the first path's name has changed to <clipping path>. The clipping path name is also underlined to indicate that it is the masking shape.

Select Stripes layer and click Make Clipping Mask button.

4 Click the triangle (▶) next to the Stripes layer name to collapse the layers in the Layers palette.

5 Choose File > Save.

Merging layers

To streamline your artwork, you can *merge* layers. Merging layers combines the contents of all selected layers onto one layer.

As a final step, you'll combine some of the artwork from the Details.ai file with your other layers.

1 In the Layers palette, click the Numbers layer to select it, and then Shift-click to select the Hands layer.

Notice the current layer indicator (◥)shows the last selected layer as the active layer. The last layer you select will determine the name and color for the merged layer.

2 Choose Merge Selected from the Layers palette menu to merge both layers into one layer called Hands.

The objects on the merged layers retain their original stacking order.

3 Now click the Highlight layer to select it, and Shift-click to select the Frame layer last.

4 Choose Merge Selected from the Layers palette menu to merge the two layers into one layer called Frame.

5 Choose File > Save.

Applying appearance attributes to layers

You can apply appearance attributes such as styles, effects, and transparency to layers, groups, and objects with the Layers palette. When an appearance attribute is applied to a layer, any object on that layer will take on that attribute. If an appearance attribute is applied only to an object on a layer, it affects only that object, not the entire layer.

You will apply an effect to an object on one layer. Then you'll copy that effect to a layer to change all objects on that layer.

1 In the Layers palette, collapse the Face layer and expand the Frame layer to reveal all of its objects. Select the bottom path in the Frame layer.

2 Click the target icon (the circle to the right of the layer name) to target the bottommost object. Clicking the target icon indicates that you want to apply an effect, style, or transparency change.

3 Choose Effect > Stylize > Drop Shadow. Leave the settings at their default values and click OK. A drop shadow appears on the outer edge of the clock.

4 Notice that the target icon is now shaded, indicating that the object has appearance attributes applied to it.

5 Click the Appearance tab to bring the palette to the front of its group. (If the Appearance palette isn't visible on-screen, choose Window > Show Appearance to display it.) Notice that Drop Shadow has been added to the list of appearance attributes for the selected shape.

Apply drop shadow effect to clock edge. *Shaded target icon indicates appearance attributes.* *Appearance palette lists selection's attributes.*

You will now use the Layers palette to copy an appearance attribute onto a layer and then edit it.

6 Expand the Face layer to reveal its contents. Drag the bottom right corner of the Layers palette to display the entire list.

7 Hold down Alt (Windows) or Option (Mac OS) and drag the shaded target icon up to the target icon of the Hands layer, without releasing the mouse button. The hand pointer with a plus sign indicates that the appearance is being copied.

8 When the target icon of the Hands layer turns light gray, release the mouse button. The drop shadow is now applied to the entire Hands layer, as indicated by the shaded target icon.

Drag target icon to copy effect.   *Result*

Now you'll edit the drop shadow attribute for the type and clock hands, to tone down the effect.

9 In the Layers palette, click the target icon for the Hands layer. This automatically selects the objects on the Hands layer and deselects the object on the Frame layer.

10 In the Appearance palette, double-click the Drop Shadow attribute. In the Drop Shadow dialog box, enter 3 points for the X and Y offsets and the Blur amount. Click OK.

11 Choose Edit > Deselect All.

12 Choose File > Save. Choose File > Close to close the file.

You have completed building a layered file.

In some cases after the artwork is complete, you may want to place all the layers of art onto a single layer and delete the empty layers. This is called *flattening* artwork. Delivering finished artwork in a single layer file can prevent accidents from happening, such as hiding layers and not printing parts of the artwork.

To flatten specific layers without deleting hidden layers, select the layers you want to flatten, and then choose Merge Layers from the Layers palette menu.

Flattening artwork

In flattened artwork, all visible layers are merged into the selected layer, and hidden layers are deleted. If you flatten a hidden layer that contains artwork, you can choose to delete the artwork along with the hidden layer, or make all artwork visible and flatten it into one layer. In most cases, you won't want to flatten a file until you finish editing individual layers.

To flatten artwork:

1. *Make sure that all the layers you want to flatten are visible.*

2. *Select the layer into which you will flatten the artwork. You cannot flatten artwork into layers that are hidden, locked, or templates. Doing this results in the topmost layer that is not hidden, locked, or a template being chosen instead. Regardless of the layer you select, the options for the layer and the stacking order of the artwork don't change.*

3. *Choose Flatten Artwork from the Layers palette menu.*

If artwork is present on a hidden layer, a dialog box prompts you to choose whether to make all artwork visible and flatten it into one layer, or delete the artwork along with the layer.

– From the Adobe Illustrator User Guide, Chapter 9

For a complete list of shortcuts that you can use with the Layers palette, see "Quick reference" in online Help or the printed *Quick Reference Card*.

Exploring on your own

When you print a layered file, only the visible layers print in the same order in which they appear in the Layers palette—with the exception of *template layers*, which do not print even if they're visible. Template layers are locked, dimmed, and previewed. Objects on template layers neither print nor export.

Now that you've learned how to work with layers, try creating layered artwork by tracing an image on a template layer. We've provided a bitmap photo image of a goldfish that you can use to practice with or use your own artwork or photo images.

1 Choose File > New to create a new file for your artwork.

Choose File > Place. In the dialog box, select the goldfish.eps, located in the Lesson10 folder, inside the Lessons folder within the AICIB folder on your hard drive; or locate your file containing the artwork or image you want to use as a template and click Place.

Illustrator adds the placed file to Layer 1.

🔲 For information on importing files, see "Importing artwork" and "Opening and placing artwork" in online Help or in Chapter 2 of the Adobe Illustrator User Guide.

2 Create the template layer by choosing Template from the Layers palette menu or choosing Layer Options and selecting the Template option in the Layer Options dialog box.

3 Click the New Layer button to create a new layer to draw on.

4 With Layer 2 active, use any of the drawing tools to trace over the template, creating new artwork.

5 Create additional layers to separate and edit various components of the new artwork.

6 If you wish, delete the template when you've finished to reduce the size of the file.

💡 *You can create custom views of your artwork with some layers hidden and other layers showing, and display each view in a separate window. To create a custom view, choose View > New View. To display each view in a separate window, choose Window > New Window.*

🔲 For information on custom views, see "Viewing artwork" in online Help or Chapter 1 in the Adobe Illustrator User Guide.

Review questions

1 Name two benefits of using layers when creating artwork.

2 How do you hide layers? Display individual layers?

3 Describe how to reorder layers in a file.

4 How can you lock layers?

5 What is the purpose of changing the selection color on a layer?

6 What happens if you paste a layered file into another file? Why is the Paste Remembers Layers option useful?

7 How do you move objects from one layer to another?

8 How do you create a layer clipping mask?

9 How do you apply an effect to a layer? How can you edit that effect?

Review answers

1 Benefits of using layers when creating artwork include: You can protect artwork that you don't want to change, you can hide artwork that you aren't working with so that it's not distracting, and you can control what prints.

2 To hide a layer, you click the eye icon to the left of the layer name; you click in the blank, leftmost column to redisplay a layer.

3 You reorder layers by selecting a layer name in the Layers palette and dragging the layer to its new location. The order of layers in the Layers palette controls the document's layer order—topmost in the palette is frontmost in the artwork.

4 You can lock layers several different ways:

• You can click in the column to the left of the layer name; a padlock icon appears, indicating that the layer is locked.

• You can choose Lock Others from the Layers palette menu to lock all layers but the active layer.

• You can hide a layer to protect it.

5 The selection color controls how selected anchor points and direction lines are displayed on a layer, and helps you identify the different layers in your document.

6 The Paste commands paste layered files or objects copied from different layers onto the active layer by default. The Paste Remembers Layers option keeps the original layers intact when the objects are pasted.

7 Select the objects you want to move and drag the square icon (to the right of the pen icon) to another layer in the Layers palette.

8 Create a clipping mask on a layer by selecting the layer and clicking the Make Clipping Mask button. The topmost object in the layer will become the clipping mask.

9 Click the target icon for the layer you want to apply an effect to. Then choose an effect from the Effect menu. To edit the effect, make sure the layer is selected and double click the name of the effect in the Appearance palette. The effect's dialog box will come up and then you can change the values.

Lesson 11

Creating Airbrush Effects

Converting shapes into gradient mesh objects lets you blend colors in multiple directions within the shapes, for a water-color or airbrush effect. It's easy to modify mesh objects. You can add or remove colors from points on the mesh, to adjust the direction and amount of color blending.

In this lesson, you'll learn how to do the following:

• Create a gradient mesh object using two methods.

• Apply colors to the mesh.

• Edit the mesh for a variety of effects.

Getting started

In this lesson, you'll convert the shapes of two butterflies into gradient meshes, paint them, and manipulate the color blending. Before you begin, you'll need to restore the default preferences for Adobe Illustrator and then you'll open the finished art file for the lesson to see what you'll be creating.

1 To ensure that the tools and palettes function exactly as described in this lesson, delete or deactivate (by renaming) the Adobe Illustrator 9.0 preferences file. See "Restoring default preferences" on page 3.

2 Start Adobe Illustrator.

3 Choose File > Open, and open the L11end.ai file in the Lesson11 folder, located inside the Lessons folder within the AICIB folder on your hard drive.

4 If you like, choose View > Zoom Out to make the finished artwork smaller, adjust the window size, and leave it on your screen as you work. (Use the hand tool (✋) to move the artwork where you want it in the window.) If you don't want to leave the image open, choose File > Close.

For an illustration of the finished artwork in this lesson, see the color section.

To begin working, you'll open an existing art file.

5 Choose File > Open, and open the L11start.ai file in the Lesson11 folder, located inside the Lessons folder within the AICIB folder on your hard drive.

6 Choose File > Save As, name the file **Buttrfly.ai**, and select the Lesson11 folder. Leave the Format option set to Adobe Illustrator® Document, and click Save. In the Illustrator Native Format Options dialog box, select Illustrator 9.0 Compatibility and click OK.

Setting Smart Guides preferences

Smart Guides are useful for working with mesh objects because they display information about the mesh without the need to select the object first. You'll set preferences for hiding the construction guides (which are useful for drawing and aligning objects) and text labels (which you won't need for this lesson), and you'll change the snapping tolerance (the distance that the pointer must be from an object before Smart Guides take effect).

1 Choose Edit > Preferences > Smart Guides.

2 In the Preferences dialog box, deselect the display options for Text Label Hints and Construction Guides, and make sure that Transform Tools and Object Highlighting are selected. Type **1 pt** in the Snapping Tolerance text box. Click OK to set the preferences.

The Transform Tools option is useful for scaling, rotating, reflecting, and shearing objects. The Object Highlighting option displays mesh lines and anchor points when the mouse is positioned over the object.

3 Choose View > Smart Guides to activate them. (A check mark in the menu indicates that they're turned on.)

Painting with the gradient mesh tool

You can convert any object into a mesh object by using the gradient mesh tool and creating one mesh point at a time. Each time you click an object using the gradient mesh tool, a new color is added to the object.

First you'll paint a color on one of the tail wings on a butterfly, and then you'll paint the other tail wing with the same color.

1 Select the zoom tool (🔍) in the toolbox and click the butterfly at the top of the artwork a few times to zoom in to 300% (as indicated in the lower left corner of the window). Then select the hand tool (✋), and use it to move the butterfly to the center of the window.

2 Click a color in the Color palette or Swatches palette to specify the current fill. (We selected the Color 2 swatch.) To display the Swatches palette, click its tab to bring it to the front of its palette group.

3 Select the gradient mesh tool (▨) in the toolbox, and click in the center of the left tail wing to apply a mesh point with the currently selected color.

The tail wing is automatically converted to a mesh object. The first time you click an object with the gradient mesh tool, the object is converted to a mesh object with one mesh point and two intersecting mesh lines.

4 Now click in the center of the right tail wing to apply a mesh point with the same color and convert it to a mesh object.

Select color.   *Click with gradient mesh tool to apply selected color.*

5 Hold down Ctrl (Windows) or Command (Mac OS), and click away from the tail wing to deselect it, and then select another color from the Color or Swatches palette. (We selected the Color 3 swatch.)

6 Click in the left tail wing to add a mesh point with the new color, and then click in the right tail wing to add one with the same color.

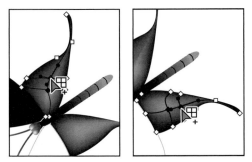

Add mesh points to mesh object with another color.

7 Ctrl-click (Windows) or Command-click (Mac OS) away from the object to deselect it, and then continue adding a few more colors and mesh points.

8 When you have finished, choose File > Save.

Specifying the number of mesh lines

When you use the gradient mesh tool to create a mesh object, two intersecting mesh lines are created for every mesh point you create. Before converting an object to a mesh object, you'll specify its number of mesh lines using the Create Gradient Mesh command.

1 Select the selection tool ( ) in the toolbox, and click the black forewing on the butterfly to select it.

2 Choose Object > Create Gradient Mesh.

3 In the Create Gradient Mesh dialog box, select the Preview option to see the changes to the selected object without closing the dialog box. Type **3** in the Rows text box; press Tab and type **4** (the default) in the Columns text box. Leave the Appearance as Flat (the default), and click OK.

The black forewing is converted to a mesh object with three rows separated by two horizontal mesh lines and four columns separated by three vertical mesh lines.

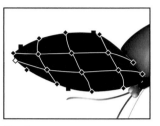

Select black forewing.   *Apply gradient mesh.*   *Result*

The mesh object is automatically selected when you create it.

4 Notice that the points in the selected object are all a solid color, indicating that they're selected. Also, the object has a mesh point at the intersection of every mesh line, anchor points at the ends of the mesh lines, and some anchor points on the segments of the outlining edge that are from the original object.

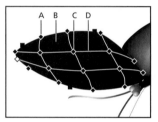

A. Anchor point **B.** Mesh patch
C. Mesh point **D.** Mesh line

For a color illustration of selected mesh objects, see figure 11-1 and figure 11-2 in the color section.

Applying colors to the mesh

You can select points on a mesh object using either the direct-selection tool or the gradient mesh tool and paint them with different colors. Now you'll practice selecting mesh points using the direct-selection tool and apply three colors to the butterfly's forewing.

1 Select the direct-selection tool ( ), and click away from the object to deselect it. Then move the pointer over the top left side of the forewing. (Smart Guides display the mesh as you move the pointer over it.)

2 Click in the center of a mesh patch to select the four mesh points where the lines intersect. (We clicked in the patch above the top horizontal line and to the right of the left vertical line.)

Position pointer over mesh patch. **A.** *Selected mesh point*
B. *Deselected mesh point*

Clicking with the direct-selection tool in a mesh patch is an easy way to select all of the mesh points and direction handles on the lines surrounding the patch. All the other points become white diamonds, indicating they're not selected.

3 Click a color in the Color palette or Swatches palette (we selected the Color 2 swatch) to apply it to the four selected points.

Select color.   *Result*

4 Select the direct select lasso tool ( ) in the toolbox.

5 With the forewing still selected, draw a selection marquee around the two left mesh points on the bottom horizontal line.

Draw selection marquee around mesh points to select them.

If you inadvertently select the wrong mesh points, draw the selection marquee again. You can also Ctrl-click (Windows) or Command-click (Mac OS) away from the artwork to deselect it, Ctrl/Command-click the artwork to reselect it, and then redraw the selection marquee.

6 Paint the two selected mesh points with a color from the Color palette or Swatches palette (we selected the Color 3 swatch).

7 Use the direct select lasso tool (🔾) to select the two middle mesh points on the right vertical mesh line. Select a third color in the Color palette or Swatches palette (we selected the Color 4 swatch) to paint the selected mesh points.

Select two right mesh points.   *Select color.*   *Result*

8 Choose File > Save.

Highlighting a mesh object

To give an object a three-dimensional appearance, you can create a gradient mesh that highlights the center or the edge of an object. Now you'll create a gradient mesh with highlighting.

1 Use the hand tool (🖑) to move the second butterfly at the bottom of the artwork to the center of the window.

2 Select the selection tool (�), and click the top forewing on the pink butterfly to select it.

3 Choose Object > Create Gradient Mesh.

4 In the Create Gradient Mesh dialog box, leave **3** entered in the Rows text box. Type **3** in the Columns text box, and make sure that the Preview option is selected.

5 For Appearance, choose To Edge in the dialog box; notice the change to the highlighting in the selected object. Then choose To Center from the pop-up menu.

To Edge creates a highlight on the edges of the object. To Center creates a highlight in the center of the object.

🌑 For a color illustration of highlighted mesh objects, see figure 11-1 in the color section.

6 Type a value between 0% and 100% in the Highlight text box (we entered 60%), and press Tab to see the change to the artwork without closing the dialog box.

A value of 100% applies a maximum white highlight to the object. A value of 0% applies no white highlight to the object.

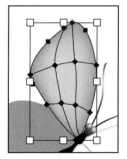

Select top forewing.   *Apply highlight and preview.*   *Result*

7 Click OK to close the dialog box, and create the highlighted mesh object.

8 Select the direct select lasso tool (🔗), and drag to draw a marquee over the tip of the forewing to select the four upper left anchor points on the mesh.

9 With the anchor points selected, click a color in the Color palette or Swatches palette to apply it to the points. (We selected the Color 4 swatch.)

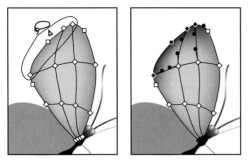

Drag direct select lasso to select mesh points.

Editing mesh points

You can use the gradient mesh tool to select, add, and delete mesh points to change the way colors blend in a mesh object. Every mesh point has a set of direction handles that let you adjust the distance and direction that a color blends with neighboring colors in the mesh object.

First, you'll use the gradient mesh tool to select a mesh point and add a color to the butterfly's forewing.

1 Select the gradient mesh tool (📰) in the toolbox and position the pointer over a mesh point. The plus sign on the pointer disappears when it's over a mesh point. Click to select the mesh point. (We selected the lower right mesh point where the right vertical line intersects with the bottom horizontal line.) Choose Edit > Undo if you add a mesh point by mistake.

2 Click a color in the Color palette or Swatches palette to apply it to the selected mesh point. (We selected the Color 5 swatch.)

Select mesh point with
gradient mesh tool.

Select color.

Result

Now you'll use the gradient mesh tool to delete a mesh point on the forewing and see how the colors and highlighting readjust.

3 Using the gradient mesh tool, hold the pointer over the top left mesh point where the top horizontal line and left vertical line intersect. Hold down Alt (Windows) or Option (Mac OS) to display a minus sign on the pointer, and click the mesh point to delete it.

Deleting a mesh point also deletes the two intersecting mesh lines.

Delete mesh point.

Result

Notice that the highlighting from the center of the object is diminished as the remaining colors on the anchor points now blend with the original base color.

4 If you want to take a look at that change again, press Ctrl+Z (Windows) or Command+Z (Mac OS) to undo the deletion, and then press Shift+Ctrl+Z (Windows) or Shift+Command+Z (Mac OS) to redo it.

Now you'll use the gradient mesh tool to add a mesh point to the tail wing on the butterfly and then change the direction that the color of the mesh point blends from the center.

5 With the gradient mesh tool selected, hold the pointer over the bottom tail wing, and click anywhere inside it to add a mesh point.

6 Click a color in the Color palette or Swatches palette (we selected the Color 5 swatch) to apply it to the new mesh point.

Click with gradient mesh   *Select color.*   *Result*
tool to add mesh point.

7 Select the direct-selection tool ( ) in the toolbox. Drag a marquee over the bottom tip of the tail wing to select the anchor points along the edge, and click a color in the Color palette or Swatches palette to apply it to the selected points. (We selected the Color 4 swatch.)

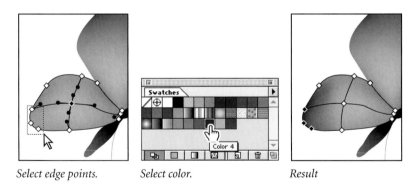

Select edge points.   *Select color.*   *Result*

8 Select the gradient mesh tool ( ) in the toolbox, and click the mesh point you created in the center of the tail wing to select it. (The plus sign on the pointer disappears when it's over a mesh point.)

The selected mesh point displays four direction points (or handles) that lie along the mesh lines until you move them. Now you'll use the handles to adjust the direction and distance of the mesh point's color.

9 Using the gradient mesh tool, select the left direction handle (don't release the mouse button) and drag it to the left about midway to the edge of the object; then release the mouse button. Notice how the mesh point's color extends further out before it starts to blend with the other colors.

10 Select another direction handle and drag it in an arc to swirl the direction of the blending colors.

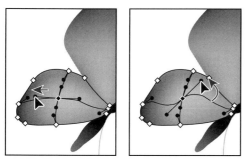

Drag direction handles to lengthen or swirl color blending.

11 Ctrl-click (Windows) or Command-click (Mac OS) away from the object to deselect it.

12 Choose File > Save.

Reflecting mesh objects

You can use the reflect tool and other tools in the toolbox on a mesh object just like any other type of object. Now you'll reflect a copy of the two wing parts to complete the butterfly.

1 Select the selection tool ( ) in the toolbox, and Shift-click to select both the tail wing and the forewing on the bottom butterfly.

2 Select the reflect tool ( ) in the toolbox, hold down Alt (Windows) or Option (Mac OS), and click in the center of the butterfly's body, midway between the selected wing parts and the wing guides on the right.

Clicking the body of the butterfly designates the point of origin from which the object will reflect. Holding down Alt/Option as you click displays the Reflect dialog box.

3 In the Reflect dialog box, select the Angle option and type **46** in the degree text box. Click Copy. (Don't click OK.)

Depending on where you clicked to set the reflecting reference point in step 2, you may need to slightly adjust the position of the reflected copy using the arrow keys—or choose Edit > Undo and repeat steps 2 and 3.

Select wing parts.   *Reflect and copy.*   *Result*

4 Ctrl-click (Windows) or Command-click (Mac OS) away from the object to deselect it. and choose File > Save to save the artwork.

Modifying mesh lines

You'll use the gradient mesh tool to reshape mesh lines by moving mesh points on them, add mesh lines with an unpainted mesh point to the mesh, and delete a single mesh line in the forewing of the first butterfly.

1 Select the hand tool (✋), and move the butterfly at the top of the artwork down to the center of your window.

2 Select the gradient mesh tool (▦), and position it over the left forewing. Select the left mesh point on the top horizontal line (don't release the mouse button), then hold down Shift, and drag the mesh point to the left.

As you drag to the left, the intersecting vertical mesh line is reshaped. Holding down Shift as you drag constrains the movement horizontally, leaving the horizontal mesh line unaffected.

3 Select the bottom mesh point on the right vertical line (don't release the mouse), and Shift-drag to move it down without affecting the vertical mesh line.

Notice how the color blending readjusts to the new position of the mesh point.

 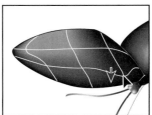

Shift-drag left to move mesh point along horizontal line. *Shift-drag down to move mesh point along vertical line.*

For a color illustration of the edited mesh point, see figure 11-2 in the color section.

You can add a mesh point to a mesh object without applying the current fill color to it or changing the existing colors in the object.

4 Ctrl-click (Windows) or Command-click (Mac OS) away from the object to deselect it.

5 Select a new color fill by clicking a color in the Color palette or the Swatches palette. (We selected the Color 6 swatch.)

6 Using the gradient mesh tool (▩), position the pointer in the center of a patch. (We chose the middle right patch; see the following illustration.) Shift-click to add a new mesh point with two intersecting mesh lines—without changing the color in the object. Notice that the Fill box in the toolbox changes to the existing color of the object where you clicked.

7 If you want to change the color of the new mesh point, click a new color in the Color palette or Swatches palette. (We selected the Color 6 swatch again.)

Shift-click to add unpainted mesh point.

New mesh point picks up underlying mesh colors.

Note: *You can add anchor points to an existing mesh line by selecting the object and using the add anchor point tool (𝄞).*

Now you'll delete a mesh line.

8 Using the gradient mesh tool, position the pointer over a mesh line and hold down Alt (Windows) or Option (Mac OS) to display a minus sign on the pointer. Alt/Option-click a segment (between two mesh points) on the mesh line to delete the line.

Notice how the color on the new mesh point spreads into the area where the line was.

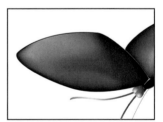

Position pointer over line to left of new mesh point.

Alt/Option-click segment to delete mesh line.

Result

You'll complete the butterfly by reflecting a copy of the forewing.

9 Click the selection tool (⬉) in the toolbox to select the bounding box of the mesh object.

10 Select the reflect tool (⬚) in the toolbox, and Alt-click (Windows) or Option-click (Mac OS) in the body of the butterfly, about midway between the existing wing and the wing guide.

11 In the Reflect dialog box, make sure that the Angle option is selected, type **36** in the degree text box, and click Copy. (Don't click OK.)

Depending on where you clicked in the body, you may have to adjust the position of the reflected copy by using the arrow keys.

Select wing.

Reflect copy.

Result

Applying transparency to a mesh

Mesh objects can be transparent or opaque just like nonmesh objects. Now you'll scroll down to the dragonfly in your lesson art. You'll create a gradient mesh in the dragonfly's wing and then you'll adjust its transparency to make it appear translucent.

1 In the Layers palette, click to the left of both the Dragonfly and Leaves layers to display the artwork on those layers. If necessary, resize the Layers palette to view all the contents.

2 Choose Edit > Deselect All to deselect the artwork.

3 Press the spacebar to get the hand tool (✋), and drag the image up until the dragonfly is visible in the center of the window.

4 Select the direct-selection tool (▷) in the toolbox, and click in the center of the lower left wing of the dragonfly.

5 Apply a gradient mesh to the dragonfly wing:

• Choose Object > Create Gradient Mesh.

• In the Create Gradient Mesh dialog box, enter **3** in the Rows text box, press Tab and type **2** in the Columns text box, and make sure that the Preview option is selected.

• For Appearance, choose To Center to highlight the center of the object. Enter a highlight of 80%. Click OK.

Select lower wing.   *Create gradient mesh with highlight.*   *Result*

6 In the Layers palette, click the triangle (▶) to the left of the Dragonfly layer to view its contents.

7 Now click the triangle to the left of the Lower Wings sublayer to expand its view. This sublayer has two paths, named <path> and <mesh>. The selection indicator (the solid square) and the target indicator (the double circle) show that the <mesh> path is selected.

8 Click the target indicator for the <path> sublayer to select the lower right wing.

Using the target indicators in the Layers palette is a quick and easy way to select objects that are in different groups or on different layers.

A. *Selection indicator*
B. *Target indicator*

9 Repeat step 5 for the lower right wing.

10 In the Layers palette, click the triangle to the left of the Lower Wings sublayer to collapse it.

11 Click the triangle to the left of the Upper Wings sublayer to expand its view. This sublayer also has two paths.

12 Now apply a gradient mesh to each of the upper right wings:

• To select the upper right wing, click the target indicator for the first <path> sublayer. Repeat step 5.

• To select the upper left wing, click the target indicator for the second <path> sublayer. Repeat step 5.

Now that the dragonfly wings are painted with a gradient mesh, you'll select them using the Layers palette and adjust their transparency.

13 In the Layers palette, click the target indicator to the right of the Upper Wings sublayer. Hold down the Shift key and click the target indicator for the Lower Wings sublayer to add the wings to the selection. All four dragonfly wings are now selected.

14 Choose Window > Show Transparency or click the Transparency palette tab to display the Transparency palette.

15 Use the Opacity slider to lower the opacity of the dragonfly wings. (We used 29%.)

Select four wings.   *Change opacity.*   *Result*

For a color illustration of the opacity change, see figure 11-3 in the color section.

Now you're ready to view the finished artwork.

16 Double-click the zoom tool (🔍) to zoom out to 100%.

17 Choose View > Hide Guides, and then choose Edit > Deselect All to clear the extra guides and selection lines.

18 Choose File > Save to save the artwork. Choose File > Close to close your file.

This completes the lesson. Now you're ready to create your own watercolor or airbrush effects. To learn about other ways to blend colors within objects, see Lesson 8, "Blending Shapes and Colors."

Tips for creating mesh objects

You can create a mesh object out of any path object, or any bitmap image (such as a photographic image imported from Adobe Photoshop). Keep these important guidelines in mind when creating mesh objects:

• *You cannot create mesh objects from compound paths, text objects, or placed EPS files.*

• *Once a mesh object has been created, it cannot be converted back to a path object.*

• *When converting complex objects, use the Create Gradient Mesh command for the best results.*

• *When converting simple objects, use either the gradient mesh tool or the Create Gradient Mesh command. However, if you want to add a highlight to a particular spot, use the gradient mesh tool and click at the point you want the highlight to appear.*

• *To create a mesh object with a regular pattern of mesh points and mesh lines, use the Create Gradient Mesh command.*

• *When converting complex objects, Illustrator can add hidden anchor points to maintain the shape of a line. If you want to edit, add, or remove one or more of these anchor points, use the add-anchor-point tool or the delete-anchor-point tool.*

• *To improve performance and speed of redrawing, keep the size of mesh objects to a minimum. Complex mesh objects can greatly reduce performance. Thus, it is better to create a few small, simple mesh objects than to create a single, complex mesh object.*

– From the Adobe Illustrator User Guide, Chapter 8

Review questions

1 Describe two methods for creating a gradient mesh.

2 How do you change a color on the mesh?

3 How do you add a mesh point to a mesh object? How do you add the mesh point without adding a color?

4 How do you delete a mesh line?

5 Describe how to move a mesh point without affecting the intersecting line.

6 How do you make a gradient mesh transparent?

Review answers

1 To create a gradient mesh, you select the gradient mesh tool and click an object; or you can select the object first, choose Object > Create Gradient Mesh, and specify the number of mesh lines and highlighting in the Create Gradient Mesh dialog box. Another way to create a gradient mesh is to select a gradient-filled object, choose Object > Expand, and select the Gradient Mesh option in the Expand dialog box to expand the gradient.

2 To change a color on the mesh, use the direct-selection tool or the gradient mesh tool to select the mesh point for the color, and then select a different color.

3 To add a mesh point to a mesh object, click in a mesh patch or on a mesh line segment with the gradient mesh tool. (You can also add anchor points to mesh lines using the add-anchor-point tool.) To add the mesh point without adding a color, hold down Shift as you click.

4 To delete a mesh line, select the gradient mesh tool, and Alt/Option-click a segment on the line.

5 To move a mesh point without affecting the intersecting line, use the gradient mesh tool to select the point without releasing the mouse button, and hold down Shift as you drag the mesh point.

6 To make a gradient mesh transparent, select the gradient mesh object and change its opacity in the Transparency palette.

Lesson 12

Drawing Cylinders and Boxes

It's easy to transform two-dimensional designs into three-dimensional cylindrical shapes and boxes. Use Smart Guides and the free transform tool to shape objects precisely. You can also use gradients to give the illusion of depth.

In this lesson, you'll learn how to do the following:

• Use bounding boxes to scale objects.

• Precisely align points using Smart Guides as you draw objects.

• Use the Pathfinder palette to create shapes.

• Use gradients to provide the illusion of depth.

• Construct and rotate objects using the free transform tool.

Getting started

In this lesson, you'll use a round and a rectangular box top as the basis for creating cylindrical and rectangular boxes. Before you begin, you'll need to restore the default preferences for Adobe Illustrator, then you'll open a file containing the finished artwork to see what you'll create.

1 To ensure that the tools and palettes function exactly as described in this lesson, delete or deactivate (by renaming) the Adobe Illustrator 9.0 preferences file. See "Restoring default preferences" on page 3.

2 Start Adobe Illustrator.

3 Choose File > Open, and open the L12end.ai file in the Lesson 12 folder, located inside the Lessons folder within the AICIB folder on your hard drive.

This file displays both the cylindrical and rectangular completed boxes. You'll create the boxes from two separate start files.

4 Choose View > Zoom Out to make the finished artwork smaller, adjust the window size, and leave it on your screen as you work. (Use the hand tool (✋) to move the artwork where you want it in the window.) If you don't want to leave the image open, choose File > Close.

For an illustration of the finished artwork in this lesson, see the color section.

To begin working, you'll open an existing art file set up for the cylindrical box.

5 Choose File > Open, and open the L12strt1.ai file in the Lesson12 folder, located inside the Lessons folder within the AICIB folder on your hard drive.

6 Choose File > Save As, name the file **Lemon.ai**, and select the Lesson12 folder. Leave the Format option set to Adobe Illustrator® Document, and click Save. In the Illustrator Native Format Options dialog box, select Illustrator 9.0 Compatibility and click OK.

Drawing three-dimensional objects

Smart Guides are very useful in creating complex shapes, such as the three-dimensional objects in this lesson. Smart Guides help you select and snap to points to create, edit, move, align, and transform objects by creating temporary guides that indicate paths, anchor and path points, and angles. You can use Smart Guides with the pen tool or the shape tools, the selection tools, and the transformation tools.

The Pathfinder palette is also helpful in creating complex shapes. Pathfinder commands combine, isolate, and subdivide shapes as part of creating complex objects. You can further modify shapes by changing their size, shape, or orientation with the free transform tool or the reflect, rotate, scale, and shear tools.

Drawing cylinders

You'll use the round box top as a basis for creating the cylindrical box.

1 Choose Edit > Select All to select all of the artwork.

You'll begin by scaling the box top to create perspective.

2 Select the selection tool (￪). Then drag the center bottom handle on the bounding box up to scale the artwork vertically.

Object selected

Drag bounding box handle up to scale object.

3 Click outside the artwork to deselect the box top.

Clicking outside the artwork with the selection tool, the direct-selection tool, or the group-selection tool deselects all selected objects.

4 Choose File > Save to save the artwork.

Creating the cylinder bottom and sides

Now you'll create the cylinder's bottom and sides, using Smart Guides to align the shapes precisely. You'll use Smart Guides to locate and join anchor points on the top and bottom ellipses.

1 Choose Edit > Preferences > Smart Guides.

Objects in artwork snap to Smart Guides when they're within the designated tolerance range. The default setting is 4 points. You'll decrease the snapping tolerance to create more precise alignment.

2 Set the Snapping Tolerance to **1 point**. (Leave other Smart Guides options at their default settings.) Click OK.

3 Choose View > Smart Guides to turn on Smart Guides. A check mark next to the command indicates that Smart Guides are turned on.

4 Use the selection tool (￪) to select the outer ellipse in the artwork.

5 Start dragging the ellipse downward; then press Alt+Shift (Windows) or Option+Shift (Mac OS), and drag a copy of the ellipse directly below the original.

The copy of the ellipse will become the bottom of the cylinder.

6 Select the pen tool ( ). Roll over the left edge of the upper ellipse until you see the Smart Guides text label for the anchor point on that edge.

Smart Guides text labels appear when you roll over anchor points or path points with the mouse. You'll use the Smart Guides text labels to locate the anchor points on the outer edges of the upper and lower ellipses, and to join the anchor points with the pen tool to create a rectangle that will become part of the cylinder barrel.

7 Click the left anchor point with the pen tool.

8 Roll over the left edge of the lower ellipse until you see the Smart Guides text label for the anchor point on that edge.

9 Shift-click the anchor point with the pen tool to create the left side of a rectangle that will join the two ellipses.

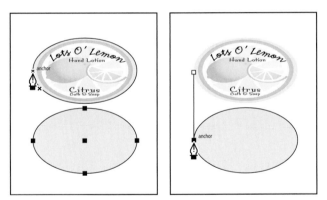

Smart Guides text labels indicate anchor points beneath tool pointer.

10 Roll over the right edge of the lower ellipse until you see the Smart Guides text label for the anchor point on that edge. Then click the anchor point with the pen tool to create the bottom side of the rectangle.

11 As you did in the previous step, use Smart Guides to locate the anchor point on the right edge of the upper ellipse, and click the anchor point with the pen tool to create the right side of the rectangle.

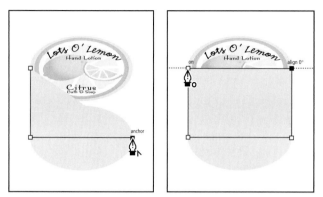

Smart Guides text labels indicate anchor and alignment points.

12 Click the anchor point on the left edge of the upper ellipse again to close the rectangle.

13 Ctrl-click (Windows) or Command-click (Mac OS) away from the artwork to deselect it. Then choose File > Save to save the file.

How Smart Guides work

When Smart Guides are turned on and you move the cursor over your artwork, the cursor looks for objects, page boundaries, and intersections of construction guides to snap to that are within the tolerance range set in Smart Guides Preferences.

You can use Smart Guides in the following ways when you create, move, and transform objects:

• *When you create an object with the pen or shape tools, use the Smart Guides to position the new object's anchor points relative to the other object.*

• *When you move an object, use the Smart Guides to align to the point on the object that you have selected. You can align to the anchor point at the corner of a selected object near the bounding box. To do so, select the object just inside the bounding box handle. If the tolerance is 5 points or greater, you can snap to the corner point from 5 points away.*

• *When the Transform Tools option is selected in Smart Guides Preferences and you transform an object, Smart Guides appear to assist the transformation.*

Note: *When Snap to Grid is turned on, you cannot use Smart Guides (even if the menu command is selected).*

– From the Adobe Illustrator User Guide, Chapter 4

Completing the cylinder

You'll use Pathfinder commands to complete construction of the cylinder, and add a gradient fill to the cylinder barrel to give the illusion of depth. Then you'll reduce the cylinder depth to complete the project.

1 Select the selection tool (ꞓ). Then Shift-click the rectangle and the bottom ellipse you created to select them.

2 Choose Window > Show Pathfinder if the Pathfinder palette is not visible. Then click the Unite button (🖫) in the Pathfinder palette (the top left button).

The Unite command creates a single object from overlapping objects.

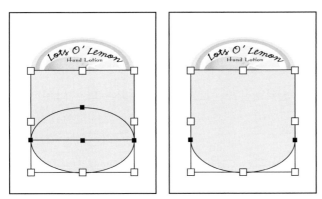

Select rectangle and bottom ellipse. Click Unite button.

3 Display the context-sensitive menu for the united shape:

• (Windows) Press Ctrl and right-click over the shape.

• (Mac OS) Press Control and then click over the shape to view the context-sensitive menu.

4 From the context-sensitive menu, choose Arrange > Send to Back.

5 With the united shape still selected, use the selection tool (ꞓ) and Shift-click to select the top ellipse.

6 In the Pathfinder palette, click the Trim button (🖫) (bottom row, second button from the left). The Trim command removes hidden parts of overlapping filled objects.

The Pathfinder palette contains many commands in addition to the Unite and Trim commands, which let you divide and combine shapes to create complex objects. You can also apply Pathfinder commands with the Effect menu. For more information on Pathfinder commands, see "Using the Pathfinder palette and Effect menu to modify shapes" in online Help or Chapter 5 in the Adobe Illustrator User Guide.

For an illustration of effects applied by the Pathfinder commands, see figure 12-1 in the color section.

Now you'll apply color and refine the shape you just created.

7 Click outside the artwork to deselect the object.

8 Select the direct-selection tool (🔓) and select the barrel of the cylinder.

You'll paint the cylinder barrel with a swatch from the Swatches palette.

9 Click the Swatches tab to bring the palette to the front of its group.

10 In the Swatches palette, click the Cylinder gradient swatch to fill the cylinder barrel.

Select cylinder with   *Click swatch to apply it.*   *Result*
direct-selection tool.

11 Click outside the artwork to deselect the cylinder barrel.

12 To reduce the depth of the cylinder, select the direct-selection tool ( ), and Shift-click or drag a marquee to select the left, bottom, and right anchor points on the bottom ellipse. Begin to drag the bottom of the cylinder up; then press Shift, and release when the cylinder height is about half the original size.

Shift-drag bottom ellipse.   *Result*

13 Click outside the artwork to deselect the object.

14 Choose File > Save to save your work, and choose File > Close to close the file.

Drawing boxes

Now you'll create a rectangular box. You'll use Smart Guides, as you did to create the cylinder, but this time you'll use the Smart Guides angle alignment guides to create precise side panels for the box.

You'll start this part of the lesson by opening a flat view (the box top). You'll use this flat view to create the box sides and then you'll decorate the sides and shear the box panels to construct the box.

1 Choose File > Open, and open the L12strt2.ai file in the Lesson12 folder, located inside the Lessons folder within the AICIB folder on your hard drive.

2 Choose File > Save As, name the file **Lime.ai**, and select the Lesson12 folder. Leave the Format option set to Adobe Illustrator® Document, and click Save. In the Illustrator Native Format Options dialog box, select Illustrator 9.0 Compatibility and click OK.

Creating box sides

You'll use Smart Guides to create sides for the box based on the dimensions of the box top.

First you'll roll the mouse over anchor points on the left side of the box top and practice using Smart Guides to find intersection points.

1 Select the pen tool ( ). Roll the pointer over the anchor points at the two left-side corners on the box top. Then roll the pointer over the artboard to the left of the box top.

Smart Guides alignment guides and text labels appear, indicating angles of alignment for the points you rolled over.

Note: If the alignment guides and text labels seem too elusive, you can change the snapping tolerance to make them easier to find. Choose Edit > Preferences > Smart Guides. Set the Snapping Tolerance to 2 pt. (Leave other Smart Guides options at their default settings.) Then click OK.

2 Roll the pointer along the alignment guides until you see the "intersect" text label. This label marks the intersection point of the points you rolled over.

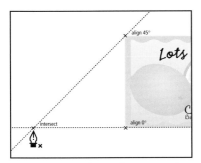

Smart Guides indicate alignment points, angles, and intersection points.

Now you're ready to use Smart Guides to draw the side panels for the box.

3 Roll the mouse pointer over the bottom left anchor point on the box top. Then click on the anchor point with the pen tool to create the first point of the longer side panel for the box.

4 Roll the pointer slowly downward from the anchor point. Use the alignment guide and the "align 90°" text label to align the pointer with the left side of the box top.

By default, Smart Guides show alignment guides and points for 0°, 45°, and 90° angles. You can change Smart Guides to show alignment guides and points for other angles.

See "Using Smart Guides" in online Help or Chapter 4 in the Adobe Illustrator User Guide.

5 Click with the pen tool along the alignment guide to create the bottom left corner point of the longer side panel (so that the side panel is about one-third the height of the box top).

Roll tool pointer to see Smart Guides.　*Click on alignment guides to draw points.*

Now you'll create the right edge of the side panel in the same manner and use the alignment guides to create the bottom edge of the side panel precisely.

6 Roll over the bottom right corner point of the box top.

7 Roll the mouse pointer slowly downward from the anchor point to view the alignment guide and the "align 90°" text label.

8 Continue rolling downward along the alignment guide until a perpendicular alignment guide and the "intersect" text label appear, marking the lower right corner of the side panel.

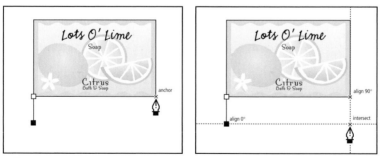

Roll over anchor points and roll along alignment guide to see intersection point.

9 Click the intersect point to create the lower right anchor point for the side panel.

Now you'll complete the side panel.

10 Roll upward and click the bottom right anchor point of the box top to create the top right anchor point for the side panel.

11 Click the upper left anchor point of the side panel to close the path.

You'll use alignment guides in a similar manner to create the shorter side panel for the box.

12 With the pen tool still selected, Shift-click the upper left anchor point of the side panel to create the upper right anchor point for the shorter side panel.

13 Roll over the upper left anchor point of the box top.

You'll use angle alignment guides and intersection points to create the top edge of the shorter panel.

14 Roll down to the left at a 45° angle to find the intersection between the 45° alignment guide of the box top upper left corner and the 0° alignment guide for the upper right corner of the shorter side panel. Then click the intersection point to create the upper left anchor point for the shorter side panel.

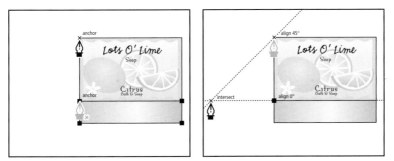

Click at point A, roll up to point B and along alignment guide to see intersection point (C).

Now you'll use alignment guides to create the left edge of the shorter panel.

15 Roll over the lower left corner of the longer side panel; then roll slowly to the left to find the intersection point between the 0° alignment guide of the longer side panel and the 90° alignment guide of the upper left corner of the shorter side panel. Then click the intersection point to create the lower left anchor point for the shorter side panel.

16 Click the lower left corner of the longer side panel to create the lower right anchor point for the shorter side panel.

Roll to see intersection point.   Click to create anchor point.

17 Click the upper right corner of the shorter side panel to close the path.

Now you'll paint the panels. By painting with various shades of color, you can create the illusion of shading and depth.

18 Select the selection tool ( ), and select the shorter side panel.

19 In the Swatches palette, click the Bright yellow-green swatch to fill the shorter panel.

20 With the selection tool, click the longer side panel to select it.

21 In the Swatches palette, click the Pale yellow-green swatch to fill the longer panel.

Select longer side panel.   Select color.

22 Click outside the artwork to deselect the side panel. Then choose File > Save to save your work.

Using brushes to decorate the panels

Next you'll use the paintbrush tool and custom brushes to add illustrations to the box's side panels.

1 Select the paintbrush tool ( ).

2 In the toolbox, click the Fill box and the None box.

Brushes apply art to the stroke of a path. Use a fill of None when painting with brushes to avoid filling the brushed path with color. For more information on applying brushes to paths, see Lesson 5, "Working with Brushes."

3 Click the Brushes tab to bring the palette to the front of its group. If necessary, resize the palette to see all of its brushes.

The Brushes palette displays the default brushes provided with the Illustrator program. The Brushes palette also includes a brush created specially for this lesson, the Lime Scatter brush. (You won't see the Lime Scatter brush when you open the Brushes palette in other lessons.)

4 In the Brushes palette, select the Lime Scatter brush.

5 Paint a wavy stroke on the shorter side panel. (Make sure that the brush stroke stays within the panel.)

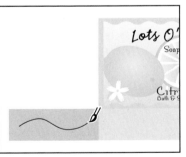

Select brush in Brushes palette.   *Draw with paintbrush tool.*

6 Use the selection tool ( ) to select the flower on the box top.

7 In the Brushes palette, select New Brush from the Brushes palette menu.

8 Select New Scatter Brush, and click OK.

9 In the Scatter Brush Options dialog box, name the brush **Flower.** Then set the following options:

• For Size, choose Random. Then enter **36%** and **70%** in the text boxes, or drag the sliders to set the size values.

• For Spacing, choose Random. Then enter **65%** and **118%** in the text boxes, or drag the sliders to set the spacing values.

• For Scatter, leave the default setting (Fixed, 0%).

• For Rotation, choose Random. Then enter **60%** and **–10%**, or drag the sliders to set the rotation values.

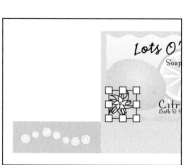

Select object to use as new brush.   Enter settings for new brush.

10 Click OK.

[?] For more information about making your own brushes, see "Creating brushes" in online Help or Chapter 3 in the Adobe Illustrator User Guide.

11 Click outside the artwork to deselect the flower.

12 In the toolbox, click the Fill box and the None box.

13 In the Brushes palette, select the new Flower Scatter brush. Then use the paintbrush tool to paint a wavy stroke on the longer side panel. (Make sure that the brush stroke stays within the panel.)

14 Select the selection tool. In the artwork, Shift-click the Lime Scatter brush stroke and the Flower Scatter brush stroke.

15 Choose Object > Expand Appearance.

The Expand Appearance command creates closed paths from stroked paths—similar to the Create Outlines command used to create closed paths from type. You must expand brushstrokes to be able to transform the paths, as you'll do in the following sections.

Select brush strokes.   Expand strokes to create closed paths.

16 Click away from the artwork to deselect it, and choose File > Save to save your work.

Constructing the box

To join the box elements into a three-dimensional object, you'll use the free transform tool and the rotate tool to shear and rotate the box top and panels.

As you'll see, you can perform the same transformation several ways. When you shear an object, you skew the object along the axis that you designate. Rotating an object turns it around a fixed point that you designate. See Lesson 6, "Transforming Objects," to learn more about the various transformation tools.

The type used in the box top artwork has been converted to outlines using the Type > Create Outlines command. Type must be converted to outlines before you can use the free transform tool to shear, distort, or change perspective in the type. If you want your type

Transforming selected objects

You can transform selected objects—that is, change their size, shape, and orientation by selecting one or more objects and then applying various transformation actions on them. For example, you can change the angle of an object by rotating it, or add perspective to an angle by shearing it.

To transform an object, you can use the free transform tool, individual transformation tools, the Transform palette, or the Transform Effect command:

* *Use the free transform tool to rotate, scale, reflect, shear, and distort objects quickly.*

* *Use the transformation tools to change the size, shape, and orientation of selected objects. The transformation tools are the rotate tool, scale tool, reflect tool, and shear tool. You can also use individual transform dialog boxes to specify numeric values, to preview the transformation before applying it, and to select other transformation options.*

* *Use the Transform palette to modify selected objects by changing information in the palette.*

* *Use the Transform Effect command to transform a selection, group, or layer without altering the original artwork.*

to remain editable while distorting it, select the type and choose Effect > Distort & Transform > Free Distort. For more information on applying editable effects see Lesson 9, "Using Appearance Attributes, Styles, and Effects."

You'll start by grouping the elements of each box panel so that you can work with each panel as a unit.

1 Select the selection tool ( ), and drag a selection marquee over the box top to select all the objects that are part of the top.

2 Choose Object > Group to group the objects in the box top.

3 Repeat steps 1 and 2 with the two side panels to select and group each panel separately.

Select and group box top.   *Select and group side panels.*

Next you'll shear and rotate the box top to give it perspective.

4 Use the selection tool to select the box top group.

5 Select the free transform tool (𝄢); then position the pointer on the center point on the right side of the box top.

6 Click, and without releasing the mouse button, press Ctrl (Windows) or Command (Mac OS), and drag the center point down to shear the box top downward.

Select object.

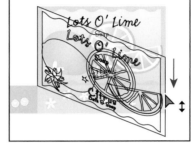

Drag bounding box handle with free transform tool to shear.

7 Select the rotate tool (◌), and click at the box top's lower left corner to set the point of origin for the rotation.

8 Hold down the Shift key, click near the right edge of the box top, and drag counter-clockwise to rotate the box top 45°. (The pointer can be inside or outside the box top when you drag.) Use the alignment guides and angle text labels to help determine the angle of rotation.

Drag with rotate tool to rotate object around point of origin.

Now you'll fit the longer side panel to the box top and shear the panel to adjust its perspective.

9 Use the selection tool to select the longer side panel.

10 Select the free transform tool; then position the pointer on the center point on the right side of the panel.

11 Click, and without releasing the mouse button, press Ctrl (Windows) or Command (Mac OS), and drag the center point up to shear the panel upward, until the upper right corner of the panel meets the lower right corner of the box top. Then release the mouse button.

To complete the box, you'll fit the shorter side panel to the box top and shear the shorter panel.

12 Press Ctrl (Windows) or Command (Mac OS) to temporarily select the selection tool, and then select the shorter side panel.

Pressing Ctrl/Command temporarily activates the selection tool (or the direct-selection or group-selection tool, whichever was used most recently) when another tool is selected in the toolbox.

13 Repeat steps 10 and 11, dragging the center point on the left side of the panel upward, until the upper left corner of the panel meets the upper left corner of the box top.

Select object.

Drag with free transform tool to shear, and join with other objects.

As a final step, you'll rotate and reposition the artwork.

14 Press Ctrl (Windows) or Command (Mac OS) to temporarily select the selection tool, and drag a marquee over the box top and side panels to select all elements in the artwork.

15 Choose Object > Group.

16 Select the selection tool from the toolbox and drag the grouped box to the center of the artboard.

17 Move the pointer near any of the four corners of the artwork until you see the rotation pointer, and then drag clockwise to rotate the artwork.

Drag outside bounding box corner to   *Result*
rotate artwork.

18 Click outside the artwork to deselect the box.

19 Choose File > Save to save the file. Choose File > Close to close the file.

Congratulations! You've now completed your box.

Review questions

1 How do you quickly scale an object using its bounding box?

2 What features of Smart Guides help you to draw an object that aligns precisely with another object in the artwork?

3 What transformations can you perform with the free transform tool?

Review answers

1 With the bounding box, you can scale objects easily by dragging the selection or a handle (one of the hollow squares surrounding the selected objects). The bounding box creates a temporary border around the selected object. You see an outline of the selection as you drag it. When you release the mouse button, the object snaps to the current border created by the bounding box, and you see the object's outline move.

2 Smart Guides have the following features to help you align objects precisely as you draw:

• Smart Guides snap objects to guides when the objects fall within a specified tolerance (distance from the guides).

• Text labels identify anchor points, intersection points, and alignment angles when the pointer is positioned over the points in the artwork.

• Alignment guides indicate alignment angles or intersection angles when you roll over one or more anchor points with the mouse, then roll away from the anchor point or points.

3 You can distort, reflect, rotate, scale, and shear objects with the free transform tool.

Lesson 13

Printing Artwork and Producing Color Separations

The quality and color of your final printed output are determined by the process you follow to prepare an image for print. Whether you're printing a draft of your work on a desktop printer or outputting color separations to be printed on a commercial press, learning fundamental printing concepts helps ensure that your printed results meet your expectations.

In this lesson, you'll learn about the following:

- Different types of printing requirements and printing devices.
- Printing concepts and printing terminology.
- Basic color principles.
- How to separate your color artwork into its component colors for output to print.
- How to use spot colors for two-color printing.
- Special considerations when outputting to print.

Printing: An overview

When you print a document from a computer, data is sent from the document to the printing device, either to be printed on paper or to be converted to a positive or negative image on film. For black-and-white, grayscale, or low quantities of color artwork, many people use desktop printers. However, if you require large quantities of printed output, such as a brochure or magazine ad, you'll need to prepare your artwork for output on a commercial printing press. Printing on a commercial press is an art that requires time and experience to perfect. In addition to close communication with a printing professional, learning basic printing concepts and terminology will help you produce printed results that meet your expectations.

Note: This lesson assumes that you have a desktop printer for use with the exercises. If you don't have a desktop printer available, read the sections and skip the step-by-step instructions.

Different printing requirements require different printing processes. To determine your printing requirements, consider the following: What effect do you want the printed piece to have on your audience? Will your artwork be printed in black and white? Color? Does it require special paper? How many printed copies do you need? If you're printing in color, is precise color matching necessary, or will approximate color matching suffice?

Take a minute to consider several types of printing jobs:

- A black-and-white interoffice newsletter, requiring a low quantity of printed copies. For this type of printing job, you can generally use a 300- to 600-dpi desktop laser printer to output the original, and then use a copy machine to reproduce the larger quantity.

• A business card using black and one other color. The term *two-color* printing typically refers to printing with black and one other color, although it may also refer to printing with two colors that are not black. Two-color printing is less expensive than four-color printing and lets you select exact color matches, called *spot* colors, which can be important for logos. For precise color matching, two-color printing is done on a printing press; if only an approximate color match is required, you might use a desktop color printer.

• A party invitation using two colors and tints of those colors. In addition to printing two solid colors, you can print tints of the colors to add depth to your printed artwork. Two-color printing is often done on colored paper that complements the ink colors and might be done on a desktop color printer or on a printing press, depending on the desired quantity and the degree of color matching required.

• A newspaper. Newspapers are typically printed on a printing press because they are time-sensitive publications printed in large quantities. In addition, newspapers are generally printed on large rolls of newsprint, which are then trimmed and folded to the correct size.

• A fashion magazine or catalog requiring accurate color reproduction. *Four-color* printing refers to mixing the four process ink colors (cyan, magenta, yellow, and black, or CMYK) for printed output. When accurate color reproduction is required, printing is done on a printing press using CMYK inks. CMYK inks can reproduce a good amount of the visible color spectrum, with the exception of neon or metallic colors. You'll learn more about color models in the next section.

About printing devices

Now that you've looked at several types of publications and different ways to reproduce them, you'll begin learning basic printing concepts and printing terminology.

Halftone screens

To reproduce any type of artwork, a printing device typically breaks down the artwork into a series of dots of various sizes called a *halftone screen*. Black dots are used to print black-and-white or grayscale artwork. For color artwork, a halftone screen is created for each ink color (cyan, magenta, yellow, and black); these then overlay one another at different angles to produce the full range of printed color. To see a good example of how individual halftone screens overlay each other at different angles on a printed page, look at a color comics page through a magnifying glass.

The size of the dots in a halftone screen determines how light or dark colors appear in print. The smaller the dot, the lighter the color appears; the larger the dot, the darker the color appears.

Screen frequency

Screen frequency (also called line screen, screen ruling, or halftone frequency) refers to the number of rows or lines of dots used to render an image on film or paper. In addition, the rows of dots are broken down into individual squares, called *halftone cells*. Screen frequency is measured in lines per inch (lpi) and is a fixed value you can set for your printing device.

As a general rule, higher screen frequencies produce finer detail in printed output. This is because the higher the screen frequency, the smaller the halftone cells, and subsequently, the smaller the halftone dot in the cell.

However, a high screen frequency alone does not guarantee high-quality output. The screen frequency must be appropriate to the paper, the inks, and the printer or printing press used to output the artwork. Your printing professional will help you select the appropriate line screen value for your artwork and output device.

Low-screen ruling (65 lpi) often used to print newsletters.

High-screen rulings (150–200 lpi) used for high-quality books.

Output device resolution

The *resolution* of a printing device describes the number of dots the printing device has available to *render*, or create, a halftone dot. The higher the output device resolution, the higher the quality of the printed output. For example, the printed quality of an image output at 2400 dots per inch (dpi) is higher than the printed quality of an image output at 300 dpi. Adobe Illustrator is resolution-independent and will always print at the printing device's highest resolution capability.

The quality of printed output depends on the relationship between the resolution of the output device (dpi) and the screen frequency (lpi). As a general rule, high-resolution output devices use higher screen frequency values to produce the highest quality images. For example, an imagesetter with a resolution of 2400 dpi and a screen frequency of 177 lpi produces a higher quality image than a desktop printer with a resolution of 300 to 600 dpi and a screen frequency of 85 lpi.

About color

Color is produced by a computer monitor and printing device using two different *color models* (methods for displaying and measuring color). The human eye perceives color according to the wavelength of the light it receives. Light containing the full color spectrum is perceived as white; in the absence of light, the eye perceives black.

The *gamut* of a color model is the range of colors that can be displayed or printed. The largest color gamut is that viewed in nature; all other color gamuts produce a subset of nature's color gamut. The two most common color models are red, green, and blue (RGB), the method by which monitors display color; and cyan, magenta, yellow, and black (CMYK), the method by which images are printed using four process ink colors.

The RGB color model

A large percentage of the visible spectrum of color can be represented by mixing three basic components of colored light in various proportions. These components are known as the *additive colors*: red, green, and blue (RGB). The RGB color model is called the additive color model because various percentages of each colored light are added to create color. All monitors display color using the RGB color model.

The CMYK color model

If 100% of red, green, or blue is subtracted from white light, the resulting color is cyan, magenta, or yellow. For example, if an object absorbs (subtracts) 100% red light and reflects green and blue, cyan is the perceived color. Cyan, magenta, and yellow are called the subtractive primaries, and they form the basis for printed colors. In addition to cyan, magenta, and yellow, black ink is used to generate true black and to deepen the shadows in images. These four inks (CMYK) are often called *process* colors because they are the four standard inks used in the printing process.

For an illustration of RGB and CMYK color models, see figure 13-3 in the color section.

Spot colors

Whereas process colors are reproduced using cyan, magenta, yellow, and black inks, spot colors are premixed inks used in place of, or in addition to, CMYK colors. Spot colors can be selected from color-matching systems, such as the PANTONE or TOYO™ color libraries. Many spot colors can be converted to their process color equivalents when printed; however, some spot colors, such as metallic or iridescent colors, require their own plate on press. Use spot color in the following situations:

• To save money on one-color and two-color print jobs. (When your printing budget won't allow for four-color printing, you can still print relatively inexpensively using one or two colors.)

• To print logos or other graphic elements that require precise color matching.

• To print special inks, such as metallic, fluorescent, or pearlescent colors.

Getting started

Before you begin, you'll need to restore the default preferences for Adobe Illustrator. Then you'll open the art file for this lesson.

1 To ensure that the tools and palettes function exactly as described in this lesson, delete or deactivate (by renaming) the Adobe Illustrator 9.0 preferences file. See "Restoring default preferences" on page 3 in the Introduction.

2 Start Adobe Illustrator.

3 Choose File > Open, and open the L13strt1.ai file in the Lesson13 folder, located inside the Lessons folder within the AICIB folder on your hard drive.

For an illustration of the finished artwork in this lesson, see the color section.

4 Choose File > Save As, name the file **Circus.ai**, and select the Lesson13 folder. Leave the Format option set to Adobe Illustrator® Document, and click Save. In the Illustrator Native Format Options dialog box, select Illustrator 9.0 Compatibility and click OK.

Color management

Although all color gamuts overlap, they don't match exactly, which is why some colors on your monitor can't be reproduced in print. The colors that can't be reproduced in print are called *out-of-gamut* colors because they are outside the spectrum of printable colors.

To compensate for these differences and to ensure the closest match between on-screen colors and printed colors, Adobe Illustrator includes a Color Management System (CMS) that lets you select profiles for your monitor and for the output device to which you'll print. Selecting a color profile controls the conversion of RGB values to CMYK values at print time. To select a color profile, you use the Color Settings command.

1 Choose Edit > Color Settings.

2 In the Color Settings dialog box, choose U.S. Prepress Defaults from the Settings menu.

In this lesson, you'll use one of the predefined sets of color management settings provided in Adobe Illustrator. Each set has corresponding color profile and conversion options designed to preserve consistent color for a particular publishing workflow under typical conditions. For more information on color management settings, see "Using predefined color management settings" in online Help or Chapter 7 in the Adobe Illustrator User Guide.

3 Leave the settings and options at their default values. Click OK.

Printing black-and-white proofs

As a general rule, you should print black-and-white proofs of all your documents at different stages of your work to check the layout and to verify the accuracy of text and graphics before preparing the document for final output.

Now you'll print a draft of the Circus.ai file.

1 In the Circus.ai file, notice the *crop marks*, the pairs of lines at each corner of the artwork. Crop marks define where the artwork is trimmed after it is printed. The crop marks indicate a *bleed*, the area of artwork that falls outside the crop marks, and which will be removed when the printed artwork is trimmed. The bleed is used to ensure that the artwork prints to the edge of the trimmed page.

[?] You can set crop marks where you want them directly in the artwork. See "Setting crop marks and trim marks" in online Help or Chapter 15 in the Adobe Illustrator User Guide.

2 If you're not connected to a black-and-white printer, go on to the next section.

3 Choose File > Print, and click OK (Windows) or Print (Mac OS).

The circus logo is printed in black, white, and shades of gray. Next, you'll soft-proof the color on your monitor screen.

Soft-proofing colors

In a color-managed work flow, you can use the precision of color profiles to soft-proof your document directly on the monitor. Soft-proofing lets you preview on-screen how your document's colors will look when reproduced on a particular output device.

The reliability of soft-proofing completely depends, however, on the quality of your monitor, your monitor profile, and the ambient lighting conditions of your workstation area. For information on creating a monitor profile, see "Creating an ICC monitor profile" in online Help or Chapter 7 in the Adobe Illustrator User Guide.

1 Choose View > Proof Setup > Custom. The profile is set to U.S. Web Coated (SWOP). Leave it set to this profile and click OK.

The View > Proof Colors option is selected by default (indicated by a check mark) so that you can view the artwork as it will look when printed to the selected standard—here, U.S. Web Coated (SWOP).

Next, you'll change the profile to see what the image will look like if printed on a different output device.

2 Choose View > Proof Setup > Custom.

3 Use the Profile menu to select Euroscale Uncoated, and click OK. Because the view is still set to Proof Colors, the image preview automatically shifts colors to display what it would look like were it printed according to the Euroscale Uncoated profile.

You'll now return the settings to the SWOP settings.

4 Choose View > Proof Setup > Custom. Set the profile to U.S. Web Coated (SWOP) and click OK.

5 Choose View > Proof Colors to turn off the soft-proofing preview.

Next, you'll work with printing color artwork.

Using the Document Info command

Before you take your color artwork to a prepress professional or begin the process of creating color separations on your own, use the Document Info command to generate and save a list of information about all the elements of your artwork file. The Document Info command displays a palette of information on the objects, linked or placed files, colors, gradients, patterns, and fonts in your document.

If you're working with prepress professionals, be sure to provide them with the Document Info list before delivering your files; they can help you determine what you'll need to include with your artwork. For example, if your artwork uses a font that the prepress house does not have, you'll need to bring or supply a copy of the font with your artwork.

1 Choose File > Document Info. The Document Info palette appears.

2 In the Document Info palette, select different subjects about the document from the palette menu in the upper right corner. The list box displays information about each subject you select.

3 If you have an object selected in the artwork, choose Selection Only from the Document Info palette menu to display information only on that selected object. A check mark indicates that the Selection Only option is turned on.

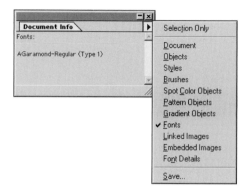

You can also view or print the entire contents of the Document Info palette by saving it and then opening it in a text editor.

4 To save the Document Info text, choose Save from the palette menu, enter a name for the Document Info file, and click Save. You can open the file in any text editor to review and print the contents of the file.

5 When you have looked through the information on the file, you can leave the Document Info palette open on-screen or close it.

Creating color separations

To print color artwork on a printing press, you must first separate the composite art into its component colors: cyan, magenta, yellow, and black, and any spot colors, if applicable. The process of breaking composite artwork into its component colors is called *color separation*.

You set separation options in the Separation Setup dialog box. It's important to note that before setting separation options, you need to discuss the specific requirements of your print job with your printing professional.

For an illustration of color separations, see figure 13-1 in the color section.

1 Make sure that the Circus.ai artwork is still open.

2 Select the selection tool ( ) in the toolbox. Then click various objects in the artwork to select them.

As you select different objects, notice that the Color palette reflects the current color's attributes. For example, if you click the flag atop the tent, a PANTONE color swatch appears in the Color palette; if you click the red or green stripe in the clown, the color is mixed using CMYK values.

Important: *To be able to continue with this section, your computer must be connected to a 370 PostScript printer. If you are connected to an ink-jet printer or not connected to a printer, the Separation Setup option will be dimmed in the File menu.*

3 Choose File > Separation Setup.

In this lesson, you'll work with the Separation Setup dialog box until you're ready to print the file.

The Separation Setup dialog box includes options for specifying how the color in the artwork should be separated into its component colors, the output device and line screen to which the artwork will be printed, and whether the separation should be a positive or negative image. Before you can see a preview of your artwork, you must select a printer description file to indicate which output device will be used to print your artwork.

Selecting a printer description file

PostScript Printer Description (PPD) files contain information about the output device, including available page sizes, resolution, available line screen values, and the angles of the halftone screens.

1 In the Separation Setup dialog box, click Open PPD.

2 Navigate to the General.ppd file, located in the Lesson13 folder, inside the Lessons folder within the AICIB folder on your hard drive. Click Open.

Note: A PostScript Printer Description file with limited selections has been placed in the Lesson13 folder for this exercise. When you install Adobe Illustrator, two PPDs are automatically installed in the Utilities folder within the Adobe Illustrator folder, and additional PPDs are provided on the Adobe Illustrator CD.

The Separation Setup dialog box is updated with general printer parameters, and a preview of your artwork is displayed on the left side of the dialog box. (The preview of your artwork depends on the page size selected in the Page Size menu. Each output device has a variety of page sizes available; select the desired page size from the Page Setup menu in the Separation Setup dialog box.)

In addition, printer's marks surround the preview of your artwork. Printer's marks help the printer align the color separations on the press and check the color and density of the inks being used. The preview also includes the crop marks and bleeds from the artwork file. The bleeds are set to 18 points, the default setting (indicated in the Options section of the Separation Setup dialog box).

A. Star target *B.* Registration mark
C. Crop mark *D.* Progressive color bar

Specifying the bleed area

Bleed is the amount of artwork that falls outside of the printing bounding box, or outside the crop marks and trim marks. You can include bleed in your artwork as a margin of error—to ensure that the ink is still printed to the edge of the page after the page is trimmed or to ensure that an image can be stripped into a keyline in a document. Once you create the artwork that extends into the bleed, you can use Illustrator to specify the extent of the bleed.

Changing the bleed moves the crop marks farther from or closer to the image; however, the crop marks still define the same size printing bounding box.

Small bleed   Large bleed

To specify bleed:

1. Choose File > Separation Setup.

2. In the Options section of the Separation Setup dialog box, enter an amount in the Bleed text box.

By default, Illustrator applies a bleed of 18 points. This means that the artwork extends 18 points beyond the crop marks on your film. The maximum bleed you can set is 72 points; the minimum bleed is 0 points.

The size of the bleed you use depends on its purpose. A press bleed (that is, an image that bleeds off the edge of the printed sheet) should be at least 18 points. If the bleed is to ensure that an image fits a keyline, it needs to be no more than 2 or 3 points. Your print shop can advise you on the size of the bleed necessary for your particular job.

3. Specify other separation options, or click OK.

– From online Help and the Adobe Illustrator User Guide, Chapter 16

Separating colors

The circus artwork is composed of process colors and spot colors, which are displayed in the Separation Setup dialog box. By default, all spot colors are converted to their process color equivalents.

🖨	▨ Process Cyan
🖨	▨ Process Magenta
🖨	☐ Process Yellow
🖨	■ Process Black
⊠	☐ PANTONE 116 CVU
⊠	▨ PANTONE 185 CVC

Indicates spot color will be separated into process color equivalents.

To the left of the process color names, a printer icon is displayed, indicating that a separation will be generated for each color. To the left of the spot color names, a process color icon is displayed, indicating that the spot colors will be converted to their process color equivalents. If you were to print color separations at this point, all the colors, including the spot colors in the artwork, would be separated onto the four process color (CMYK) plates or pieces of film.

Composite image

Cyan separation

Magenta separation

Yellow separation

Black separation

As you learned earlier, you can print separations using process colors or spot colors, or you can use a combination of both. You'll convert the first spot color (PANTONE 116 CVC) to a process color because a precise color match isn't necessary. The second spot color, PANTONE 185 CVC, will not be converted to a process color because a precise color match is desired.

To modify how individual spot colors are separated, you must first deselect the Convert to Process option in the Separation Setup dialog box.

1 In the Separation Setup dialog box, deselect the Convert to Process option.

2 To convert the first spot color (PANTONE 116) to a process color, click the printer icon next to its name in the list of colors.

If you were to print at this point, five separations would be generated: one each for the cyan, magenta, yellow, and black plates (including the spot color converted to a process color); and a single plate for the PANTONE 185 CVC spot color. (This job would require a more specialized press, capable of printing five colors, or the paper would have to be sent back through the press to print the fifth color.)

Composite image

Cyan separation

Magenta separation

Yellow separation

Black separation

Spot separation

Specifying the screen frequency

At the beginning of this lesson, you learned that the relationship between the output device resolution and the screen frequency determines the quality of the printed output. Depending on the output device you select, more than one screen frequency value may be available. Your printing professional will direct you to select the screen frequency appropriate to your artwork.

1 In the General.ppd section of the Separation Setup dialog box, choose 60 lpi/300 dpi from the Halftone menu. The first value, 60, represents the screen frequency (lpi), and the second value, 300, represents the output device resolution (dpi).

Additional separation options, such as Emulsion Up/Down and Positive or Negative film, should be discussed with your printing professional, who can help you determine how these options should be set for your particular job.

2 Click OK to exit the Separation Setup dialog box.

🔲 For more information, see "Step 5: Set separation options" in online Help or Chapter 16 in the Adobe Illustrator User Guide.

Printing separations

Before printing your separations to a high-resolution output device, it's a good idea to print a set of separations, called *proofs*, on your black-and-white desktop printer. You'll save time and money by making any needed corrections to your files after reviewing the black-and-white proofs.

1 Choose File > Print.

2 In Mac OS, choose Adobe Illustrator 9.0 from the pop-up menu.

3 In Windows and Mac OS, choose Separate from the Output menu.

4 In Mac OS, select Printer in the Destination section of the Print dialog box.

5 Click OK (Windows) or Print (Mac OS) to print separations. Five pieces of paper should be printed—one each for cyan, magenta, yellow, and black, and one for the spot color.

6 Choose File > Save. The Separation Setup settings you entered are saved with your artwork file.

7 Close the Circus.ai file.

Working with two-color illustrations

As you learned earlier, two-color printing generally refers to black and one spot color, but may also refer to two spot colors. In addition to printing the two solid colors, you can print tints, or *screens*, of the colors. Two-color printing is much less expensive than four-color printing and lets you create a rich range of depth and color when used effectively.

Editing a spot color

In this section, you'll open a two-color version of the circus illustration containing black, a spot color, and tints of the spot color. Before you separate the illustration, you'll replace the current spot color with another from the PANTONE color library. Illustrator lets you make global adjustments to spot colors and tints of spot colors using a keyboard shortcut.

1 Choose File > Open, and open the L13strt2.ai file in the Lesson13 folder, located inside the Lessons folder within the AICIB folder on your hard drive.

Because you have set up Illustrator to work with a color management profile, you will be prompted each time you open a new file if you want to change how that file is color managed.

2 At the prompt, select Assign Current Working Space, and click OK.

3 Choose File > Save As, name the file **Twocolor.ai**, and select the Lesson13 folder. Leave the Format option set to Adobe Illustrator® Document, and click Save. In the Illustrator Native Format Options dialog box, select Illustrator 9.0 Compatibility and click OK.

4 Make sure that the Color palette and the Swatches palette are open and visible; if they aren't, use the Window menu to display them. Click the Swatches tab to bring the palette to the front of its group.

5 Select the selection tool ( ) in the toolbox. Then click any colored part of the circus tent. Notice the PANTONE 116 CVC swatch in the Color palette.

Next, you'll replace every instance of the spot color (including any tints of the color) with another spot color.

6 Choose Edit > Deselect All to deselect the artwork.

7 Choose Window > Swatch Libraries > PANTONE Coated. The PANTONE swatch library appears.

You can choose new spot colors from the swatch library by typing the number of the color you want to use.

8 Click in the Find text box of the PANTONE Coated palette and type **193**. PANTONE 193 CVC is selected in the palette.

Next you'll replace the current PANTONE color with the new PANTONE color.

9 If necessary, drag the title bar of the PANTONE Coated swatch library to view the Swatches palette.

10 Hold down Alt (Windows) or Option (Mac OS), and drag the PANTONE 193 CVC swatch from the PANTONE Coated swatch library onto the PANTONE 116 CVC swatch in the Swatches palette.

The PANTONE 193 CVC replaces the PANTONE 116 CVC swatch in the Swatches palette, and the artwork is updated with the new PANTONE color.

PANTONE Coated swatch library.   Replacing PANTONE color swatch in the Swatches palette.

Notice that the updated red swatch still is named PANTONE 116 CVC. You need to rename the updated swatch to avoid confusion about the spot color when your artwork is printed by a commercial press.

11 In the Swatches palette, double-click the updated swatch (still named PANTONE 116 CVC), and rename the swatch to match its color, PANTONE 193 CVC.

Separating spot colors

As you learned in "Separating colors" on page 370, you can convert spot colors to their process color equivalents, or you can output them to their own separation. When you're working with a two-color illustration, separating spot colors into their process color equivalents is less cost-effective than outputting the spot color to its own separation (converting to four CMYK plates versus one plate for each individual spot color). You'll deselect the Convert to Process option in the Separation Setup dialog box to output each spot color to its own separation.

Composite image   *Separation 1: Black*   *Separation 2: Spot color*

1 Choose File > Separation Setup.

2 Deselect the Convert to Process option. Notice that Process Black and the spot color PANTONE 193 CVC now have printer icons to their left in the list of colors for the artwork. The printer icon indicates that a single separation will be printed for each color. No icons appear next to cyan, magenta, and yellow in the list of separations, because the artwork contains no cyan, magenta, or yellow values.

	Process Cyan
	Process Magenta
	Process Yellow
🖨	Process Black
🖨	PANTONE 116 CVU

3 Click OK to exit the Separation Setup dialog box.

4 Choose File > Save to save the separation settings with your file.

5 Close the Twocolor.ai file.

Creating a trap

Trapping is used to compensate for any gaps or color shifts that may occur between adjoining or overlapping objects when printing. These gaps or color shifts are the effect of *misregistration*, which happens if the paper or the printing plates become misaligned during printing. Trapping is a technique developed by commercial print shops to slightly overprint the colors along common edges.

Gap created by misregistration

Gap removed by trapping

About traps

When overlapping painted objects share a common color, trapping may be unnecessary if the color that is common to both objects creates an automatic trap. For example, if two overlapping objects contain cyan as part of their CMYK values, any gap between them is covered by the cyan content of the object underneath. When artwork does contain common ink colors, overprinting does not occur on the shared plate.

There are two types of traps: a spread, in which a lighter object overlaps a darker background and seems to expand into the background; and a choke, in which a lighter background overlaps a darker object that falls within the background and seems to squeeze or reduce the object.

You can create both spreads and chokes in the Adobe Illustrator program.

Spread: Object overlaps background.

Choke: Background overlaps object.

It is generally best to scale your graphic to its final size before adding a trap. Once you create a trap for an object, the amount of trapping increases or decreases if you scale the object (unless you deselect the Scale line weight option in the Scale dialog box). For example, if you create a graphic that has a 0.5-point trap and scale it to five times its original size, the result is a 2.5-point trap for the enlarged graphic.

–From online Help and the Adobe Illustrator User Guide, Chapter 16

Although trapping sounds simple enough, it requires a thorough knowledge of color and design and an eye for determining where trapping is necessary. You can create a trap in Adobe Illustrator using two methods: by applying the Trap filter or Trap effect, for simple artwork whose parts can be selected and trapped individually; and by setting a Stroke value for individual objects you want to trap. Like printing, creating a trap is an art that requires time and experience.

For more information on creating a trap, see "Step 3: Create a trap to compensate for misregistration on press" in online Help or Chapter 16 in the Adobe Illustrator User Guide.

Now you'll practice creating a simple kind of trap called overprinting.

Overprinting objects

When preparing an image for color separation, you can define how you want overlapping objects of different colors to print. By default, the top object in the Illustrator artwork *knocks out*, or removes the color of, underlying artwork on the other separations and prints with the color of the top object only. Misregistration may occur when you knock out colors.

Composite image   *First plate*   *Second plate*

You can also specify objects to *overprint*, or print on top of, any of the artwork under them. Overprinting is the simplest method you can use to prevent misregistration (gaps between colors) on press. The overprinted color automatically traps into the background color.

Composite image

First plate

Second plate

For an illustration of overprinting, see figure 13-2 in the color section.

You'll select an object in the circus illustration and apply the overprint option. Then you will preview the overprint on-screen.

1 Choose File > Open. Locate and open the Circus.ai file, which you saved in the Lesson13 folder, inside the Lessons folder within the AICIB folder on your hard drive.

The color version of the circus illustration appears.

2 Choose View > Zoom In to zoom in on the lion. You'll be able to see the overprint lines better if you magnify the view of the image. (We zoomed in to 400%.)

3 Select the selection tool ( ) in the toolbox. Then click the lion to select it.

4 Click the Attributes tab to bring the palette to the front of its group. (If the Attributes palette isn't open, choose Window > Show Attributes.)

5 In the Attributes palette, select Overprint Fill.

Now you'll see an approximation of how overprinting and blending will appear in the color-separated output.

6 Choose View > Overprint Preview to see the effect of the overprinted objects.

If an object has a stroke, you can also select the Overprint Stroke option to make sure that the stroke overprints on the object below it as well. Next you'll add a stroke to an object to create a trap.

7 With the selection tool ( ), select the yellow flag to the left of the lion.

8 Click the Color tab to bring the palette to the front.

9 In the Color palette, drag the yellow fill swatch onto the Stroke box to stroke the flag with the same color as its fill.

10 Click the Attributes tab to bring the palette to the front of its group. Select the Overprint Stroke option.

Drag the fill swatch onto   *Result*   *Select Overprint Stroke option.*
the Stroke box.

Depending on what you have discussed with your printing professional, you may want to change the amount of trap specified. You'll try out changing the specified trap now.

11 Select the shape with the overprint stroke.

12 Click the Stroke tab to bring the palette to the front of its group. Change the Stroke Weight, and then choose View > Overprint Preview to see the results.

No Overprint preview

Overprint preview

Note: *Strokes are centered over the object's path. This means that if an object is stroked with the same color as its fill, only half of the stroke weight actually overprints. For example, if your printing professional wants a .5-point trap added to the yellow flag, you would use a 1-point Stroke Weight to achieve the trap. Half the stroke will appear inside the fill area and half will appear outside the fill area.*

13 Choose File > Save. Choose File > Close to close the file.

You've finished the lesson. In an ordinary workflow situation, you would now be ready to send your artwork to a commercial press to be printed. Include proofs of color separation setups when you send your electronic file to a printer. Also tell your printer about any traps you created in the artwork. Keep in mind that you must remain in close communication with your printing professional for each print job. Each print job has unique requirements you must consider before you begin the process of color separation.

Review questions

1 How do the RGB and CMYK color gamuts affect the relationship between on-screen colors and printed colors?

2 How can you create a closer match between your on-screen colors and printed colors?

3 What is the benefit of printing interim drafts of your artwork to a black-and-white desktop printer?

4 What does the term *color separation* mean?

5 What are two ways to output spot colors?

6 What are the advantages of one- or two-color printing?

7 What is trapping?

8 What is a simple method you can use to create trap?

Review answers

1 Each color model has a gamut of color that overlaps, but does not precisely match the others. Because monitors display color using the RGB color gamut and printed artwork uses the smaller CMYK color gamut, there may be times when a printed color cannot precisely match an on-screen color.

2 You can select one of Illustrator's built-in color management profiles to better simulate the relationship between on-screen colors and printed colors. You can choose View > Proof Setup and select an output device profile. Then choose View > Proof Colors to get an on-screen version of how the artwork will look when printed to the selected device.

3 It's a good idea to print black-and-white drafts of your artwork on a desktop printer to check the layout and the accuracy of text and graphics in your publication before incurring the expense of printing to a color printer or imagesetter (for separations).

4 Color separation refers to breaking down composite artwork into its component colors—for example, using the four process colors (cyan, magenta, yellow, and black) to reproduce a large portion of the visible color spectrum.

5 You can convert a spot color to its process color equivalents if a precise color match is not required, or you can output a spot color to its own separation.

6 One- or two-color printing is less expensive than four-color printing, and you can use spot colors for precise color matching.

7 Trapping is a technique developed by commercial print shops to slightly overprint the colors along common edges, and it is used to compensate for any gaps or color shifts that may occur between adjoining or overlapping objects when printed.

8 You can specify objects to overprint, or print on top of, any of the artwork under them. Overprinting is the simplest method you can use to create trap, which compensates for misregistration on press.

Lesson 14

Combining Illustrator Graphics and Photoshop Images

ANNUAL DIGITAL CHESS TOURNAMENT
CONVENTION CENTER
WEST WING

You can easily add an image created in an image-editing program to an Adobe Illustrator file. This is an effective method for seeing how a photograph looks incorporated with a line drawing or for trying out Illustrator special effects on bitmap images.

In this lesson, you'll learn how to do the following:

- Differentiate between vector and bitmap graphics.
- Place embedded Adobe Photoshop graphics in an Adobe Illustrator file.
- Create a clipping mask from compound paths.
- Make an opacity mask to display part of the image.
- Sample color in a placed image.
- Replace a placed image with another and update the document.
- Export a layered file to Adobe Photoshop and edit the type.

Combining artwork

You can combine Illustrator artwork with images from other graphics applications in a variety of ways for a wide range of creative results. Sharing artwork between applications lets you combine continuous-tone paintings and photographs with line art. Even though Illustrator lets you create certain types of raster images, Photoshop excels at many image-editing tasks; once done, the images then can be placed in Illustrator.

To illustrate how you can combine bitmap images with vector art and work between applications, this lesson steps you through the process of creating a composite image. In this lesson, you will add photographic images created in Adobe Photoshop to a postcard created in Adobe Illustrator. Then you'll adjust the color in the photo, mask the photo, and sample color from the photo to use in the Illustrator artwork. You'll update a placed image and then export your postcard to Photoshop to complete the type treatment.

Vector versus bitmap graphics

Adobe Illustrator creates *vector graphics*, also called draw graphics, which are made up of shapes based on mathematical expressions. These graphics consist of clear, smooth lines that retain their crispness when scaled. They are appropriate for illustrations, type, and graphics such as logos that may be scaled to different sizes.

Bitmap images, also called raster images, are based on a grid of pixels and are created by image-editing applications such as Adobe Photoshop. In working with bitmap images, you edit groups of pixels rather than objects or shapes. Because bitmap graphics can represent subtle gradations of shade and color, they are appropriate for continuous-tone images such as photographs or artwork created in painting programs. A disadvantage of bitmap graphics is that they lose definition and appear "jagged" when scaled up.

Logo drawn as vector art

Logo rasterized as bitmap art

In deciding whether to use Illustrator or a bitmap image program such as Photoshop for creating and combining graphics, consider both the elements of the image and how the image will be used. In general, use Illustrator if you need to create art or type with clean lines that will look good at any magnification. In most cases, you will also want to use Illustrator for laying out a design, because Illustrator offers more flexibility in working with type and with reselecting, moving, and altering images. You can create raster images in Illustrator but its pixel-editing tools are limited. Use Photoshop for images that need pixel-editing, color correcting, painting, and other special effects.

Getting started

Before you begin, you'll need to restore the default preferences for Adobe Illustrator. Then you'll open the finished art file for this lesson to see what you'll create.

1 To ensure that the tools and palettes function exactly as described in this lesson, delete or deactivate (by renaming) the Adobe Illustrator 9.0 preferences file. See "Restoring default preferences" on page 3.

2 Start Adobe Illustrator.

3 Choose File > Open, and open the L14end.ai file in the Lesson14 folder, located inside the Lessons folder within the AICIB folder on your hard drive.

4 Choose View > Zoom Out to make the finished artwork smaller, adjust the window size, and leave it on-screen as you work. (Use the hand tool ($^{\text{🖑}}$) to move the artwork where you want it in the window.) If you don't want to leave the image open, choose File > Close.

For an illustration of the finished artwork in this lesson, see the color section.

Now you'll open the start file to begin the lesson.

5 Choose File > Open, and open the L14strt.ai file.

The file has been prepared with three layers: the Text layer, and two additional layers, Layer 1 and Checkerboard, on which you'll place images. Checkerboard also contains objects that you'll make into a mask.

6 Choose File > Save As, name the file **Postcard.ai**, and select the Lesson14 folder. Leave the Format option set to Adobe Illustrator® Document, and click Save. In the Illustrator Native Format Options dialog box, select Illustrator 9.0 Compatibility and click OK.

Placing an Adobe Photoshop file

You'll begin by placing a Photoshop file in the Illustrator document as an *embedded* file. Placed files can be embedded or *linked*. Embedded files are added to the Illustrator file, and the Illustrator file size increases to reflect the addition of the placed file. Linked files remain separate, external files, with a link to the placed file in the Illustrator file. (The linked file must always accompany the Illustrator file, or the link will break and the placed file will not appear in the Illustrator artwork.)

1 In the Layers palette, select the Checkerboard layer.

Whichever layer is selected is the layer that the placed image will reside on. Eventually you will be making a mask for the placed image. The artwork for that mask is on the Checkerboard layer, so you will add the image to the Checkerboard layer as well.

2 Choose File > Place.

3 Navigate to the Chess.psd file (in the Lesson 14 folder inside the Lessons folder in the AICIB folder on your hard drive), and select it.

4 Click Link to deselect the option.

Placed files are linked by default. Deselecting the Link option embeds the placed file and makes it part of the Illustrator file.

The advantage of embedding a file is that the file is permanently included in the Illustrator artwork, and no link can be broken. The advantage of linking a file is that the Illustrator file size does not become as large (because the linked file is not included in the Illustrator file).

5 Click Place.

6 In the Photoshop Import dialog box, select the Convert Photoshop Layers to Objects option. Click OK.

Rather than flatten the file, you want to convert the Photoshop layers to objects because the Chess.psd file contains two layers and one layer mask. You will use them later in the lesson.

Now you'll move the placed image, using the guides in the artwork to place the image precisely.

7 Select the selection tool ( ) in the toolbox. Grab the placed image at its edge (but don't grab a bounding box handle or the image will be resized), and drag the image onto the guides provided in the artwork.

The pointer turns white when you align the pointer with the guide.

8 Release the mouse button when you have aligned the image with the guides.

The placed image covers up the squares in the Checkerboard layer. The placed image was added as a sublayer to the Checkerboard layer because it was selected when you chose the Place command. Now you will move the image below the squares and duplicate it.

9 Choose File > Save.

Placing files

*The Place command places files from other applications into Adobe Illustrator. Files can be **embedded**, or included, in the Illustrator file, or they can be linked to the Illustrator file. **Linked** files are those that are independent of the Illustrator file, resulting in a smaller Illustrator file; when the artwork in the linked file is edited or changed, the linked image in the Illustrator file is automatically changed.*

By default, the Link option is selected in the Place dialog box. If you deselect the Link option, the artwork is embedded in the Adobe Illustrator file, resulting in a larger Illustrator file. The Links palette lets you identify, select, monitor, and update objects in the Illustrator artwork that are linked to external files.

Placed bitmap images can be modified using transformation tools and image filters; placed vector artwork is converted to Illustrator paths (embedded images only).

If you place a Photoshop file and deselect the Link option, the Photoshop Import dialog box appears. For information on options in the Photoshop Import dialog box, see "Opening files" in online Help or in Chapter 2 of the Adobe Illustrator User Guide.

– From the Adobe Illustrator User Guide, Chapter 2

Duplicating a placed image

You can duplicate placed images just as you do other objects in an Illustrator file. The copy of the image can then be modified independently of the original.

Now you'll reposition and duplicate the Chess.psd image in the Layers palette.

1 Click the Expand triangle (▷) to the left of the Checkerboard layer to expand it. If necessary, enlarge the Layers palette so that you can see all the contents of the Checkerboard layer.

2 Drag the Chess.psd layer down the list until it is at the bottom of the Checkerboard layer, and then release the mouse button when the indicator bar appears between the last <path> layer and Layer 1.

Indicator bar   Chess.psd layer moved

3 Click the triangle to the left of the Chess.psd layer to expand it. Notice that the Chess.psd layer has two sublayers, Masked King and Background. You will now duplicate the Background layer.

4 To duplicate the Background layer, drag its thumbnail onto the New Layer button at the bottom of the Layers palette. Another layer called Background is created.

5 Double-click the lower Background layer and rename it **Blue Chess.psd.** Click OK. You will change the color of this image later in the lesson.

Duplicate Background layer.   *Rename layer.*

6 Choose File > Save.

Adjusting color in a placed image

You can use filters to modify colors in placed images in a variety of ways. You can use filters to convert to a different color mode (such as RGB, CMYK, or grayscale) or to adjust individual color values. You can also use filters to saturate or desaturate (darken or lighten) colors, or invert colors (create a color negative).

For information on color modes and modifying colors with filters, see "Color modes and models" and "Using filters to modify colors" in online Help or Chapter 6 in the Adobe Illustrator User Guide.

In this section, you'll adjust colors in the Background layer. Later in the lesson, you'll apply a mask to this image and then adjust colors in the Blue Chess.psd layer so that the two layers appear in contrasting colors through the mask.

For an illustration of color filters, see figure 14-1 in the color section.

1 In the Layers palette, select the Background layer.

2 Click in the eye column to the far left of the Masked King layer to hide it.

When you hide a layer, all objects on that layer are deselected and hidden.

3 In the Layers palette, click the selection column to the far right of the Background layer to select its contents quickly.

Masked King layer hidden and contents of Background layer selected

4 Choose Filter > Colors > Adjust Colors.

5 Drag the sliders or enter values for the CMYK percentages to change the colors in the image. You can press Tab to move between the text boxes. (We used the following values to create an orange cast: Cyan = –23, Magenta = 20, Yellow = 74, and Black = –52.)

6 When you are satisfied with the color in the image, click OK.

7 Click outside the artwork to deselect the Background image, and then choose File > Save.

▣ Besides using filters to adjust colors, you can also use filters to apply special effects to images, distort images, produce a hand-drawn appearance, and create other interesting effects. See "Using filters and filter effects on bitmap images" in online Help or Chapter 11 in the Adobe Illustrator User Guide.

◉ For an illustration of filters used to apply special effects, see figure 14-2 in the color section.

Masking an image

Masks crop part of an image so that only a portion of the image appears through the shape of the mask. You can make a mask from a single path or a compound path. You can also import masks made in Photoshop files.

Creating compound path and opacity masks

In this section, you'll create a compound path from the checkerboard pattern on the Checkerboard layer and create an opacity mask from the compound path, so that the Background layer appears through the mask. Then you'll adjust the colors in Blue Chess.psd to contrast with the Background layer. You'll also use an opacity mask that was created in Photoshop and saved as a layer mask.

1 Select the selection tool (▸) in the toolbox.

2 Using the selection tool, Shift-click all the black squares in the checkerboard pattern to select them. This action selects the Checkerboard layer and deselects the Background layer.

3 Choose Object > Compound Paths > Make.

Notice how all the squares have been placed onto one layer in the Layers palette called <compound path>.

The Compound Paths command creates a single compound object from two or more objects. Compound paths act as grouped objects. The Compound Paths command lets you create complex objects more easily than if you used the drawing tools or the Pathfinder commands.

4 With the Checkerboard layer still selected, in the Layers palette Shift-click the selection column to the far right of the Background layer to select it. (The selection indicator will appear and the Background layer will be added to the selection.)

Both the masking object and the object to be masked must be selected in order to create a mask.

Checkerboard layer and <compound path> selected

5 Click the Transparency palette tab to bring it to the front of its group. (If the Transparency palette isn't visible on-screen, choose Window > Show Transparency.)

6 From the Transparency palette menu, choose Show Options to expand the palette fully.

Now you'll mask the Background layer with an opacity mask that lets you use the change luminosity in the overlying checkerboard to affect the Background. Similar to a clipping mask, an opacity mask lets you make color and other fine adjustments that you can't make with a clipping mask.

7 From the Transparency palette menu, choose Make Opacity Mask.

Dotted line indicates mask.   *Preview includes opacity mask.*

The checkerboard pattern is assigned a fill and stroke of None, and the Background layer is masked with the checkerboard pattern, as indicated by the dotted underline beneath the layer name. The Blue Chess.psd layer appears through the masked sections of the Background layer.

Now you'll apply the Adjust Colors filter to the Blue Chess.psd layer to create a stronger contrast between the two images.

8 In the Layers palette, click the selection indicator for the Blue Chess.psd layer to select only its contents.

9 Choose Filter > Colors > Adjust Colors.

The most recently used filter (in this case, Adjust Colors) appears at the top of the Filter menu, letting you easily reapply the filter. (Choosing Filter > Apply Adjust Colors would apply the filter with the same settings used on the Background layer.)

10 Click Preview to preview changes in the artwork.

11 Drag the sliders for the CMYK values to change the colors in the image. (We used the following values to create a blue cast: Cyan = 12, Magenta = –10, Yellow = –74, and Black = –31.) You can compare the color in Blue Chess.psd to that in the Background layer, to choose a color that contrasts effectively.

12 When you are satisfied with the color, click OK. Click outside the artwork to deselect the Blue Chess.psd image.

13 Choose File > Save.

Editing an imported mask

You've made an opacity mask from artwork created in Illustrator. Now you'll use a mask that was created in Photoshop and imported when you placed the Chess.psd file. You'll experiment with changing the color of the image and then adjusting the transparency of the opacity mask to tone down the effect.

1 In the Layers palette, click the eye icon to show the Masked King layer.

2 Click the selection indicator for the Masked King layer to select its contents. (The dotted line under its layer name indicates that the Masked King layer has an opacity mask applied to it.)

3 Choose Filter > Colors > Adjust Colors.

4 Click Preview to preview changes in the artwork.

Drag the sliders for the CMYK values to change the colors in the image. (We used the following values to create a strong purple cast: Cyan = 60, Magenta = 60, Yellow = –46, and Black = –60.) Click OK.

5 In the Transparency palette, change the opacity setting to 75% for the Masked King layer.

Mask opacity set to 75%   *Result*

For a dramatic effect you will now invert the opacity mask. This will subdue the Background and Blue Chess.psd layers and make the Masked King layer pop visually.

6 In the Transparency palette, select the Invert Mask option to reverse the effect of the opacity mask.

Mask inverted   *Result*

7 Click outside the artwork to deselect the Masked King layer.

8 Choose File > Save.

Sampling colors in placed images

You can *sample*, or copy, the colors in placed images, to apply the colors to other objects in the artwork. Sampling colors enables you to easily make colors consistent in a file combining Photoshop images and Illustrator artwork.

Copying paint attributes between objects

You can use the eyedropper tool to copy colors from any object in an Illustrator file—from a paint swatch or from anywhere on the desktop, including from another application. You can then use the paint bucket tool to apply the current paint attributes to an object. Together these tools let you copy the paint attributes from anywhere on-screen to other objects.

By default, the eyedropper and paint bucket tools affect all paint attributes of an object. You can use the tool's options dialog box to change the object's attributes. You can also use the eyedropper tool and paint bucket tool to copy and paste type attributes.

– From the Adobe Illustrator User Guide, Chapter 6

In this section, you'll use the eyedropper tool to sample colors from the placed image, and apply the colors to selected type on the Text layer.

1 Use the selection tool (▶) to click in the text at the bottom of the artwork to select the entire text block.

2 Select the eyedropper tool (✐), and Shift-click in the image to sample a color to be applied to the selected text. (We chose a medium-purple color near the center of the image, between the king and queen chess pieces.)

The color you sample is applied to the selected text.

Now you'll color part of the text a different color.

3 In the Layers palette, click in the eye column to the far left of Masked King and Blue Chess.psd to hide those layers.

You hide these layers in order to sample a color from the Background layer. Hiding a layer makes it easier to work with artwork on other layers, without changing the artwork on the hidden layer.

4 Select the type tool (T) and drag over the text *DIGITAL CHESS TOURNAMENT* in the artwork to select the text.

Next you'll choose a color from the artwork to apply to the selected text. Text selected with the text tool is reverse highlighted, so you'll have to deselect the text after you apply the color to be able to view the color.

5 Select the eyedropper tool ( ), and Shift-click in the Background layer to sample a color to be applied to the selected text. (We chose a reddish orange color from the lower left corner of the image.)

Sampling color from selected text

6 Press Ctrl (Windows) or Command (Mac OS), and click outside the artwork to deselect the text and view the new color.

Pressing Ctrl/Command temporarily activates the selection tool (or the direct-selection or group-selection tool, whichever has been used most recently) when another tool is selected in the toolbox.

7 In the Layers palette, click in the eye column to the far left of Masked King and Blue Chess.psd to display the layers.

8 Choose File > Save.

Replacing a placed image

You can easily replace a placed image with another image to update a document. The replacement image is positioned exactly where the original image was, so you don't have to align the replacement image. (If you scaled the original images, you may have to resize the replacement image to match the original image.)

Now you'll replace the Blue Chess.psd image with the Chess2.psd image to create a new version of the postcard.

1 Choose File > Save As, name the file **Postcard2.ai**, and select the Lesson14 folder. Leave the Format option set to Adobe Illustrator® Document, and click Save. In the Illustrator Native Format Options dialog box, select Illustrator 9.0 Compatibility and click OK.

2 Click the Links tab to bring the Links palette to the front of its group. (If the Links palette isn't visible on-screen, choose Window > Show Links.)

3 Click the last link in the Links palette to select it. (These links don't have names because we embedded them instead of linking them.)

4 Click the Replace Link button at the bottom of the Links palette.

5 In the Place dialog box, navigate to the Chess2.psd image in the Lesson14 folder and select it. Click Place to replace the Blue Chess.psd image with the new one.

6 In the Photoshop Import options dialog box, click OK to flatten the image and place it.

The replacement image appears in the Chess.psd layer with no color adjustments applied. When you replace an image, color adjustments you made to the original image are not applied to the replacement. However, masks applied to the original image are preserved. Any layer modes and transparency adjustments you've made to other layers also may affect the image's appearance.

Select image in Links palette.   *Click Replace Link button to replace with new image.*

7 Choose File > Save.

You have completed the lesson. If you want to learn how to open and manipulate a layered Illustrator file in Photoshop, continue. If not, skip to "Exploring on your own" on page 406.

Exporting a layered file to Photoshop

Not only can you open layered Photoshop files in Illustrator, but you can also save layered Illustrator files and then open them in Photoshop. Working with layered files between Illustrator and Photoshop is very help when creating and editing Web graphics. You can preserve the hierarchical relationship of the layers by selecting the Write Nested Layers option when saving your file. You can also open and edit type objects.

Now you'll adjust the Text layer and change the file's color mode to RGB. Then you'll export the file and save it in layered Photoshop format so that you can edit it in Photoshop.

1 Click the Layers tab to bring the palette to the front of its group.

2 In the Layers palette, click the triangle (▶) to the left of the Text layer to expand its list.

3 Drag the ANNUAL DIGITAL CHESS sublayer out of and above the Text layer. It is now its own layer instead of a sublayer nested in the Text layer.

Note: *To keep the Illustrator type layer editable when opened in Photoshop, the type layer must reside on its own layer and not be nested inside another layer.*

Select sublayer.   Drag out of nested hierarchy to own layer.

4 Choose File > Document Color Mode > RGB Color.

5 Choose File > Export.

6 Navigate to the folder where you'll save the file, and name the file **Postcard2.psd**. Changing the file name preserves your original Illustrator file.

7 Choose Photoshop 5 (PSD) from the Save as Type (Windows) or Format (Mac OS) pop-up menu, and click Save (Windows) or Export (Mac OS).

8 In the Photoshop Options dialog box, select Screen (72 dpi) for Resolution, and make sure that Anti-alias, Write Layers, and Editable Type options are selected. Click OK.

The Anti-alias option removes jagged edges in the artwork. The Write Layers option lets you export each Illustrator top-level layer as a separate Photoshop layer. Nested layers are flattened into the top-level layer during export, unless you've also selected the Nested Layers option. You're not exporting any nested layers from the Postcard file.

9 Launch the Adobe Photoshop application.

10 Open the Postcard2.psd file.

You'll edit the text you just exported to shorten it and increase its type size.

11 In the Layers palette, double-click the ANNUAL DIGITAL CHESS type layer to open the Type Tool dialog box.

12 Choose Select > All or drag to select all of the text.

13 Edit the text in the Type Tool dialog box:

• Change the point size to 36 points.

• Change the Leading to 36 points.

• Click the Flush Left button

• Select and delete the *CONVENTION CENTER WEST WING* text.

14 Click OK to apply the changes.

15 In the image, use the selection pointer to move the type so that its left edge aligns with the left edge of the image.

16 Choose File > Save. Choose File > Close to close the file.

You've completed the lesson on combining Illustrator graphics and Photoshop images, and learned how easy it is to work between the two applications.

Exploring on your own

Now that you know how to place and mask an image in an Illustrator file, you can place other images and apply a variety of modifications to the images. You can also create masks for images from objects you create in Illustrator. For more practice, try the following:

• Repeat the lesson using the Chess2.psd image in place of the Chess.psd image. In addition to adjusting color in the copies of the image, apply transformation effects, such as shearing or rotating, or filters or effects, such as one of the Artistic or Distort filters/effects, to create contrast between the two images in the checkerboard pattern.

• Use the basic shapes tools or the drawing tools to draw objects to create a compound path to use as a mask. Then place the Chess.psd image into the file with the compound path, and apply the compound path as a mask.

• Create large type and use the type as a mask to mask a placed object.

Review questions

1 Describe the difference between linking and embedding a placed file in Illustrator.

2 How do you create an opacity mask for a placed image?

3 What kinds of objects can be used as masks?

4 What color modifications can you apply to a selected object using filters?

5 Describe how to replace a placed image with another image in a document.

Review answers

1 A linked file is a separate, external file connected to the Illustrator file by an electronic link. A linked file does not add significantly to the size of the Illustrator file. The linked file must accompany the Illustrator file to preserve the link and ensure that the placed file appears in the Illustrator file. An embedded file is included in the Illustrator file. The Illustrator file size reflects the addition of the embedded file. Because the embedded file is part of the Illustrator file, no link can be broken. Both linked and embedded files can be updated using the Replace button in the Links palette.

2 You create an opacity mask by placing the object to be used as a mask on top of the object to be masked. Then you select the mask and the objects to be masked, and choose Make Opacity Mask from the Transparency palette menu.

3 A mask can be a simple or compound path. You can use type as a mask. You can import opacity masks with placed Photoshop files. You can also create layer clipping masks with any shape that is the topmost object of a group or layer.

4 You can use filters to change the color mode (RGB, CMYK, or Grayscale) or adjust individual colors in a selected object. You can also saturate or desaturate colors or invert colors in a selected object. You can apply color modifications to placed images, as well as to artwork created in Illustrator.

5 To replace a placed image, select the placed image in the Links palette. Then click the Replace Links button, and locate and select the image to be used as the replacement. Then click Place. The replacement image appears in the artwork in place of the original image.

Lesson 15

Preparing Graphics for Web Publication

The style of your artwork determines the file format you use to export the file for publication on the World Wide Web. For example, flat-color artwork is typically exported to GIF or PNG-8 format, and continuous-tone artwork containing photos or gradients is typically exported to JPEG or PNG-24 format. When preparing images for Web distribution, the goal is to create the smallest possible file while maintaining the integrity of the artwork.

In this lesson, you'll learn how to do the following:

• Determine which file format to use to publish different styles of artwork on the Web.

• Use Web-safe colors in your artwork.

• Link objects to URL addresses for an image map.

• Export different styles of artwork to GIF and JPEG formats.

• Create artwork for a simple animation and export it to Flash (SWF) format.

Optimizing images for the Web

Creating small graphics files is key to distributing images on the World Wide Web. With smaller files, Web servers can store and transmit images more efficiently, and viewers can download images more quickly. You decrease file size by saving your artwork in one of several compressed file formats. For basic optimization tasks, you can export artwork in Illustrator as a GIF, JPEG or PNG-8 file.

You can also export your files for the Web in other formats such as the vector-based Flash SWF, format for interactive, animated Web graphics, and the SVG and SVGZ (Scalable Vector Graphics and compressed SVG) formats, which work well with HTML and JavaScript. For more informations on exporting images for the Web, see "About exporting artwork" in online Help or Chapter 14 of the Adobe Illustrator User Guide.

There's always a trade-off between image quality and amount of compression: Higher quality images use less compression (and thus take longer to download) than lower quality images. The JPEG format uses a *lossy* compression method, in which data is discarded during compression. The JPEG compression method can degrade sharp detail in an image, such as type and line drawings. You specify the amount of compression to be applied by choosing a quality setting. A higher quality setting results in less data being discarded.

Note: Data is discarded from a JPEG image each time you save the file. You should always save JPEG files from the original artwork, not from a previously saved JPEG file.

The GIF format uses a *lossless* compression method, in which no data is discarded during compression. You can save a GIF file multiple times without discarding data. However, because GIF files are 8-bit color, optimizing an original 24-bit image (artwork created on a system displaying millions of colors) as an 8-bit GIF can degrade image quality.

The PNG-8 format is similar to the GIF format in that it is lossless and uses 8-bit color. It uses a more advanced compression scheme than GIF and depending on the image's color patterns, some PNG-8 files can be 10–30% smaller than GIF files. The disadvantage to using PNG-8, however, is that not all browsers support it. Therefore, it may be advisable to avoid this format if your image needs to be accessible to the widest possible audience.

Most images viewed on the Web are created using 24-bit color displays, but many Web browsers are on computers using only 8-bit color displays, so that Web images often contain colors not available to many Web browsers. Computers use a technique called *dithering* to simulate colors not available in the color display system. Dithering adjusts adjacent pixels of different colors to give the appearance of a third color. (For example, a blue color and a yellow color may dither in a mosaic pattern to produce the illusion of a green color that does not appear in the color palette.)

Dithering can occur when you export artwork to GIF or PNG-8 formats if Illustrator attempts to simulate colors that appear in the original artwork but don't appear in the color palette you specify. It can also occur in GIF or JPEG images when a Web browser using an 8-bit color display attempts to simulate colors that are in the image but not in the browser's color palette. You can minimize dithering by shifting individual or groups of colors to their closest Web-palette equivalent. You can also control dithering done by Web browsers by painting your artwork with Web-safe colors from the Web palette. Web-safe colors can be displayed by any browser that uses an 8-bit or 24-bit color display.

For an example of dithering that occurs in a GIF image that has not been painted with Web-safe colors compared to a GIF image that has been painted with them, see figure 15-1 in the color section.

Getting started

In this lesson, you'll create a GIF image, a JPEG image, an image map with three buttons, and a simple animation for a Web page. Before you begin, you'll need to restore the default preferences for Adobe Illustrator and then you'll open the finished art file for this lesson to see what you'll be creating.

1 To ensure that the tools and palettes function exactly as described in this lesson, delete or deactivate (by renaming) the Adobe Illustrator 9.0 preferences file. See "Restoring default preferences" on page 3.

2 Start Adobe Illustrator.

3 Choose File > Open, and open the L15comp.ai file in the L15Start folder, located in the Lesson15 folder, inside the Lessons folder within the AICIB folder on your hard drive.

The artwork in this file is a design mock-up of a Web home page. The design for the completed page includes several styles of artwork, including flat-color, continuous-tone, and gradient-filled artwork.

4 Notice the various styles of artwork in the design:

• Logo. The Swing Classes logo in the top left corner of the page is flat-color artwork with a transparency option applied to it, allowing the background to show through the cutout areas around the objects.

• Buttons. The three shoe prints at the right side of the page are flat-color artwork made into buttons on an image map by linking each to a separate URL address.

• Placed photograph. The photograph is a continuous-tone bitmap image imported from Adobe Photoshop.

• Gradients. The background of the design is a tiled pattern, with each tile containing a number of shapes filled with a gradient.

The following table describes the file formats generally recommended for displaying specific types of artwork on the Web. Keep in mind, however, that the file format you choose for your artwork may also be determined by the quality and size of the image you want to place on the Web.

Graphic	Export to
Flat color	GIF or PNG-8
Full color (continuous-tone)	JPEG, or PNG-24 if multilevel transparency is required
Gradient-filled	JPEG, PNG-8, GIF, SVG
Grayscale (continuous-tone)	JPEG
Animation layers	SWF or SVG

5 If you like, choose View > Zoom Out to make the design mock-up smaller, adjust the window size, and leave it on your screen as you work. (Use the hand tool (✋) to move the artwork where you want it in the window.) If you don't want to leave the artwork open, choose File > Close.

For an illustration of the finished artwork in this lesson, see the color section.

Now you'll open individual files that contain the artwork for the various parts of the Web page.

Exporting flat-color artwork

Flat-color artwork with repetitive color and sharp detail, such as line art, logos, or illustrations with type, should be exported to GIF or PNG-8 format. Flat-color artwork appears best on the Web without any *dithering*—mixing colors to approximate those not present in the palette. To prevent computers from dithering colors, use Web-safe colors in your artwork. Then export the artwork to GIF using the Save for Web feature.

Painting with Web-safe colors

You'll start by painting the flat-color Swing Classes logo with Web-safe colors and then save it in GIF format.

1 Choose File > Open, and open the L15strt1.ai file in the L15Start folder, located in the Lesson15 folder, inside the Lessons folder within the AICIB folder on your hard drive.

2 Choose File > Save As, name the file **LogoArt.ai**, and select the L15Start folder. Leave the Format option set to Adobe Illustrator® Document, and click Save. In the Illustrator Native Format Options dialog box, select Illustrator 9.0 Compatibility and click OK.

You'll select multiple objects and paint them with Web-safe colors.

3 Choose View > Zoom In to zoom in on the artwork.

4 Choose View > Pixel Preview to see the artwork as it will look in a Web browser. Notice that graphics that appeared smooth in the Preview view are now pixelated in the Pixel Preview. This is how your graphic will appear when it is placed in a Web page.

You've been looking at a zoomed-in view of the graphic. Web browsers don't allow you to zoom in on graphics so let's look at the graphic at the actual size to see how much the pixelization will really show.

5 Choose View > Actual Size to get a 100% view of the artwork.

Preview   *Pixel preview*

6 Using the selection tool (▶), select the letter *S* in the word Swing. Choose Edit > Select > Same Fill Color to select all the objects in the artwork that are painted the same color as the selected object.

7 In the Color palette, choose the Web Safe RGB option from the palette menu in the upper right corner.

Select letter S.   *Auto-select objects with*
                                      same fill color.

Change Color palette to Web Safe RGB.

The Web palette contains 216 RGB colors that are shared by both Windows and Mac OS platforms, so they can be viewed by anyone who has a system displaying at least 256 colors. If you have used a color that is not Web-safe, the Color palette displays a cube below the stroke and fill boxes in the Color palette and a small color swatch next to the cube containing the closest Web-safe color.

Now you'll select and correct the colors in the artwork that are not Web-safe.

8 In the Color palette, click the Out of Web Color Warning cube to change the fill color to the nearest Web-safe color.

Click Out of Web Color Warning button to substitute nearest Web-safe color.

9 Now select the letter *C* in the word Classes, and choose Edit > Select > Same Fill Color to select all the objects with the same color (including the blue ellipse).

10 In the Color palette, click the Out of Web Color Warning cube to change the fill color to the nearest Web-safe color.

11 Choose File > Save to save the changes to the artwork.

Setting GIF export options

The remaining objects in the artwork are already painted with Web-safe colors. Now you're ready to export the artwork to GIF format.

1 Choose File > Save for Web.

The View options in the Save for Web dialog box let you switch easily between optimized and original (nonoptimized) versions of an image and view up to four versions of an optimized image simultaneously. This lets you try out different settings before saving an optimized version.

Now you'll select one of the predefined optimization settings available in Illustrator.

2 In the Settings pop-up menu, choose GIF Web Palette.

3 Notice that the background display is now transparent, as indicated by the checker-board, because the Transparency option has been selected. Leave this option selected. You'll create a background later in this lesson with transparency to reveal "holes" in this image.

The Transparency option applies transparency to all unpainted areas around the image and to any cutout areas within the image. Transparency is useful for showing through a colored or tiled background on your Web page.

Note: In Illustrator, you cannot specify which areas to make transparent; transparent areas are set by the unpainted areas of the artwork.

4 Click OK, name the optimized image file **logo.gif**, and click Save.

You can now open this file in any Web-authoring application or any browser.

You can also create your own custom settings. For more information on creating custom settings see "Applying optimization settings" in online Help or Chapter 13 in the Adobe Illustrator User Guide.

5 Close the LogoArt.ai file.

Exporting continuous-tone and gradient artwork

Continuous-tone artwork and artwork containing gradients are generally saved to the JPEG image file format. Illustrator saves JPEG files using different compressions based on the image quality you specify. The compression option you choose for the image deter-mines how the color information in the artwork is preserved, which affects the size and quality of the image.

Note: Although JPEG is the recommended file format for retaining the quality of continuous-tone artwork, you can also export continuous-tone artwork to PNG-24 format—for example, to use background transparency or background matting with an image. The PNG-24 format uses the same lossless compression method as the PNG-8 format, in which no data is discarded. As a result, the same image in PNG-24 format usually is larger than in JPEG format. Not all browsers support PNG-24 format.

You'll export the artwork containing the background tile to JPEG format and compare two different compression options.

1 Choose File > Open, and open the L15strt2.ai file in the L15Start folder, located in the Lesson15 folder, inside the Lessons folder within the AICIB folder on your hard drive.

 For information on how to create tile patterns like this one, see "Constructing patterns with irregular textures" in online Help.

2 Choose File > Save for Web. In the Save for Web dialog box, click the 4-Up tab to view four different optimized versions of the file.

3 Click the upper right version and choose the JPEG High setting from the Settings menu.

4 Click the lower right version and choose the JPEG Medium setting from the Settings menu.

5 Click the lower left version and choose the JPEG Low setting from the Settings menu.

6 Notice the difference in image quality between the four versions, particularly around the edges of the shapes where the colors are blurred. To compare the versions better, use the zoom tool in the dialog box to enlarge the previews.

In this example, the file size of the JPEG High version is approximately 2.87K, the JPEG Medium version is about 1.31K, and the JPEG Low version is only 934 bytes. The JPEG Low version will download more quickly than the JPEG High or Medium versions, but like the JPEG Medium version, is seriously compromised. Only the JPEG High version maintains the image quality.

Now you'll compare the image quality and file size for the PNG-24 setting.

7 Click the lower left version if it is not already selected. Choose PNG-24 from the Settings pop-up menu.

Notice that the image quality of the PNG-24 version is very good, but the file size is now 7.607K. Even though the image quality is slightly better than the JPEG High version, the increased file size will considerably slow down the Web site download time.

8 Choose the JPEG High setting from the Settings pop-up menu.

9 Click OK, name the file **tile.jpg**, and then click Save.

10 Close the L15strt2.ai file.

Linking objects in an image map to URLs

Any object you create in Adobe Illustrator can be linked to a Uniform Resource Locator (URL) address, transforming the object into a button that links to an Internet Web site. This feature is useful when designing image maps for Web pages, letting you preattach links to individual objects in an illustration before importing the artwork into a Web-page design application.

You'll open a file containing artwork for an image map with three buttons, add URL links to the buttons using the Attributes palette, and then save the file in GIF format.

1 Choose File > Open, and open the L15strt3.ai file in the L15Start folder, located in the Lesson15 folder, inside the Lessons folder within the AICIB folder on your hard drive.

All of the objects in this artwork are painted with Web-safe colors.

2 Choose File > Save As, name the file **Footstep.ai**, and select the L15Start folder. Leave the Format option set to Adobe Illustrator® Document, and click Save. In the Illustrator Native Format Options dialog box, select Illustrator 9.0 Compatibility and click OK.

You'll select each shoe print with its corresponding type to create a button and link it to a URL address.

Note: You can assign the image map shape as a rectangle or as a free-form polygon that follows the outline of the selected object.

3 Using the selection tool ( ), Shift-click to select the objects for the top button (the shoe print and the words "Our Hep Hoppers").

4 Click the Attributes tab to bring the palette to the front of its group. (If the palette isn't open, choose Window > Show Attributes to display it.)

5 In the Attributes palette, choose Rectangle from the Image Map menu. In the URL text box, type the URL for the destination of the link (we used **http://www.adobe.com**), and press Enter or Return to apply it.

Select objects for button.   *Enter URL address for link's destination.*

6 Select the second button (the shoe print and the words "Sessions & Sets"). Repeat step 5 to link the image map to a second destination URL. You can also select a URL from the pop-up menu.

7 Select the third button (the shoe print and the words "Slide to Sign-up"), and repeat step 5 to link the image map to a URL.

Note: After assigning the URLs to the buttons, you can verify that each URL is valid by using the Launch Browser button in the Attributes palette if your computer has a Web browser (such as Netscape® Navigator or Microsoft Internet Explorer®). Clicking the Launch Browser button automatically connects to the URL you have defined as the object's link.

8 To export the image map to GIF format, choose File > Save for Web. In the Save for Web dialog box, choose GIF Web Palette.

9 Click OK, name the file **map.gif**, and click Save.

10 Close the Footstep.ai file.

Creating a Flash animation

Now you'll animate the footsteps by expanding the artwork and placing each step on its own layer. Each footstep then will become a separate frame in the animation.

The Release to Layers command instantly distributes all of the objects on one layer into separate, individual layers. You can use this feature to prepare files for Web animation applications that support layers, such as Macromedia Flash™. For example, you can prepare different frames of an animation by first applying blend options to objects or by using the scatter brush to paint repeated copies of an object along a path. You can then release each object in the blend or scattered path to a separate layer and export the file as a Flash (SWF) file or to Adobe Photoshop 5.5 to set up the animation.

1 Choose File > Open, and open the L15strt5.ai file in the L15Start folder, located in the Lesson15 folder, inside the Lessons folder within the AICIB folder on your hard drive.

2 Choose File > Save As, name the file **Feet.ai**, and select the L15Start folder. Leave the Format option set to Adobe Illustrator® Document, and click Save. In the Illustrator Native Format Options dialog box, select Illustrator 9.0 Compatibility and click OK.

3 Using the selection tool (⬉), select the stroke painted with the Footsteps art brush.

4 Choose Object > Expand Appearance to expand the art brush into separate objects.

Select the stroke.

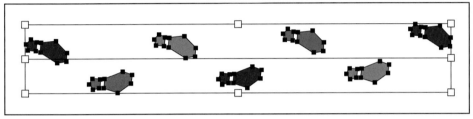

Apply Expand Appearance command to convert the brush stroke to outlined paths.

Now you will remove the path on which the footsteps were painted. You won't need the path in the final animation.

5 Make sure that the artwork is still selected.

6 In the Layers palette, click the triangle (▶) next to the Footsteps layer to display the new group that has been created. (If the Layers palette isn't open, choose Window > Show Layers.)

7 Click the triangle (▶) next to the new group layer to reveal its contents. That layer contains another group and a path.

8 Click the sublayer named <path> to select it, and click the Trash button at the bottom of the Layers palette to delete the path.

Using the Layers palette is a quick and easy way to select or delete paths, groups, and objects within groups without having to ungroup or change selection tools.

Select the <path> sublayer and delete it using the Layers palette.

To make each footstep a different frame in an animation, each footstep must be on its own layer. Now you'll release each footstep to its own layer. To more easily understand the layers and grouping, you will ungroup the set of footsteps to remove two levels of grouping. (It's not necessary to remove sublayers before releasing to layers, but it makes the layer hierarchy easier to understand.)

9 Click the triangle (▷) next to the last group layer to reveal its contents. If necessary, resize the Layers palette so that you can see all of its contents.

Notice the long list of groups that represent each footstep. Each footstep is a group of the sole and the heel shapes.

10 Select the Footsteps layer and choose Object > Ungroup. One level of grouping has been removed.

11 Choose Object > Ungroup again to remove another level of grouping.

Ungroup twice to simplify the hierarchy.

12 Make sure that the footsteps are still selected.

13 In the Layers palette, choose Release to Layers from the palette menu. Each footstep is now on its own layer, and all layers have been named and numbered. You'll also notice that each layer has been assigned a different selection color.

Apply Release to Layers command to place all footsteps on named and numbered layers.

Now you're ready to export the layered file to SWF format. You can then open the animation in a browser and see the dancing feet.

14 Choose File > Export, and choose Flash (SWF) for the format. Select the L15Start folder, name the file **feet.swf**, and click Save (Windows) or Export (Mac OS).

15 In the Flash Format Options dialog box, choose AI Layers to SWF Frames from the Export As menu. Adjust the Frame Rate and Resolution if desired (we used a frame rate of 12 fps and a resolution of 72 ppi). Click OK.

16 Save the Feet.ai file and close it.

17 To view the Flash animation, drag and drop the feet.swf file into your browser, or import it into the Flash application for further editing.

You've completed the Web graphics lesson.

For more practice, you can try your hand at creating the Savoy Stomp Web page with the images and files provided—the "Savoy Stomp presents" text, the Hop on HOME button, and the Jumpcat Mavens photo image. The finished Web page, called Swnghome.htm, also is included. These files, along with versions of the files you created in this lesson, are located in the L15Web folder in the Lesson15 folder.

🔆 *If you plan to convert several files to Web images or want to create animations from your artwork, consider Adobe ImageReady™, Adobe GoLive™ or Adobe Live Motion™—all programs for optimizing your graphics for the Web. For more information on these Adobe products and capabilities, visit the Adobe Web site at www.adobe.com.*

Exploring on your own

You can recreate the Jumpcat Mavens image for a Web page, or adjust its appearance. This photo was created in Adobe Illustrator and Adobe Photoshop. Follow the steps in this section to replicate the image for a Web page.

1 In Illustrator, choose File > Open, and open the L15strt4.ai file in the L15Start folder, located in the Lesson15 folder, inside the Lessons folder within the AICIB folder on your hard drive.

Notice the Jumpcat Mavens flat-color artwork is separated into five separate layers: type, musical note, purple rings, orange oval, and rings back. All of the objects in the artwork have been painted with Web-safe colors.

2 Choose File > Export to export the artwork to Photoshop format. In the dialog box, choose Photoshop 5 from the Save as Type (Windows) or Format (Mac OS) menu, name the file **Jumpcat.psd**, and click Save (Windows) or Export (Mac OS).

3 In the Photoshop Options dialog box, choose RGB for Color Model and Screen (72 dpi) resolution. Leave the Anti-Alias and Write Layers options selected, and click OK.

For the rest of this exercise, you'll work in the Adobe Photoshop 5.5 application.

4 Start Adobe Photoshop.

5 In Photoshop, open the new exported file, Jumpcat.psd.

Notice how the layers in the artwork remain intact in the exported file.

6 Open the Dancers.psd file. This file contains the bitmap image of the two people dancing.

7 Choose Select > All, and then choose Edit > Copy to copy the image to the Clipboard.

8 In the Jumpcat.psd file, choose Edit > Paste to paste the photo image into the Jumpcat Mavens artwork.

Notice a new Layer 1 has been added to the bottom of the Layers palette.

9 In the Layers palette, drag Layer 1 up between the Musical Note and Purple Rings layers.

10 Select the move tool and position the photo in the center of the olive-colored oval in the artwork.

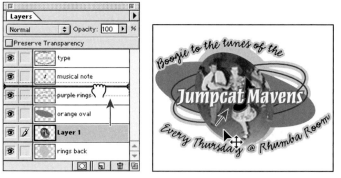

Move Layer 1.   Reposition photo.

11 With Layer 1 (the dancers) active, choose Image > Adjust > Hue/Saturation. In the Hue/Saturation dialog box, select the Colorize option, and drag the sliders to adjust the Hue (we selected 30) and the Saturation (we selected 20). Click OK.

12 Choose Layer > Effects > Bevel and Emboss to apply a filter to the image. In the Effects dialog box, change the Depth to **4** pixels and the Blur to **4** pixels, and then click OK.

13 Choose File > Save to save the Jumpcat.psd file.

Now you'll create an optimized version for the Web.

14 Choose File > Save for Web.

15 Click the 2-Up tab and choose GIF 128 Dithered from the Settings pop-up menu.

16 Click OK to save the file. In the dialog box, name the file **jumpcat.gif**, and click Save.

Review questions

1 What determines the file format you should use when saving images for Web publication?

2 Name three styles of artwork that require different file formats for publication on the Web.

3 What is the benefit of selecting the Web palette when preparing images for publication on the World Wide Web?

4 What does the transparency option in a GIF file format do?

5 Describe how to select multiple objects and paint them with the same Web-safe colors.

Review answers

1 The style of artwork you're working with determines the file format you should use to save an image for publication on the Web. In addition, file size and image integrity may also affect which file format you use. In general, you should attempt to maintain the integrity of the image and keep the file size down.

2 Different styles of artwork include the following:

• Flat color (such as line art, logos, or illustrations with type).

• Full-color continuous-tone (such as bitmap images).

• Gradient-filled.

• Continuous-tone grayscale.

• Black and white.

• Animation.

• Artwork with URL links embedded in it for an image map.

3 Selecting the Web palette ensures that your images are displayed using the same color palette, regardless of the platform on which the image is displayed.

4 Transparency makes all the unpainted areas of the artwork transparent in a Web browser. You cannot select specific areas to be transparent; only the unpainted areas are defined as transparent.

5 Select an object and choose Edit > Select > Same Fill Color/Stroke Color/Paint Style to select the fill, stroke, or both of all the objects in the artwork that are painted the same color. Then choose Web Safe RGB from the Color palette menu, and click a color to apply it to the selection. You can also click the Out of Web color warning cube in the Color palette to automatically switch to the nearest Web-safe color.

Index

Production Notes

This book was created electronically using Adobe FrameMaker®. Art was produced using Adobe Illustrator, Adobe ImageReady, and Adobe Photoshop. The Minion® and Frutiger® families of typefaces are used throughout the book.

Photography Credits

Photographic images intended for use with tutorials only.

Adobe Image Library: Lesson 7 (figure of woman, from Exercise and Wellness, EWE_095; clouds, from Endless Skies, ESK_076); Lesson 15 (chess pieces, from Business Symbols, BSY_058 and BSY_066).

National Archives and Records Administration: Lesson 14 (couple dancing).

The Adobe Image Library contains compelling images to make your ideas stand out in any media. For more information, visit the U.S. Web site at http://www.adobestudios.com.

Adobe Typefaces Used

Lesson 6: Bossa Nova™, pkg. 447

Lesson 8: Sassafras™, pkg. 398

Lesson 9: Penumbra™, pkg. 377

Lesson 12: Bossa Nova™, pkg. 447; Emmascript™, pkg. 447

Lesson 14: Mezz™ MM, pkg. 370

Lesson 15: Block Berthold®, pkg. 325

The Adobe Type Library

Adobe Certification Programs

 Adobe® Certified Expert

 Adobe® Certified Training Provider

What is an ACE?

An Adobe Certified Expert (ACE) is an individual who has passed an Adobe Product Proficiency Exam for a specified Adobe software product. Adobe Certified Experts are eligible to promote themselves to clients or employers as highly skilled, expert level users of Adobe Software. ACE certification is a recognized standard for excellence in Adobe software knowledge.

ACE Benefits

When you become an ACE, you enjoy these special benefits:

- Professional recognition
- An ACE program certificate
- Use of the Adobe Certified Expert program logo

What is an ACTP?

An Adobe Certified Training Provider (ACTP) is a Training professional or organization that has met the ACTP program requirements. Adobe promotes ACTPs to customers who need training on Adobe software.

ACTP Benefits

- Professional recognition
- An ACTP program certificate
- Use of the Adobe Certified Training Provider program logo
- Listing in the Partner Finder on Adobe.com
- Access to beta software releases when available
- Classroom in a Book in Adobe Acrobat PDF
- Marketing materials
- Co-marketing opportunities

For more information on the ACE and ACTP programs, go to partners.adobe.com, and look for these programs under the Join section.